The UN Security Council and the International Criminal Court

ELGAR INTERNATIONAL LAW

This important series will present high quality monographs that analyse current thinking and research across the field of international law, rigorously examining key concepts as well as provoking debate and questions for further research. Some volumes will draw on insights from disciplines other than law, such as economics and politics, in an attempt to arrive at a genuinely inter-disciplinary perspective. Seeking to attract original thinking and new, challenging research, proposals are encouraged that primarily engage with new and previously under-developed themes in the field, or alternatively offer an innovative analysis of areas of uncertainty in the existing law.

Titles in this series include:

Epistemic Forces in International Law
Foundational Doctrines and Techniques of International Legal Argumentation
Jean d'Aspremont

International Claims Commissions
Righting Wrongs after Conflict
Lea Brilmayer, Chiara Giorgetti and Lorraine Charlton

The Paradigm of State Consent in the Law of Treaties
Challenges and Perspectives
Vassillis Pergantis

The UN Security Council and the International Criminal Court
The Referral Mechanism in Theory and Practice
Gabriel M. Lentner

The UN Security Council and the International Criminal Court

The Referral Mechanism in Theory and Practice

Gabriel M. Lentner

Assistant Professor, Danube University Krems, Austria and Fellow, Stanford University, USA

ELGAR INTERNATIONAL LAW

Edward Elgar PUBLISHING

Cheltenham, UK • Northampton, MA, USA

Published by
Edward Elgar Publishing Limited
The Lypiatts
15 Lansdown Road
Cheltenham
Glos GL50 2JA
UK

Edward Elgar Publishing, Inc.
William Pratt House
9 Dewey Court
Northampton
Massachusetts 01060
USA

A catalogue record for this book
is available from the British Library

Library of Congress Control Number: 2018946006

This book is available electronically in the **Elgar**online
Law subject collection
DOI 10.4337/9781788117326

MIX
Paper from
responsible sources
FSC® C013056

ISBN 978 1 78811 731 9 (cased)
ISBN 978 1 78811 732 6 (eBook)

Printed and bound in Great Britain by TJ International Ltd, Padstow

Dieses Buch sei meiner Familie gewidmet

Contents

Acknowledgements

First and foremost, I wish to thank Professor Ursula Kriebaum for the extensive and critical feedback, comments and suggestions on an earlier version of the manuscript, as well as Professors August Reinisch and Stephan Wittich, who offered additional feedback and comments towards publication. I would also like to thank my academic mentor, Professor Siegfried Fina, for his constant support and encouragement over the years. Additionally, I would like to express my sincerest gratitude to Vice-Rector Professor Thomas Ratka, for his generous support and inspiration at the Danube University Krems. I am also grateful for the thought-provoking discussions on legal reasoning with Professor Dieter Krimphove, and his kind support and friendship.

I would also like to thank Dr Sarah Nouwen who challenged me on my theory with constructive criticism and valuable feedback, including during my time as Visiting Scholar at the Lauterpacht Centre for International Law at the University of Cambridge in 2016. I am thankful to Teresa Weber for feedback on an earlier draft of Chapter 3, to Fabiane Baxewanos for the insightful discussions on international law and critical theory, and all other friends and colleagues who helped me along the way (you know who you are!).

Abbreviations

AMIS	African Union Mission in Sudan
art/arts	article/s
ASP	Assembly of States Parties of the ICC
AU	African Union
ECHR	European Convention of Human Rights
ECtHR	European Court of Human Rights
FRD	Friendly Relations Declaration
GA	UN General Assembly
ICC	International Criminal Court
ICJ	International Court of Justice
ICL	International Criminal Law
ICRC	International Committee of the Red Cross
ICTR	International Criminal Tribunal for Rwanda
ICTY	International Criminal Tribunal for the former Yugoslavia
ILC	International Law Commission
RA	Negotiated Relationship Agreement between the UN and the ICC
Res	Resolution
SC	United Nations Security Council
SCSL	Special Court for Sierra Leone
SOFA	Status of Forces Agreement
STL	Special Tribunal for Lebanon
UN	United Nations

1. Introduction

1.1 SETTING THE SCENE

The United Nations Security Council (SC) referral to the International Criminal Court (ICC) is arguably the most fundamental operational relationship between the United Nations (UN) and the ICC.[1] It allows the Court to exercise jurisdiction over situations in states not parties to the Rome Statute of the ICC[2] (the Statute, Rome Statute) provided for in art 13(b) of the Statute.[3] In contrast to referrals by states parties (art 14) or the Prosecutor acting *proprio motu* (art 15), where jurisdiction is conferred to the ICC through the ratification of the Rome Statute,[4] the SC referral would confer jurisdiction to the ICC over situations which it otherwise could not lawfully exercise.[5]

---

[1] Kenneth S. Gallant, 'The International Criminal Court in the System of States and International Organizations' (2003) 16(3) *Leiden Journal of International Law* 553, 571.

[2] *Rome Statute of the International Criminal Court*, UN Doc. A/CONF.183/9, 17 July 1998 (Text of the Rome Statute circulated as UN Doc. A/CONF.183/9 of 17 July 1998 and corrected by procès-verbaux of 10 November 1998, 12 July 1999, 30 November 1999, 8 May 2000, 17 January 2001 and 16 January 2002). The Statute entered into force on 1 July 2002.

[3] The jurisdiction of the ICC is not based on the principle of universality: see Office of the Prosecutor of the International Criminal Court, 'Situation in Palestine' (3 April 2012), para 4 available at http://www.icc-cpi.int/NR/rdonlyres/C6162BBF-FEB9-4FAF-AFA9-836106D2694A/284387/SituationinPalestine030412ENG.pdf (accessed 5 March 2018); Louise Arbour and Morten Bergsmo, 'Conspicuous Absence of Jurisdictional Overreach' in Herman von Hebel, J. G. Lammers and Jolien Schukking (eds), *Reflections on the International Criminal Court: Essays in Honour of Adriaan Bos* (T.M.C. Asser Press; Kluwer Law International 1999) 19; Olympia Bekou and Robert Cryer, 'The International Criminal Court and Universal Jurisdiction: A Close Encounter?' (2007) 56(1) *International & Comparative Law Quarterly* 50.

[4] Article 1 Rome Statute provides that '[t]he jurisdiction and functioning of the Court shall be governed by the provisions of this Statute'. Pursuant to art 12(1) Rome Statute provides 'A State which becomes a party to this Statute thereby accepts the jurisdiction of the Court with respect to the crimes referred to in Art. 5'.

[5] Note that the ICC (with the exception of the SC referral) only has jurisdiction over offences committed when a state that has nationality or territorial jurisdiction over the offence is a state party to the Rome Statute (see art 12 Rome Statute); see also Jennifer

Its inclusion proved to be one of the most contentious issues during the preparatory work as well as at the conference in Rome. Legal issues were raised, particularly regarding the power of the SC to refer a situation involving a state not party to the ICC. In fact, when the proposed Statute for the ICC was put to a vote at the end of the negotiations in Rome on 17 July 1998, the Head of the Indian delegation, Dilip Lahiri, issued a statement explaining the rejection of the Statute by India. He delivered ruthless criticism of the final draft and pointed out that

> it was odd, for instance, that the draft adopted a definition of crimes against humanity with which the representatives of over half of humanity did not agree. And we are now about to adopt a Statute to which the Governments who represent two-thirds of humanity would not be a party.

He criticized the fact that, in his view, 'the Statute gives to the Security Council a role in terms that violate international law' because

> [t]he power to bind non-States Parties to any international treaty is not a power given to the Council by the Charter. Under the Law of Treaties, no state can be forced to accede to a treaty or be bound by the provisions of a treaty it has not accepted . . . Why wait now for signature and ratificating [*sic*]? The permanent members of the Security Council could have got together with the like-minded and cobbled together a Statute with which the rest of the world in any case has no option but to comply if the Security Council, acting under Chapter VII, demands it.[6]

Trahan, 'The Relationship Between the International Criminal Court and the U.N. Security Council: Parameters and Best Practices' (2013) 24(4) *Criminal Law Forum* 417, 419; Dapo Akande, 'The Effect of Security Council Resolutions and Domestic Proceedings on State Obligations to Cooperate with the ICC' (2012) 10(2) *Journal of International Criminal Justice* 299, 301; Luca Schicho, 'The Security Council and the International Criminal Court: An Awkward Partnership?' (2008) 13 *Austrian Review of International and European Law* 115, 116. On the similar powers of the UN ad hoc tribunals, see Danesh Sarooshi, 'The Powers of the United Nations International Criminal Tribunals' in Jochen A. Frowein, Rüdiger Wolfrum and Christiane Philipp (eds), *Max Planck Yearbook of United Nations law* (Kluwer Law International 1998).

6 Dilip Lahiri, 'Explanation of Vote by Mr. Dilip Lahiri, Head of Delegation of India, on the Adoption of the Statute of the International Criminal Court' (17 July 1998). For an analysis of the Indian position regarding the ICC, see e.g. U. Ramanathan, 'India and the ICC' (2005) 3(3) *Journal of International Criminal Justice* 627. For a rebuttal of the legal arguments presented by India (and the US) against the adoption of the Rome Statute, see an early commentator: Diane F. Orentlicher, 'Politics by Other Means: The Law of the International Criminal Court' (1999) 32(3) *Cornell International Law Journal* 489. For a more recent review and evaluation of India's position see Dilip Lahiri, 'Should India continue to stay out of ICC?' Observer Research Foundation (24 November 2010) available at http://www.orfonline.org/research/should-india-continue-to-stay-out-of-icc/ (accessed 28 March 2018).

And while the Rome Statute was eventually adopted by 120 votes in favour and only 7 votes against (with 21 states abstaining), questions with respect to the legal nature and the legal justification for such SC referral remained unresolved.[7] Aside from art 13(b), the Rome Statute does not include any detailed provision on this referral mechanism.[8] A discussion regarding the referral's legal nature did not take place. One of the reasons for the lack of such debate is that the legal justification for such referral powers of the SC were simply assumed to exist due to its political expedience and feasibility. This widespread understanding is exemplified by the fact that the referral power was also supported in the name of the ICC acting as a permanent version of the ad hoc tribunals.[9] The power of the SC to establish ad hoc tribunals was being challenged at the time. But their legality was later confirmed in the Appeals Chamber's judgment of the International Criminal Tribunal for the Former Yugoslavia (ICTY) in *Tadic* and has not been seriously contested since.[10]

However, as this study will demonstrate, essential differences exist between the confirmed legality of the establishment of ad hoc tribunals and the questions regarding the legality of SC referrals involving situations in the territory of states not parties to the Rome Statute. These differences bring to bear the fact that the legal nature of SC referrals cannot be equated to that of the establishment of the ad hoc tribunals. Hence the need for a detailed analysis of the SC referral mechanism.

These issues are not merely an academic exercise but are important for answering the legal questions raised by the SC referral practice, especially due to the ambiguous SC Res 1593 (2005)[11] and Res 1970 (2011)[12] in which the SC

---

7 Morten Bergsmo, 'Occasional Remarks on Certain State Concerns about the Jurisdictional Reach of the International Criminal Court, and Their Possible Implications for the Relationship between the Court and the Security Council' (2000) 69 *Nordic Journal of International Law* 87, 111.

8 Luigi Condorelli and Santiago Villalpando, 'Referral and Deferral by the Security Council' in Antonio Cassese, Paola Gaeta and John R. Jones (eds), *The Rome Statute of the International Criminal Court* (Oxford University Press 2002) 629.

9 Bruce Broomhall, *International Justice and the International Criminal Court: Between Sovereignty and the Rule of Law* (Oxford University Press 2004) 79. See further on this below in Chapter 4.1.

10 William Schabas, *The International Criminal Court: A Commentary on the Rome Statute* (Oxford commentaries on international law, Oxford University Press 2010) 294; *Tadic Case* (Decision on the Defence Motion for Interlocutory Appeal on Jurisdiction) ICTY-IT-94-l-A (2 October 1995) confirmed subsequently by the ICTR in *Kanyabashi Case* (Decision on the Defence Motion on Jurisdiction) ICTR-96-15-T (18 June 1997). See also *Milosevic Case* (Decision on Preliminary Motions) ICTY-IT-99-37-PT (8 November 2001).

11 UNSC Res 1593 (31 March 2005) UN Doc S/RES/1593.

12 UNSC Res 1970 (26 February 2011) UN Doc S/RES/1970.

referred the situations concerning Darfur and Libya respectively to the ICC. Question arise, for instance, whether and what legal effects the jurisdictional exemption for certain categories of nationals of states not parties to the ICC has, or whether or not personal immunities under customary international law still apply. Other issues include whether the SC referral can refer situations retroactively or only prospectively, and with what if any temporal limitations. Indeed, it will be demonstrated that a firm theoretical foundation of the legal nature of SC referrals is essential for the analysis of the operation and exercise of the ICC's jurisdiction and powers to answer these and other questions.

To that end, I proceed by first introducing the hypotheses of this study and describing the analytical and methodological framework as well as the terminology adopted. Next, Chapter 2 examines the legislative history of the SC referral as included in the Rome Statute of the ICC to bring to bear the inherent contradictions and unresolved issues surrounding its legal basis and conceptualization under international law. Against this historical backdrop, Chapter 3 analyzes the legal nature of the SC referral, arguing that it constitutes a conferral of powers from the SC to the ICC. On this basis, the powers of the SC under the UN Charter are analyzed in Chapter 4 to establish potential limits to SC referrals and their conditions. Chapter 5 then addresses the legal consequences for the ICC acting on the SC referral, followed by Chapter 6 which introduces the actual practice of the SC and Chapter 7 which applies the findings of this study to the key issues raised by it. Finally, Chapter 8 concludes by evaluating the findings of this study and assessing the usefulness of considering the ICC a Janus-faced institution.

It is important to note that this study is only concerned with the SC referral and the resulting exercise of criminal jurisdiction by the ICC over a situation in the territory of a state which is neither a party to the Rome Statute nor otherwise consenting to this exercise of jurisdiction.

1.2 HYPOTHESES

This study focuses on the relationship between the SC and the ICC, as others have already done in detail.[13] The present inquiry is distinct from previous

[13] Jakob Pichon, *Internationaler Strafgerichtshof und Sicherheitsrat der Vereinten Nationen: Zur Rolle des Sicherheitsrats bei der Verfolgung völkerrechtlicher Verbrechen durch den IStGH* (Max-Planck-Gesellschaft zur Förderung der Wissenschaften e.V 2011); Robert Frau, *Das Verhältnis zwischen dem ständigen Internationalen Strafgerichtshof und dem Sicherheitsrat der Vereinten Nationen: Art. 13 lit. b) IStGH-Statut und der Darfur-Konflikt vor dem Gerichtshof* (Schriften zum Völkerrecht Band 192, Duncker & Humblot 2010); Michael E. Kurth, *Das Verhältnis des Internationalen Strafgerichtshofes zum UN-Sicherheitsrat: Unter besonderer*

accounts of this relationship in that it exclusively deals with the legal nature of SC referrals to the ICC involving non-party states to present a comprehensive legal analysis of the SC's referral practice. In doing so, this study provides a more detailed account of the legal nature of such referrals in the context of non-party states from the law of international organizations.

Against this background the following hypotheses have directed this study. The first working hypothesis was that by applying the law of international organizations to the institutional relationship between the SC and the ICC, important solutions are provided to the normative problems arising out of the SC's practice.

Second, this study puts forward the hypothesis that the legislative history of the SC referral reveals the inherent contradictions and paradoxes of the Rome Statute and that this proves the continuation of a double standard applied in international criminal law, in which powerful states subject other, weaker states to the jurisdiction of an international tribunal, but are not willing to subject themselves to such jurisdiction. The SC referral is the legal epitome of this reality.

Third, at the core of this study is the hypothesis that the legal nature of the SC referral is significantly different from the precedents set by the establishment of the ad hoc tribunals (ICTY and International Criminal Tribunal for Rwanda (ICTR)). This is the reason why I carefully analyze the legal differences between the SC referral and the creation of the ad hoc tribunals.

Fourth, I hypothesize that while it is not unbound by law, the SC enjoys broad discretionary powers and it is not easy to establish binding limits to SC measures under Chapter VII.

Finally, the last hypothesis that this study wishes to validate is the fact that the ICC is bound by the jurisdictional exemptions included in the SC referrals since the ICC is not authorized to exercise jurisdiction over situations in non-party states that goes beyond the conferred jurisdictional authority as included in the SC referral.

1.3 ANALYTICAL APPROACH AND METHODOLOGY

The analytical approach and methodology of this study can be defined in terms of what literature and theory it primarily analyzes, uses and employs, what

---

Berücksichtigung von Sicherheitsratsresolution 1422 (2002) (Nomos 2006); Daniela Stagel, *Sicherheitsrat und Internationaler Strafgerichtshof: Zur Abgrenzung ihrer Kompetenzen nach der Charta der Vereinten Nationen und dem Römischen Statut* (Schriftenreihe Studien zum Völker- und Europarecht Bd. 41, Kovač 2008).

emphasis it puts on the value of court decisions for the determination of rules of international law, as well as the author's normative commitment.

First, this study uses a broad literature base. It is important to note that it not only consults 'mainstream' international criminal law (ICL) scholarship but also ties in the arguably nascent critical scholarship of ICL. Still, this study confines itself to the legal analysis of the issues at hand and can therefore not be considered critical legal scholarship in the sense of critical legal studies. Most importantly, however, this study departs from current accounts of ICL in that it analyzes the institutional relationship between the SC and the ICC from the perspective of the law of international organizations.

Second, as regards the legal nature of the SC referral, this study is primarily based on the theory of conferral of powers. This theory has been successful in the analysis of the delegation of Chapter VII powers of the SC to UN member states, regional arrangements, subsidiary organs and the UN Secretary-General.[14]

Third, the author's normative commitment is to realism, which describes a concern with what *actually is*.[15] As Sarah Nouwen puts it:

> This is a realism that acknowledges the importance of big ideas and great ideals, but believes that they should start from what a matter of fact *is*, for them not to become dangerous; a realism that is idealistic precisely because it works towards ideals from a difficult *status quo*, as opposed to an idealism that proceeds on the basis of assumptions that do not reflect reality.[16]

---

[14] Dan Sarooshi, *The United Nations and the Development of Collective Security: The Delegation by the UN Security Council of its Chapter VII Powers* (Clarendon Press; Oxford University Press 1999).

[15] Sarah M. H. Nouwen, *Complementarity in the Line of Fire: The Catalysing Effect of the International Criminal Court in Uganda and Sudan* (Cambridge studies in law and society, Cambridge University Press 2013) 27.

[16] Ibid. [emphasis in the original]. It must be noted in this respect that particularly in the field of international criminal law, it is important not to confuse the law as it *is*, with a concept of justice, i.e. a (subjective) conviction of what the law *should* be. This has been pointed out by Koskenniemi, who stated that '[t]he dilemma of rules and standards undermines the ability of the mode of control to establish behavioural hierarchies by reference to the "lawful"/"illegal" scheme. It pits "law" against "justice" in a fashion that reverses the hierarchy between the two. We can no longer assume that we find social justice by applying the law. We now seem able to find the law only by applying justice. This, however, seems fatal to the legal project altogether. We have recourse to law in the control of social behaviour precisely to avoid reference to principles of justice that we assume to be subjective, undemonstrable [*sic*] and open to misuse by those in power. If now we are required to know justice before we can know the law, then we must either give up the ideal of control or assume that justice is not so subjective and undemonstrable [*sic*] after all. Though more appealing, the latter alternative, however, deprives the point in knowing the law: we are already able to set up the perfect

An example of implications of the realist commitment adopted in this study is the analysis of the powers of the SC. Realism in this sense views much of the writing about the actions of the SC, which asserts that many such actions are ultra vires, beyond its powers under the Charter, or otherwise unlawful, as rather unconvincing. Upon close examination, this part of the literature is neither based on state practice nor on the practice of the organs of the UN, nor on decisions of courts and tribunals.[17]

1.4 TERMINOLOGY

The ICC is collectively identified in art 1 of the Rome Statute as 'the Court' encompassing all its organs enumerated in art 34 (the Presidency, an Appeals Division, a Trial Division and a Pre-Trial Division, the Office of the Prosecutor, the Registry), along with the Assembly of States Parties (art 112). The word 'Court' is used throughout the Statute as signifying the vestee of judicial, prosecutorial or administrative functions of the ICC.[18] Without any specific mention of certain organs of the ICC, this study uses the term 'ICC' in reference to the ICC as the international organization established by its constituent treaty, i.e. the Rome Statute of the ICC.[19]

1.5 THE ICC AS AN INTERNATIONAL ORGANIZATION

The argument presented here is based on the classification of the ICC as an international organization with international legal personality distinct from its member states. The general criteria for the determination of an entity as being an international organization under international law do not appear to pose any problems. It is established through a multilateral treaty between sovereign states, is equipped with organs, and its legal powers and purpose are distinguished from those of its members.[20] However, treating international

society!' Martti Koskenniemi, 'Hierarchy in International Law: A Sketch' (1997) 8 *European Journal of International Law* 566, 575.

[17] Michael Wood, 'The Law of Treaties and the UN Security Council: Some Reflections' in Enzo Cannizzaro (ed), *The Law of Treaties Beyond the Vienna Convention* (Oxford University Press 2011) 247.

[18] Georghios M. Pikis, *The Rome Statute for the International Criminal Court: Analysis of the Statute, the Rules of Procedure and Evidence, the Regulations of the Court and Supplementary Instruments* (Nijhoff 2010) 45–46.

[19] On the question of the ICC as an international organization, see below.

[20] Tarcisio Gazzini, 'Personality of International Organizations' in Jan Klabbers (ed), *Research Handbook on the Law of International Organizations* (Edward Elgar 2011) 35. See also art 2 of the International Law Commission (ILC) Draft Articles on

courts as international organizations may be 'awkward'.[21] Nevertheless, the ICC is the 'overt' example, since it must be understood as being governed by an Assembly of States Parties.[22]

Regarding the related question of international legal personality of the ICC, two main theories have emerged as to how international organizations acquire international legal personality. First, the so-called will theory sees the intent of the contracting parties as being determinant for international legal personality.[23] This intent may be expressly established, or inferred from the constituent instrument containing no specific provision.[24] Following the will theory, the intention of the founders of the organization decides the organization's legal personality.[25] Article 4 of the Rome Statute sets out the legal status and powers of the court, according to which '[t]he Court shall have international legal personality. It shall also have such legal capacity as may be necessary for the exercise of its functions and the fulfilment of its purposes'. Accordingly, the express reference in art 4 establishes the international legal personality of the ICC. The problem with this view is, however, that art 4 cannot legally bind third states: for them art 4 is *res inter alios acta*.[26]

On the other hand, under the objective theory of personality, legal personality is established once it exists as a matter of law, i.e. meeting the legal requirement of international law for 'organizationhood'.[27] It is therefore a factual, objective question and not the provisions of the constitution or the intention of its framers which establishes the international personality of an international organization.[28] As a main requirement, the organization must possess a *volonté distincte* or 'distinct will of its own'. It must be a 'collectivity of States established by treaty, with a constitution and common organs, having a personality distinct from that of its member-States'.[29]

---

the Responsibility of International Organizations: '"international organization" means an organization established by a treaty or other instrument governed by international law and possessing its own international legal personality'.

21 Jan Klabbers, 'Unity, Diversity, Accountability: The Ambivalent Concept of International Organisation' (2013) 14 *Melbourne Journal of International Law* 1, 9–10.

22 Ibid.

23 Gazzini (n 20) 34.

24 Ibid.

25 Jan Klabbers, *An Introduction to International Organizations Law* (3rd edn, Cambridge University Press 2015) 47.

26 Danilenko G. M., 'ICC Statute and Third States' in Cassese (n 8) 1873; see generally Gazzini (n 20) 35.

27 Klabbers (n 25) 48–49.

28 Finn Seyersted, 'Objective International Personality of Intergovernmental Organizations' (1964) 34 *Nordisk Tidsskrift for International Ret* 1, 39–40.

29 ILC, 'Report by G. G. Fitzmaurice, Special Rapporteur' (14 March 1956) UN Doc A/CN.4/101, 108. The International Law Commission defines 'International

The ICC fulfils these requirements of organizationhood for the following reasons. First, the ICC is established by the Rome Statute, which is an international treaty. Second, the Rome Statute is the constitution of the ICC in that it confers and governs the powers of the various organs of the ICC. These organs are the Assembly of States Parties (art 112), the Presidency, an Appeals Division, a Trial Division and a Pre-Trial Division; The Office of the Prosecutor; and The Registry (art 34). It has international legal personality distinct from that of its member states (art 4(1)). And it concluded the Relationship Agreement (RA) with the UN and other agreements with states (for example, the host state agreement with the Netherlands).[30] In conclusion, the ICC is an international organization.[31]

Organization' in its draft articles on the responsibility of international organizations as 'an organization established by a treaty or other instrument governed by international law and possessing its own international legal personality. International organizations may include as members, in addition to States, other entities.' See art 2 of ILC, 'Draft Articles on the Responsibility of International Organizations' 2011, adopted by the International Law Commission at its sixty-third session, in 2011, and submitted to the General Assembly as a part of the Commission's report covering the work of that session (A/66/10, para 87). For a discussion of this definition and an overview of the other authoritative definitions adopted in the literature see e.g. Stephen Bouwhuis, 'The International Law Commission's Definition of International Organizations' (2012) 9(2) *International Organizations Law Review* 451.

[30] Headquarters Agreement between the International Criminal Court and the Host State (entry into force 1 March 2008) ICC-BD/04-01-08.

[31] See also Alain Pellet, 'Applicable Law' in Cassese (n 8) 1053.

2. Legislative history of the referral mechanism

2.1 INTRODUCTION

To understand the underlying and inherent issues with the SC referral, a critical analysis of its legislative history is insightful.[1] This chapter seeks to demonstrate that the controversies surrounding the SC referral and its legal nature can be explained by the general tension between the ideal of the establishment of a universal and permanent institution to end impunity on the one hand, and the realities of international relations as reflected by the legal limitations stemming from political interests and power.[2] As a preliminary remark, there are many histories of ICL[3] and this chapter makes no claim of comprehensiveness. It does however provide an overview of the historical development leading up to the establishment of the ICC in Rome.

From the outset, it is important to note that any historical narrative is in some way distorted. In the words of legal historian Samuel Moyn: 'If the past is read as preparation for a surprising recent event, both are distorted. The past is treated as if it were simply the future waiting to happen. And the surprising recent event is treated as less surprising that it really is.'[4] The same can be said

---

1 A careful and sober analysis seems particularly apt with respect to an institution that seeks to 'guarantee lasting respect for and the enforcement of international justice' (Preamble of the Rome Statute). As Friedrich Nietzsche famously put it, 'Distrust all those who talk much of their justice!' See Friedrich Nietzsche, *Also sprach Zarathustra: Ein Buch für Alle und Keinen* (Ernst Schmeitzner 1883), Chapter 40 (translated by the author), cited from Friedrich Nietzsche, Giorgio Colli and Mazzino Montinari, *Sämtliche Werke: Kritische Studienausgabe in 15 Bänden* (Deutscher Taschenbuch Verlag; W. de Gruyter 1980).

2 For an insightful political science study into the relationship between power and principle in the ICC and its development and its institutional design, see Christopher Rudolph, *Power and Principle: The Politics of International Criminal Courts* (Cornell University Press 2017).

3 Robert Cryer, *Prosecuting International Crimes: Selectivity and the International Criminal Law Regime* (Cambridge University Press 2005) 9 (with further references).

4 Samuel Moyn, *Last Utopia: Human Rights in History* (Harvard University Press 2010) 11; cf the moral outrage (in a different context) of Jacob Burckhardt at those

of the establishment of the ICC, which is often portrayed in a way that gives the impression of the ICC as a logical and necessary historical consequence of the Nuremberg trials.

In recognition of this distortion, the following historical review should not be read as a continuous and gradual development from the first attempts at an international criminal court to the entry into force of the Rome Statute establishing the ICC in July 2002. It is also not the purpose of this chapter to give a comprehensive account of these developments. Rather, this chapter points to the most important historical events that may help us to understand the current legal issues of the SC referral in their historical context.

To this end, this chapter begins with an analysis of the negotiations in the different fora to identify the divergent opinions regarding the SC referral, and on what legal grounds this was debated. It closes with a critical evaluation confronting the general legal-historical narrative with the realities of ICL to draw conclusions that help explain the compromise reached during the negotiations of the Rome Statute.

2.2 THE NEGOTIATIONS CONCERNING THE SC REFERRAL LEADING UP TO ROME

The role of the SC in a future ICC was much debated throughout the negotiations, carried out in various UN fora: the International Law Commission (ILC), which produced two versions of the draft Statute, the General Assembly's Sixth Committee, the Ad Hoc Committee on the Establishment of an International Criminal Court and the Preparatory Committee on the Establishment of an International Criminal Court (including its working groups).

2.2.1 Historical Background and Development

The Nuremberg trials provided important impetus for the establishment of an international criminal court. In 1946, an international congress met in Paris calling for the adoption of an international criminal code and the establishment of a permanent international criminal court.[5] The Convention on the

---

viewing history as no more than a vast preparation for the way things are, and the way people think, right now: 'Each man regards all times as fulfilled in his own, and cannot see his own as one of many passing waves. Just as if the world and its history had existed merely for our sakes!' Jacob Burckhardt, *Force and Freedom: Reflections on History* (Pantheon Books 1943) 358.

[5] Claudia Tofan and R. van der Wolf, *The Long and Winding Road to … Rome: A Brief History of the ICC* (published and distributed by the International Courts Association by Wolf Legal Publishers 2011) 1.

Prevention and Punishment of the Crime of Genocide (Genocide Convention) was adopted by the UN General Assembly (GA) on 9 December 1948 and entered into force on 12 January 1951.[6] This convention obliged the states parties to adopt domestic legislation punishing genocide. It also envisioned in art VI that '[p]ersons charged with genocide . . . shall be tried by a competent tribunal of the State in the territory of which the act was committed, or *by such international penal tribunal as may have jurisdiction with respect to those Contracting Parties which shall have accepted its jurisdiction*'.[7] Accompanying the resolution adopting the Genocide Convention, the GA invited the ILC to 'study the desirability and possibility of establishing an international judicial organ for the trial of persons charged with genocide or other crimes over which jurisdiction will be conferred upon that organ by international conventions'.[8]

In 1950, the ILC ultimately voted in favour of the desirability and feasibility of creating an international criminal court.[9] The ILC voted 8–1 in favour of desirability and 7–3 in favour of its possibility.[10] However, the ILC was in fact deeply divided on this subject: in the two separate reports submitted to the

---

6 UN Doc A/64/Add. 1. 31 January 1947, UNTS 1951/278.

7 Emphasis added. For a discussion of the draft history of that phrase, see e.g. ILC Report by Special Rapporteur Ricardo Alfaro on the Question of International Criminal Jurisdiction, UN Doc A/CN.4/15 (3 March 1950) paras 46–49 reprinted in International Law Commission, 'Documents of the second session including the report of the Commission to the General Assembly' (1950) 2 *Yearbook of the International Law Commission*.

8 UN General Assembly, Third Session, Resolution adopted by the General Assembly 260 B (III), 'Study by the International Law Commission of the Question of an International Criminal Tribunal' (179th plenary meeting 9 December 1948), available at http://www.un-documents.net/a3r260b.htm (accessed 11 May 2016).

9 See *Yearbook of the International Law Commission*, 1950, vol II, document A/1316, paras 128–45, available at http://legal.un.org/ilc/publications/yearbooks/Ybkvolumes%28e%29/ILC_1950_v2_e.pdf (accessed 11 May 2016).

10 Report of the International Law Commission to the General Assembly, UN Doc A/1316: Report of the International Law Commission covering its second session, 5 June–29 July 1950, paras 140–41, reprinted in *Yearbook of the International Law Commission*, 1950, vol II, 379.

Commission, one[11] supported the court's establishment and the other[12] rejected it.[13]

It is interesting to note that even at this early stage it was recognized by the special rapporteur that a consent-based system would have its problems. The special rapporteur noted:

> The competence of the Court will be restricted to parties having submitted by convention to its jurisdiction. No organization does exist to enforce an appearance before the Court or the execution of its judgements, and it seems difficult to establish such an organization. The jurisdiction therefore is likely to be limited and brought into action in a haphazard way. There are great risks that culprits will not always be brought before the Court.

On the whole it was felt that the jurisdiction would be exercised in an arbitrary way. The Court's deterring effect would thus be very doubtful, if any.[14]

In the subsequent work of the ILC on the matter, the discussions and written comments, especially from major powers,[15] clearly indicated that the project had no chance of acceptance and was politically premature.[16] Most importantly, the major powers did not reach consensus on this jurisdiction.[17] However, because these states did not want to assume political responsibility for the demise of a permanent international criminal court within only five and six years, respectively, of the Nuremberg judgments, the Committee's mandate was extended, with some membership changes, and in 1953 it produced a revised text.[18]

---

[11] Ricardo J. Alfaro, Question of International Criminal Jurisdiction, UN Doc No A/CN.4/15 (1950), reprinted in [1950] 2 *Yearbook of the International Law Commission* 1, UN Doc A/CN.4/SER.A/1950/Add.1.

[12] Emil Sandström, Question of International Criminal Jurisdiction, UN Doc No A/CN.4/15 (1950), reprinted in [1950] 2 *Yearbook of the International Law Commission* 18, UN Doc A/CN.4/SER.A/1950/Add.1.

[13] Leila N. Sadat, *The International Criminal Court and the Transformation of International Law: Justice for the New Millennium* (International and comparative criminal law series, Transnational Publishers 2002) 33–34.

[14] Sandström (n 12) para 34.

[15] See e.g. Report of the Sixth Committee, UN GOAR, 7th Sess., UN Doc A/2275 (1952).

[16] Cherif M. Bassiouni, *The Legislative History of the International Criminal Court* (International and comparative criminal law series, Transnational Publishers 2005) 55–60.

[17] Ibid. 57.

[18] See Report of the Committee on International Criminal Jurisdiction, UN GOAR 7th Sess., Supp. No. 12 at 21, UN Doc A/26645 (1954).

In 1954, the ILC at its sixth session submitted to the GA the 'Draft Code of Offences against the Peace and Security of Mankind'.[19] Subsequently, the GA vested the question of enforcement of the Draft Code[20] to a commission composed of representatives of 17 member states,[21] which found it first desirable to establish the court as an organ of the UN, but then recommended its establishment by a multilateral convention due to the practical and legal difficulty in establishing such a court by a GA resolution or by amending the UN Charter.[22] For example, doubts were raised that the legal powers of the GA under the Charter were not sufficient to enable it to establish a court by resolution.[23] Eventually, by eight votes to two, with three abstentions, the Committee decided that the best method of establishing an international criminal court would be by means of a convention prepared by an international diplomatic conference convened under the auspices of the UN.[24]

For the next 20 years, the Cold War paralyzed all efforts to move the preparations for a permanent international criminal court forward.[25] In 1974, the GA agreed on a definition of aggression, a minor sign of life of a future ICC.[26] Finally in 1989, with the end of the Cold War, the idea to establish the ICC became more viable.

2.2.2 The Referral in Negotiations up to Rome

In 1989, the GA instructed the ILC to again deal with the question of a permanent international criminal court.[27] In 1991, the ILC provisionally adopted the Draft Code of Crimes and created a working group[28] on an international

---

19 *Yearbook of the International Law Commission* (1954), vol II.

20 Draft Code of Offences Against the Peace and Security of Mankind of 1954.

21 International Criminal Jurisdiction, GA Res 489 (V), available at http://legal.un.org/docs/?symbol=A/RES/489%28V%29 (accessed 11 May 2016).

22 Report of the Committee on International Criminal Jurisdiction on its Session Held from 1 to 31 August 1951, UN GAOR, 7th Sess., Supp. (No11), UN Doc A/2136 (1952) 3.

23 International Law Commission, 'Report of the Committee on International Criminal Jurisdiction' [1953] UN Doc A/2645, para 39.

24 Ibid. para 49.

25 Antonio Cassese, 'From Nuremberg to Rome: International Military Tribunals to the International Criminal Court' in Antonio Cassese, Paola Gaeta and John R. W. D. Jones (eds), *The Rome Statute of the International Criminal Court: A Commentary* (Oxford University Press 2002) 10.

26 Tofan and Wolf (n 5) 1.

27 UN General Assembly Resolution 44/39 (1989) UN Doc A/RES/44/39 (4 December 1989).

28 On the basis of the mandate of the General Assembly in Resolution 47/33 (1992) UN Doc A/RES/47/33 1992.

criminal court in 1992.[29] In regard to the definition of crimes and the jurisdiction of the court, the Working Group of the ILC suggested that customary international law and treaties were to be incorporated by references, rather than codified therein.[30] A possibility for a SC referral was not included in the Draft Code of Crimes Against the Peace and Security of Mankind, but was discussed. In his comments, Special Rapporteur Doudou Thiam wrote that a SC referral would 'exceed the powers vested in the Council by the Charter of the United Nations'.[31] Nevertheless, in 1994 the ILC adopted its draft Statute (hereinafter '1994 Draft Statute').[32] Article 23 entitled 'Action by the Security Council' provided:

> 1. Notwithstanding article 21 [preconditions to the exercise of jurisdiction], the Court has jurisdiction in accordance with this Statute with respect to crimes referred to in article 20 as a consequence of the referral of a matter to the Court by the Security Council acting under Chapter VII of the Charter of the United Nations.
> 2. A complaint of or directly related to an act of aggression may not be brought under this Statute unless the Security Council has first determined that a State has committed the act of aggression which is the subject of the complaint.
> 3. No prosecution may be commenced under this Statute arising from a situation which is being dealt with by the Security Council as a threat to or breach of the peace or an act of aggression under Chapter VII of the Charter, unless the Security Council otherwise decides.[33]

Generally, the jurisdiction of the court relied on the so-called 'opting-in procedure', which meant that the state does not automatically accept the competence of the Court by becoming a party, but must do this by way of a special decla-

---

[29] Sadat (n 13) 37–38.

[30] Report of the Working Group on the question of an international criminal jurisdiction, in report of the ILC on the work of its forty-fourth session, 47 UN GAOR Supp (No. 10), 106–107, UN Doc No 1/47/10 (1992).

[31] 'Ninth report on the Draft Code of Crimes against the Peace and Security of Mankind, by Mr. Doudou Thiam, Special Rapporteur', UN Doc. A/CN.4/435 & Corr. 1 and Add. 1 & Corr. 1, para 57. This related only to the jurisdiction of the Court over the crime of aggression. See also William Schabas, *The International Criminal Court: A Commentary on the Rome Statute* (Oxford commentaries on international law, Oxford University Press 2010) 293–94.

[32] ILC Report of 1994, vol II, Part II, UN Doc A/49/10.

[33] ILC, 'Report of the International Law Commission on the work of its forty-sixth session, 2 May–22 July 1994, Official Records of the General Assembly, Forty-ninth session, Supplement No. 10', 43–44.

ration either at the time of becoming a party or subsequently and with respect to specified crimes.[34]

Therefore, as a result of the operation of the phrase 'notwithstanding Article 21', it appears that where the Court has jurisdiction by virtue of a referral of a matter by the SC, the two major conditions stipulated in art 21 may be dispensed with. This means that there is no requirement for the prior lodging of a complaint by a state under art 25(2), and this is clearly stated in art 25(4).[35]

It was generally agreed that the ICC should be brought into a close relationship with the UN. The need for involvement of the SC in the work of the ICC more specifically was based on the recognition that the Court's jurisdiction over the most serious crimes of concern to the international community as a whole were similarly of concern to the SC, as such crimes most likely constitute threats to international peace and security. And the maintenance of international peace and security is the primary responsibility of the SC under the UN Charter.[36] Initially the ILC had envisioned a court that was perfectly subordinated to the SC and operating within the UN Charter.[37]

This raised the issue of whether the SC possessed the competence under Chapter VII to refer a matter to the ICC. As is evident from the 1994 Report

---

[34] Vera Gowlland-Debbas, 'The Relationship between the Security Council and the projected International Criminal Court' (1998) 3 *Journal of Conflict and Security Law* 97, 101.

[35] Ibid. This was not uncontested: discussions relating to art 25(1) of the 1994 ILC Draft Statute suggest that a referral from the Council would override the need for state consent. But it is not clear from the discussions whether this would apply to the exercise of jurisdiction or in relation to obligations to cooperate (see in particular, ILC 1994 Session, 2332nd Meeting, paras 1 and 49). During deliberations at the Rome Conference on the role of the Council (draft arts 10(1) and 10(3)), delegations which supported the Council's power to initiate proceedings were of the view that the enforcement powers of the Council bind 'all members of the United Nations'. See Lionel Yee, 'The International Criminal Court and the Security Council' in Roy S. Lee (ed), *The International Criminal Court: The Making of the Rome Statute; Issues, Negotiations, Results* (Kluwer Law International 2002) 147. But the intended effects of a referral were ambiguously explained. In his presentation to the Rome Conference, intervening on behalf of the ILC, James Crawford was of the view that a referral by the SC would serve as a 'substitute of consent' (Rome Conference, Official Records, Vol II, 2nd Plenary Meeting, para 106); D. R. Verduzco, 'The Relationship between the ICC and the United Nations Security Council' in Carsten Stahn (ed), *The Law and Practice of the International Criminal Court* (Oxford University Press 2015).

[36] See art 24(1) ILC Draft Statute.

[37] Mahnoush H. Arsanjani, 'The Rome Statute of the International Criminal' (1999) 93 *American Journal of International Law* 22; William Schabas, 'United States Hostility to the International Criminal Court: It's All About the Security Council' (2004) 15 *European Journal of International Law* 701.

of the International Law Commission,[38] the legality of the SC referral was doubted. The ILC sidelined this question. In its commentary, the Commission felt 'that such a provision [providing for SC referrals] was necessary in order to enable the Council to make use of the court, as an alternative to establishing *ad hoc* tribunals and as a response to crimes which affront the conscience of mankind'.[39] However, '[s]ome members of the Commission expressed concern at the possibility of the Security Council referring a particular case to the court in any circumstances at all.'[40] Most importantly, concern was expressed by some members at the 'linkage between the Security Council as a principal organ of the United Nations and a treaty body established by a certain number of States'.[41] The Commission eventually adopted the paragraph providing for the referral, concluding, however, that

> the Commission is not to be understood as taking any position as to the extent of the powers of the Security Council under Chapter VII of the Charter of the United Nations or otherwise, or as to the situations in which it is proper that these powers should be exercised.[42]

The possibility for the GA to refer cases was discussed, particularly for circumstances in which a situation is not referred to the ICC due to a veto in the SC, but was eventually rejected due to the non-binding nature of GA resolutions.[43]

The project was given further impetus by the establishment of the ad hoc tribunals ICTY (1993)[44] and ICTR (1995).[45] Their creation emphasized the need for a permanent international institution addressing serious violations

---

[38] Report of the International Law Commission on the work of its forty-sixth session (2 May–22 July 1994) UN Doc A/49/10, printed in *Yearbook of the International Law Commission* (1994) Report of the Commission to the General Assembly on the work of its forty-sixth session, vol II, part 2, A/CN.4/SER.A/1994/Add.1 (Part 2).

[39] Adding that '[o]n the other hand it did not intend in any way to add to or increase the powers of the Council as defined in the Charter, as distinct from making available to it the jurisdiction mechanism created by the statute'. Report of the International Law Commission on the work of its forty-sixth session (2 May–22 July 1994) UN A/CN.4/SER.A/1994/Add.l, part 2, 44, commentary 1 on art 23.

[40] Ibid. commentary 3.

[41] Ibid. commentary 4.

[42] Ibid. commentary 6.

[43] Ibid. commentary 5; see also Eighth Report on the Draft Code of Crimes Against the Peace and Security of Mankind (Doudou Thiam, Special Rapporteur) UN Doc A/CN.4/430 and Add.l (42nd session of the ILC (1990)) para 89.

[44] UNSC Res 808 (1993).

[45] UNSC Res 955 (1994).

of international humanitarian law.[46] These ad hoc tribunals were established through SC resolutions as subsidiary organs of the SC pursuant to art 29 of the UN Charter.[47] The leading ICL scholar Bassiouni thus concluded in 1998 that

> [t]he history and record of international criminal investigation and adjudication bodies, from the Treaty of Versailles to the International Criminal Court for Rwanda, clearly demonstrate the need to establish a permanent international criminal court. In the absence of such a court, not only have many atrocities gone unpunished, but every one of the *ad hoc* tribunals and investigations that has been created has suffered from the competing interests of politics or the influence of a changed geopolitical situation. As the history of the United Nations' efforts to establish a permanent international criminal court and a code of crimes evince, this task is controversial and complex. Nevertheless, the lessons of the past seventy-five years dictate its fundamental importance.[48]

Indeed, most judges of the ICTY voiced their support for the establishment of a permanent international criminal court by treaty in a plenary session.[49]

2.2.3 The Ad Hoc Committee 1995

Following the acceptance of the final report of the ILC, the GA established an ad hoc committee to prepare the international conference for the adoption of the Statute of the Court.[50] The role of the SC was still hotly debated. A majority of states supported the SC referral provided that the ICC had the option to accept or reject such referrals, while the US insisted that the Court should only have jurisdiction if interested states had consented to the exercise of such jurisdiction (supported by China, Russia and Middle Eastern states), others firmly rejecting such an approach.[51]

In April 1995, the Ad Hoc Committee identified, among other issues, the role of the SC as one of the most challenging to resolve. It was again suggested that the power to refer was not consistent with the SC's powers under the UN

---

[46] Sadat (n 13) 39–40.

[47] Dan Sarooshi, The United Nations and the Development of Collective Security: The Delegation by the UN Security Council of its Chapter VII Powers (Clarendon Press; Oxford University Press 1999) 95.

[48] Cherif M. Bassiouni, 'From Versailles to Rwanda in Seventy-Five Years: The Need to Establish a Permanent International Criminal Court' (1997) 10 *Harvard Human Rights Journal* 11, 11.

[49] Gowlland-Debbas (n 34) 97.

[50] General Assembly Res 49/53 (1994) UN Doc A/RES/49/53 (1 December 1994).

[51] Fanny Benedetti, Karine Bonneau and John L. Washburn, *Negotiating the International Criminal Court: New York to Rome, 1994–1998* (Martinus Nijhoff Publishers 2014) 29–31.

Charter.[52] The developments regarding the establishment of the ad hoc tribunals by virtue of SC resolutions under Chapter VII of the UN Charter certainly influenced this debate. In its report, the Ad Hoc Committee stated that

> several delegations were of the view that the Security Council should be authorized to refer matters to the court to obviate the need for the creation of additional ad hoc tribunals and to enhance the effectiveness of the court as a consequence of referrals made under Chapter VII of the Charter of the United Nations. The role envisaged for the Security Council was described as consistent with its primary responsibility for the maintenance of international peace and security and its existing powers under the Charter as reflected in recent practice. The Council, it was observed, would merely refer a general matter or situation to the court, as opposed to bringing a case against a specific individual – which would preserve the independence and autonomy of the court in the exercise of its investigative, prosecutorial and judicial functions. In this regard, reference was made to the modus operandi of the two ad hoc Tribunals established by the Security Council. The view was expressed that the intervention of the Security Council in triggering the jurisdiction of the court under the paragraph under consideration would be particularly relevant if the jurisdiction of the court were limited to the most serious crimes that might threaten international peace and security . . . It was also suggested that the elimination of the Council's role as envisaged in that paragraph would necessitate a more complex State consent regime, which would have the further drawback of resting on the political agenda of individual States rather than on the collective decision of the Security Council. There were different views as to whether a Security Council referral should obviate the need for State consent, as envisaged by the phrase 'notwithstanding article 21' as well as the commentary to the article.[53]

In this respect, the critics of such an approach pointed to the fact that a distinction should be drawn between the ad hoc tribunals instituted by the SC under Chapter VII and the future permanent court to be established on a consensual basis by the states parties to its statute.[54] However, most delegations regarded the SC referral as a simple recognition of the existing powers of the SC under the UN Charter and valuable for the effectiveness of the ICC.[55]

The prevailing view of delegations supporting the SC referral pointed to the removal of a need for the creation of ad hoc tribunals in future situations.[56]

---

[52] Report of the Ad Hoc Committee on the Establishment of an International Criminal Court 1995, UN Doc A/50/22 (6 September 1995) para 121.

[53] Report of the Ad Hoc Committee on the Establishment of an International Criminal Court UN Doc A/50/22 (1995) para 120.

[54] Ibid. para 121.

[55] Philippe Kirsch and Darryl Robinson, 'Reaching Agreement at the Rome Conference' in Cassese (n 25) 82–83.

[56] Yee (n 35) 146; Mauro Politi, 'The Rome Statute of the ICC: Rays of Light and Some Shadows' in Mauro Politi and Giuseppe Nesi (eds), *The Rome Statute of the International Criminal Court: A Challenge to Impunity* (Ashgate 2001) 13.

Important for the US[57] was the affirmation of the SC's role and the inclusion of art 16, which allows the SC to halt an investigation for a renewable term of one year acting under Chapter VII of the Charter.[58]

The work of the Ad Hoc Committee was continued in the Preparatory Committee from 1996–98. During the preparatory negotiations, the discussions focused on whether the SC could refer a 'case' or more broadly a 'matter' to the Court. The Preparatory Committee ultimately decided to exclude the referral of 'cases' to preserve the ability and independence of the Court to decide on prosecutions. The draft article discussed in the Rome Diplomatic Conference left open two more options for the referral of a matter or situation: the referral of a matter giving more direction on the prosecutions and the referral of a situation leaving the Court entirely free to decide upon which investigations to open.[59] The other part of the SC's mandate, the power to veto an investigation or prosecution, raised a particularly high degree of controversy. In August 1997, the Singapore proposal provided a basis for compromise. The proposal stated that on the basis of Chapter VII, the ICC could act unless the SC expressly decided otherwise.[60] The delegation of Canada proposed that the SC be permitted to defer a decision for a period of 12 months. This type of 'veto' would be, in practice, much more difficult to achieve as the investigation or prosecution would already be ongoing. As member of the Like-Minded Group, the UK was the first veto-yielding member[61] of the SC to accept the compromise and specify a new draft to be discussed at the Rome Diplomatic Conference.

2.3 THE NEGOTIATIONS IN ROME

The issues surrounding the SC referral were still not resolved at the beginning of the Diplomatic Conference in Rome. Indeed, it was not until the final days of the Diplomatic Conference in Rome that these issues were resolved.[62] States were still divided in Rome between those in favour of the ILC Statute (mainly the remaining four permanent members of the SC) and those supporting the

---

[57] David J. Scheffer, 'Staying the Course with the International Criminal Court' (2001–2002) 35 *Cornell International Law Journal* 47, 90–91.

[58] Ibid. 73.

[59] Draft Statute for the International Criminal Court and Draft Final Act (14 April 1998) ICC Doc A/CONF.183/2/Add.1, draft article 10.

[60] Singapore Proposal, A/AC.249/WP.51.

[61] On the political background for the UK to accept the compromise, see Rudolph (n 2) 94–102.

[62] Benedetti, Bonneau and Washburn (n 51) 29. For the political background of France accepting the compromise, see Rudolph (n 2) 102–106.

Singapore proposal, as well as the delegations opposing any role whatsoever for the SC.[63] The latter delegations put forward the argument that a role of the SC in the ICC would subject the functioning of the Court to the decisions of a political body and therefore undermine the Court's independence and credibility. Some felt that such a provision was unacceptable in that the SC referral would only be used against states other than the permanent members of the SC, due to their veto powers.[64]

A majority of states eventually recognized the responsibility of the SC in the field of international criminal justice and its involvement a necessary concession to the permanent members of the SC. Most delegations accepted the SC powers to do so, particularly referencing the precedent of the Appeals Chamber Judgment of the ICTY in the *Tadic* case.[65]

The final version of art 13 Rome Statute, as it stands today, thus reflects the result of profound compromises and intense bargaining between those who 'wanted a judicial body completely independent from any political influence, and those espousing the idea of a judicial institution subordinated to some form of political control'.[66] The referral power was eventually accepted because the political authority of the SC could empower international justice, by de facto extending its jurisdiction to non-member states.[67]

In all, arts 12 and 13 provide the Court with jurisdiction on the basis of territory or nationality of a state party, and theoretically with jurisdiction in non-member states by virtue of the SC referral. At the Rome Conference not all delegations supported giving the Council such powers, among their arguments being the view that as a political body the SC would undermine the ICC's independence and credibility.[68]

Important for the understanding of the SC referral as it stands is the fact that a proposal to endow the ICC with universal jurisdiction was rejected at the Diplomatic Conference in Rome. A proposal to this effect by the German

---

63 A/CONF.183/C.1/L.53.

64 Yee (n 35) 146–47.

65 *Tadic Case* (Decision on the Defence Motion for Interlocutory Appeal on Jurisdiction) ICTY-IT-94-l-A (2 October 1995).

66 Rosa Aloisi, 'A Tale of Two Institutions: The United Nations Security Council and the International Criminal Court' (2013) 13(1) *International Criminal Law Review* 147, 148.

67 Ibid. 149.

68 Yee (n 35) 146–47.

delegation[69] was rejected at the Rome Conference.[70] The formulation of art 12 was probably the only way out of the impasse.[71] According to art 12, in the sense of extending its jurisdiction, the Court will be allowed to proceed even against the nationals of states not parties to the Statute, without the consent of these states, when the crime is committed in the territory of another state that has accepted the Statute or explicitly recognized the Court's jurisdiction. This was one of the fundamental reasons for the opposition of the United States.[72] As a result, the ICC system was based on state consent, a concession to the sovereignty of states.[73]

When it became apparent that the final draft of the Rome Statute would include territorial jurisdiction as well as nationality jurisdiction, the US called for a vote in the very last hours of the Conference to eliminate territorial jurisdiction from the draft, but lost the vote by an overwhelming majority.[74] As a concession to those states who would have preferred more SC control, in particular the US, a compromise floated by Singapore was incorporated into the Rome Statute, which is now art 16 of the Statute providing for the power of the SC to halt investigations for a renewable period of 12 months.[75]

As a result, the US achieved its major objectives during the negotiations, namely a role preserved for the SC, including the affirmation of its powers to halt the ICC's work.[76] Other states such as India – as mentioned – rejected the final version of the Rome Statute because of the SC referral, arguing that the

---

69 The Jurisdiction of the International Criminal Court: An Informal Discussion Paper presented by Germany, UN Doc. A/AC 249/1998/DP 2. This proposal only enjoyed the firm support of some 25–30 states in Rome; see Hans-Peter Kaul, 'The International Criminal Court: Jurisdiction, Trigger Mechanism and Relationship to National Jurisdictions' in Politi (n 56) 61.

70 Gerhard Werle, *Völkerstrafrecht* (2nd edn, Mohr Siebeck 2007) 183. The Korean proposal was close to the idea of universal jurisdiction but could similarly not guarantee a wide support; Politi (n 56) 14. In favour see UN Doc. A/CONF.183/SR.3, para 21 (Czech Republic), para 42 (Latvia), para 76 (Costa Rica); UN Doc. A/CONF.183/SR.4, para 12 (Albania), paras 20–21 (Germany); UN Doc. A/CONF.183/SR.6, para 4 (Belgium), para 69 (Luxembourg); UN Doc. A/CONF.183/SR.8, para 18 (Bosnia and Herzegovina), para 62 (Ecuador). Rejecting the legality of such an approach see e.g., UN Doc. A/CONF.183/SR.9, para 28 (United States), para 37 (China).

71 Politi (n 56) 14.

72 Ibid. 14.

73 Sadat (n 13) 118.

74 Claudia Fritsche, 'Security Council Resolution 1422: Peacekeeping and the International Criminal Court' in Jochen A. Frowein (ed), *Verhandeln für den Frieden: Negotiating for Peace: liber amicorum Tono Eitel* (Beiträge zum ausländischen öffentlichen Recht und Völkerrecht vol 162 Springer 2003) 110.

75 Ibid. 112.

76 Scheffer (n 57) 73.

power to refer is unnecessary and unacceptable.[77] Finally, 120 states voted in favour, 7 states voted against the adoption of the Rome Statute, and 21 states abstained.[78]

2.4 DOUBLE STANDARDS AND THE SC REFERRAL

Despite the ideal of the ICC to end impunity and deliver equal justice, the SC referral mechanism of the ICC (coupled with the rejection of conferring universal jurisdiction to the Court) appears to be in some ways a continuation of applying a double standard in ICL. The permanent members of the SC not party to the ICC are put in a position to impose international criminal jurisdiction before an international criminal court, while not being subject to the same jurisdiction themselves. The ensuing limitations in practice are the consent-based system of its establishment and the SC referral mechanism.

First, the ICC was established as a consent-based system. This means that it is not likely that states that would be subjected to ICC jurisdiction against their will, would join the Court. In fact, David Bosco showed in his study that major powers have not joined the ICC, including the US, China, Russia, India and regional powers including Turkey, Egypt, Israel, Saudi Arabia, Pakistan and Indonesia.[79] Together, states not parties to the ICC account for almost three-quarters of the world's armed forces.[80] Historically this is not surprising because states have traditionally been very reluctant to 'internationalize' the processes of accountability for serious violations of humanitarian law.[81]

It is therefore interesting to note that from such a perspective, the establishment of the ICC appears to depart from the traditional international relations

---

[77] Dilip Lahiri, 'Explanation of Vote by Mr. Dilip Lahiri, Head of Delegation of India, on the Adoption of the Statute of the International Court' (Rome Conference, 17 July 1998). For the political background behind this, see Rudolph (n 2) 57–112.

[78] Official Records, United Nations Diplomatic Conference of Plenipotentiaries on the Establishment of an International Criminal Court Rome, (15 June–17 July 1998) A/CONF.183/1.

[79] David Bosco, *Rough Justice: The International Criminal Court in a World of Power Politics* (Oxford University Press 2014) 5. In a similar vein, see Stephen Hopgood, *The Endtimes of Human Rights* (Cornell University Press 2013) 14. See also Rudolph (n 2) 89–112.

[80] Bosco (n 79) 5.

[81] See Antonio Cassese, 'On the Current Trends Towards Criminal Prosecution and Punishment of Breaches of International Humanitarian Law' (1998) 9(1) *European Journal of International Law* 2, 6. One explanation might be found in the phenomenon called 'move to institutions'; for the most authoritative voices on this, see e.g. Martti Koskenniemi, *The Gentle Civilizer of Nations: The rise and Fall of International Law, 1870–1960* (Cambridge University Press 2002); David Kennedy, 'The Move to Institutions' (1987) 8 *Cardozo Law Review* 841.

accounts of how international organizations work.[82] International Relations scholars have generally assumed that international organizations are, in principle, the product of major-power interests. As Kenneth Abbot and Duncan Snidal have written, 'powerful states structure [international] organizations to further their own interests but must do so in a way that induces weaker states to participate'.[83] In case of the ICC, these major power structures do not seem to be visible in the organization.

However, the inclusion of the SC referral mechanism must be viewed as exactly that element of powerful states structuring the ICC to serve their interest.[84] The legislative history clearly demonstrates that the SC referral was a concession to major powers.[85] Scholarship has demonstrated that acting through international organizations may provide political advantages to powerful states.[86] The US delegate to the Rome Conference noted that, in fact, the objectives of the US Government in shaping the ICC were achieved.[87] The

---

[82] Major powers were always sceptical of the idea of a permanent international criminal court; see Bosco (n 79) 5; Rudolph (n 2) 20–39.

[83] Kenneth W. Abbott and Duncan Snidal, 'Why States Act through Formal International Organizations' (1998) 42(1) *Journal of Conflict Resolution* 3.

[84] See further, Gabriel M. Lentner, 'Victor's Justice in Disguise? UN Security Council Referrals and the International Criminal Court' (2016), available at http://voelkerrechtsblog.org/victors-justice-in-disguise/ (accessed 1 January 2018). See also B. S. Chimni, 'International Institutions Today: An Imperial Global State in the Making' (2004) 15(1) *European Journal of International Law* 1, 13–14; he points out that 'powerful states are unlikely to be the subject of [the Court's] attention . . . It is extremely unlikely that the leaders and armed personnel of Northern states would ever be dragged before the ICC'. Chimni also highlights the structural issues, fearing that international criminal tribunals, including the ICC, 'may be used to (a) threaten third world leaders who dare to question and oppose hegemonic states; and (b) give a humane and cathartic dimension to the ravages of global capitalism for it does not involve attention to the *international* causes of internal conflicts in third world societies, whose manifestation in unspeakable violence is their real subject'.

[85] Rudolph (n 2) 85–86.

[86] Alexander Thompson, 'Coercion Through IOs: The Security Council and the Logic of Information Transmission' (2006) 60(1) *International Organization* 1.

[87] Scheffer (n 57) 73. Further on the US position see J. P. Cerone, 'Dynamic Equilibrium: The Evolution of US Attitudes toward International Criminal Courts and Tribunals' (2007) 18(2) *European Journal of International Law* 277; Jennifer K. Elsea, 'U.S. Policy Regarding the International Criminal Court', CRS Report for Congress, American Law Division (updated 29 August 2006); Caroline Fehl, *Living with a Reluctant Hegemon: Explaining European Responses to US Unilateralism* (Oxford University Press 2011); Lee Feinstein and Tod Lindberg, *Means to an End: U.S. Interest in the International Criminal Court* (Brookings Institution Press 2009); Thomas M. Franck and Stephen H. Yuhan, 'The United States and the International Criminal Court: Unilateralism Rapant' (2003) 35 *International Law and Politics* 519; G. Hafner, 'An Attempt to Explain the Position of the USA towards the ICC' (2005) 3(2) *Journal of*

absence of compulsory jurisdiction over states not parties to the ICC limits the Court's independence particularly with respect to the permanent members of the SC: whether or not the ICC will gain jurisdiction over cases otherwise not covered by the Court's jurisdiction depends on them.[88] It must be further noted that even if powerful states are subject to the ICC's jurisdiction, the lack of any police force or other significant enforcement powers means that without the cooperation of the government concerned, prosecutions against the interest of a powerful government are almost impossible.[89] Indeed, it is interesting to note scholarship that has shown that international tribunals are more effective when they are not independent.[90]

International Criminal Justice 323; Robert C. Johansen, 'The Impact of US Policy toward the International Criminal Court on the Prevention of Genocide, War Crimes, and Crimes Against Humanity' (2006) 28(2) *Human Rights Quarterly* 301; Mark D. Kielsgard, *Reluctant Engagement: U.S. Policy and the International Criminal Court* (Studies in intercultural human rights v. 2, Martinus Nijhoff Publishers 2010); Harold Koh, 'On American Exceptionalism' (2003) 55 *Stanford Law Review* 1479; Jason G. Ralph, *Defending the Society of States: Why America Opposes the International Criminal Court and Its Vision of World Society* (Oxford University Press 2007); Leila N. Sadat, 'Summer in Rome, Spring in the Hague, Winter in Washington?: U.S. Policy Towards the International Criminal Court' (2003) 21 *Wisconsin International Law Journal* 557.

88 Yuval Shany (ed), *Assessing the Effectiveness of International Courts* (Oxford University Press 2014) 241.

89 The failed cases against the President and Vice-President of Kenya for their role in international crimes committed in the aftermath of the elections in 2007 are a case in point. On 5 April 2016, Trial Chamber V(A) decided, by majority, that the case against William Samoei Ruto and Joshua Arap Sang was to be terminated. In the Kenyatta case the confirmation of charges hearing took place from 21 September to 5 October 2011. Charges were withdrawn due to insufficient evidence; Marlise Simons and Jeffrey Gettleman, 'International Criminal Court Drops Case Against Kenya's William Ruto', *New York Times*, 5 April 2016, available at http://www.nytimes.com/2016/04/06/world/africa/william-ruto-kenya-icc.html?smid=tw-share&_r=0 (accessed 11 May 2016). Uganda is another example, as the Government refuses to cooperate with the court with respect to allegations of crimes committed by government forces in the conflict with the Lord's Resistance Army; see Sarah M. H. Nouwen, *Complementarity in the Line of Fire: The Catalysing Effect of the International Criminal Court in Uganda and Sudan* (Cambridge studies in law and society, Cambridge University Press 2013) 114ff.

90 See Eric A. Posner and John C. Yoo, 'Judicial Independence in International Tribunals' (2005) 93(1) *California Law Review* 1. For an overview on this debate see e.g. Tom Ginsburg, 'Political Constraints on International Courts' (2013) *Chicago Public Law and Legal Theory Working Paper* 484, 486, available at http://ssrn.com/abstract=2369970 (accessed 1 May 2018). Contra this view see e.g. Laurence R. Helfer and Anne-Marie Slaughter, 'Why States Create International Tribunals: A Response to Professors Posner and Yoo' (2005) 93 *California Law Review* 899. But see Eric A.

The SC referral mechanism ensures the influence of powerful states in that it breaks from the otherwise consent-based system of the ICC.[91] The SC may refer situations in states not parties to the Rome Statute to the jurisdiction of the ICC. In practice, the permanent members of the SC are given the power to veto or otherwise influence any such referral.[92] In other words, the SC referral gives these permanent members of the SC (which are not members of the ICC, namely China, Russia and the US) the power to refer situations to the ICC, without themselves necessarily being subjected to its jurisdiction.[93] As the ICC's 'selective geography of intervention' has demonstrated, prosecuting international crimes is an inherently political undertaking.[94] Hence, SC referrals are equally unlikely to involve a state where a P5 member has an interest in not bringing it before the ICC (see for example the situation involving Syria[95] or North Korea[96]) as the SC has no obligation to refer a case in which crimes under the statute appear to be committed.[97]

Posner and John C. Yoo, 'Reply to Helfer and Slaughter' 93 *California Law Review* 957.

91 In a similar vein, see Sara Kendal, 'Critical Orientations: A Critique of International Criminal Court Practice' in Christine E. J. Schwöbel (ed), *Critical Approaches to International Criminal Law: An Introduction* (2014) 58.

92 Regarding the jurisdictional exemptions included in the SC referrals, this study will show that the major powers will ensure they are exempted from the jurisdiction of the ICC through other means.

93 While the Rome Statute grants the ICC jurisdiction over nationals accused of crimes under the statute of non-state parties in cases in which the victims are nationals of a state party, the US pre-emptively secured their interest via art 98 agreements preventing any possible extradition of US nationals to the ICC. The ICC has no enforcement powers itself, and the legal obligation to hand over the accused in that scenario is neither clear nor undisputed.

94 Kendal (n 91) 58. See also Sarah M. H. Nouwen and W. G Werner, 'Doing Justice to the Political: The International Criminal Court in Uganda and Sudan' (2010) 21(4) *European Journal of International Law* 941. This is also what led political scientist Judith Shklar to conclude, writing in 1986 about the Nuremberg trials, 'that there was no political system resembling that of nation-states within which judicial institutions exist was clear enough. The Nuremberg Trial took place in a social vacuum. There was and is no system of international criminal law, just as there are no international community and no international political institutions to formulate or regularly enforce criminal laws. The U.N. was not even a going concern at that time, and its existence since then has not contributed anything to creating those social conditions on which criminal law must rest to be effective.' Judith N. Shklar, *Legalism: Law, Morals, and Political Trials* (Harvard University Press 1986) 157.

95 On Syria see particularly Rudolph (n 2) 160–71. See further Chapter 6.4.

96 Rudolph (n 2) 130–31.

97 Some authors claim that there is an obligation due to the *jus cogens* nature of the crimes, but this appears to be the case only *de lege ferenda* and not reflecting international law as it presently stands (*de lege lata*). For the argument that once the

All this is, of course, in stark contrast to the ICC's goal to end impunity. However, double standards in dealing with war crimes have deep roots. It was general practice and undisputed in ancient Greece and in ancient Rome that the victors had the right to enslave prisoners of war as punishment.[98] This probably led to the often-quoted passage in which Thrasymachus says in Plato's *Republic* that 'everywhere justice is the same thing, the advantage of the stronger'.[99]

Yet, the ideal behind a permanent international criminal court was precisely to end such double standards.[100] Indeed, the *raison d'être* of such a permanent institution lies in the fact that only through such an institution is it possible to depart from the double standard. The German philosopher Immanuel Kant realized that in the state of war, 'where no tribunal empowered to make judgments supported by the power of law exists', judgment would rest on power: 'neither party can be declared an unjust enemy (since this already presupposes a judgment of right) and the outcome of the conflict (as if it were a so-called "judgment of God") determines the side on which justice lies.'[101] The establishment of the ICC should overcome these problems and epitomize the ideal of actual international justice.

Whether the SC referral as it was included in the Rome Statute represents this ideal of justice is seriously questionable. This is because, as Hans Kelsen wrote in the aftermath of World War II,

> [i]t is not compatible with the idea of international justice that only the vanquished States should be obliged to surrender their subjects to the jurisdiction of international tribunal for the punishment of war crimes. The victorious States, too, should

---

responsibility to protect attains the status of a binding legal rule under international law, the SC and its members would be under the obligation to authorize or to take sufficiently robust action in situations that would fall under the concept of responsibility to protect, see Anne Peters, 'The Security Council's Responsibility to Protect' (2011) 8(1) *International Organizations Law Review* 15.

98 Karl-Heinz Ziegler, 'Vae victis – Sieger und Besiegte im Lichte des Römischen Rechts' in Otto Kraus (ed), *"Vae victis!" Über den Umgang mit Besiegten: Referate gehalten auf der Tagung der Joachim Jungius-Gesellschaft der Wissenschaften Hamburg am 31. Oktober und 1. November 1997* (Veröffentlichung der Joachim Jungius-Gesellschaft der Wissenschaften Hamburg Nr. 86. Vandenhoeck & Ruprecht 1998) 45. See also references to the practice of executing prisoners of war in Hugo Grotius, *De iure belli ac pacis libri tres* (trans. Walter Schätzel, Mohr Siebeck 1950) 508 (3, 11, 7).

99 Plato, *Republic* (Alan Bloom trans. book 1, Basic Books 1968), 339a, 16.

100 Sandström (n 12) 38–38a.

101 Immanuel Kant, *To Perpetual Peace: A Philosophical Sketch* (Ted Humphrey trans., Hackett Publishing 2003) 5. For the original German, see e.g. Immanuel Kant, *Zum ewigen Frieden: Ein philosophischer Entwurf* (Reclam 2008) 7–8.

> be willing to transfer jurisdiction over their own subjects who have offended the laws of warfare to the same independent and impartial international tribunal. *Only if the victors submit themselves to the same law which they wish to impose upon the vanquished States will the idea of international justice be preserved.*[102]

This points to the troubling conclusion that all the relevant and plausible justifications for adjudicative jurisdiction of an international criminal court to try defendants for legal wrongs committed during armed conflict are, in fact, not valid in case of the jurisdiction of the ICC. International adjudication is generally justified because states will often be unwilling to prosecute individuals, and even if they do, they are likely to prosecute low-ranking personnel while high-ranking officials most responsible are likely to enjoy impunity.[103] With a consent-based system, those states that are not willing to have their personnel subjected to international jurisdiction will refrain from joining the court or would not cooperate even when joining. The ICC is not in a position to hold trials without cooperation from the territorial state where the crimes in question took place, and where the suspects, witnesses and physical evidence are present.[104] Second, international adjudication is justified because states that prosecute enemy forces may impose (or appear to impose) 'victor's justice'.[105] As pointed out, with the SC referral mechanism the ICC may be subject to the same claims of double standards. Indeed, the jurisdictional exemptions provided for certain categories of nationals of non-party states could at least be framed as such.[106] Furthermore, the selective nature of SC referrals means that some situations are subject to criminal proceedings (e.g. Darfur and Libya) while other no less serious situations are not (e.g. Syria, North Korea). It is clear that such a selective approach rests on political considerations and not on a strict and universal enforcement of ICL.[107] In sum, the general justifications

---

[102] Hans Kelsen, *Peace through Law* (University of North Carolina Press 1944) 114–15 (emphasis added).

[103] Sigall Horovitz, Gilad Noam and Yuval Shany, 'The International Criminal Court' in Yuval Shany (ed), *Assessing the Effectiveness of International Courts* (Oxford University Press 2014) 223.

[104] Ibid. 245.

[105] Adil A. Haque, 'International Crime: in Context and in Contrast' in R. A. Duff et al (eds), *The Structures of the Criminal Law* (Oxford University Press 2011) 109–10.

[106] See further in Chapter 7.1.

[107] Horovitz, Noam and Shany (n 103) 223. Indeed, as regards US policy in decisions on transitional justice concerning Germany and Japan after World War II, the 1988 bombing of Pan Am flight 103, the 1990–1991 Iraqi offenses against Kuwaitis, the atrocities in the former Yugoslavia in the 1990s, and the 1994 Rwandan genocide, a recent study demonstrates that political and pragmatic factors have been more important than normative beliefs of the US Government: Zachary D. Kaufman, *United States Law and Policy on Transitional Justice: Principles, Politics, and Pragmatics* (Oxford

offered for international adjudication for an international criminal court are hardly fulfilled at the ICC.[108]

At the same time, the fact that international trials almost always concern highly political events, such as international or internal armed conflict, is a dilemma.[109] As Martti Koskenniemi put it:

> [Such a trial] will necessarily involve an interpretation of the context which is precisely what is disputed in the individual actions that are the object of the trial. To accept the terms in which the trial is conducted – what deeds are singled out, who is being accused – is to already accept one interpretation of the context among those between which the political struggle has been waged . . . [T]he context is always a part of the dispute itself. To understand the German bombing of Coventry and Birmingham in November 1940, with their over 1200 victims as a war crime, but not to see one in the carpet bombing of Germany that resulted in perhaps 600,000 civilian deaths is possible only if one already accepts the truth of the Allied view. Not to condemn Germany, and only Germany, would have put to question the justice of the Allied cause itself. The Nuremberg idiom presumed that the war had been launched as Axis aggression and that every atrocity came about as a consequence of it.[110]

University Press 2016). On the question of equality of states and individuals see also Sarah M. H. Nouwen, 'Legal Equality on Trial: Sovereigns and Individuals before the International Criminal Court' (2013) 43 *Netherlands Yearbook of International Law* 151–81. Voicing similar concerns regarding international criminal law, see Richard A. Falk, *Humanitarian Intervention and Legitimacy Wars: Seeking Peace and Justice in the 21st Century* (Global horizons vol 14, Routledge 2014) 36 ('the implementation of international criminal law is undertaken only against individuals on the losing side who are indeed responsible for substantive wrongdoing, while exempting individuals on the winning side').

[108] Similarly Hans Köchler, who views the systemic crisis of the ICC as rooted in both structural (related to Statute and ratification status) as well as performance-related issues: Hans Köchler, 'Justice and Realpolitik: The Predicament of the International Criminal Court' (2017) 16(1) *Chinese Journal of International Law* 1.

[109] Awareness of the shortcomings of the theory of international criminal law is, however, slowly growing; see Kai Ambos, 'Punishment without a Sovereign? The Ius Puniendi Issue of International Criminal Law: A First Contribution towards a Consistent Theory of International Criminal Law' (2013) 33(2) *Oxford Journal of Legal Studies* 293, 294. For a general critique of the theoretical shortcomings of the ICL project see also C. F. Stuckenberg, 'Völkerrecht und Staatsverbrechen' in J. Menzel, T. Pierlings and J. Hoffmann (eds), *Völkerrechtsprechung* (Mohr Siebeck 2005) 768, 772. See also generally on the lack of critique in ICL, Christine E. J. Schwöbel, 'The Comfort of International Criminal Law' (2013) 24(2) *Law Critique* 169, 170. For an overview of the philosophy of international criminal law, see Robert Cryer, 'The Philosophy of International Criminal Law' in Alexander Orakhelashvili (ed), *Research Handbook on the Theory and History of International Law* (Research handbooks in international law, Edward Elgar 2011) 232–67.

[110] Martti Koskenniemi, 'Between Impunity and Show Trials' in Jochen A. Frowein and Rüdiger Wolfrum (eds), *Max Planck Yearbook of United Nations Law* (vol 6 Kluwer Law International 2002) 16–17.

That is the reason why the political scientist Judith Shklar concluded that '[i]t is not the political trial itself but the situation in which it takes place and the ends that it serves which matter. It is the quality of the politics pursued in them that distinguishes one political trial from another'.[111] Ultimately, as Judith Shklar correctly points out, it is the political results that count.[112]

2.5 CONCLUSION

The historical development of the SC demonstrates the difficulties of the international community to reconcile the sometimes diverging interests of international criminal justice on the one hand, and the interests of major powers on the other. As was pointed out by the ICTY's comments, the Rome Statute 'presents an underlying tension between State sovereignty and the demands of international justice', a tension which 'may also be described as a contrast between consensualism and community interests'.[113]

What is striking is the absence of any mechanism for the prevention of international crimes. The ICC Statute mentions in its preamble the determination to prevent such crimes. The absence of any role for the SC to use its coercive powers for the prevention of international crimes is, of course, symptomatic for the problematic focus on accountability rather than prevention. As Michael Reisman correctly points out, this also has its historical roots in the Nuremberg trials. He points out that

> Nuremberg has, however, set one ironic precedent. In each of those mass murders, little or no effort was made to prevent or arrest them; on the contrary, the preferred strategy has always been 'Nurembergian' – to wait for the mass killings to play themselves out and *then* to establish criminal tribunals.[114]

---

[111] Shklar (n 94) 145.

[112] Ibid. 151.

[113] See Ad Hoc Committee on the Establishment of an International Criminal Court (3–13 April 1995) Comments received pursuant to paragraph 4 of General Assembly Resolution 49/53 on the Establishment of an International Criminal Court, Report of the Secretary-General (20 March 1995) UN Doc A/AC.244/1, 26–27.

[114] W. M. Reisman, 'Acting before Victims Become Victims: Preventing and Arresting Mass Murder' (2007–2008) 40 *Case Western Reserve Journal of International Law* 57, 60. In fact, as Saira Mohamed pointed out, the establishment of the ICTY/ICTR must also be understood as efforts to absolve the international community of its own sins of inaction: Saira Mohamed, 'Deviance, Aspiration, and the Stories We Tell: Reconciling Mass Atrocity and the Criminal Law' (2015) 124 *Yale Law Journal* 1628, 1685.

Also, there is only negligible evidence that international criminal accountability has a deterrent effect.[115]

In an overall assessment, the clear victory for international criminal justice and its fight against impunity for international crimes appears to be rather doubtful. The major powers were not ready to subordinate themselves to the jurisdiction of a strong, permanent international criminal court.[116] The threat of still ending up effectively applying a double standard in the enforcement of ICL was thus not overcome despite the general rhetoric to this effect in the preamble of the ICC.

The compromise reached in Rome reflects this paradox and leaves open a set of difficult questions that – as will be shown in the next chapter – are not answerable by mere treaty interpretation of the provisions included in the Statute. Indeed, what the historical analysis cannot deliver is a detailed account of the actual legal basis upon which the SC referral was justified under the rules of international law.

---

[115] Hopgood (n 79) 14. See also Immi Tallgren, 'The Sensibility and Sense of International Criminal Law' (2002) 13(3) *European Journal of International Law* 561, 569ff, 590 ('[e]verybody knows that prevention does not work, even if one hopes it might one day').On the evidence see Leslie Vinjamuri, 'Deterrence, Democracy, and the Pursuit of International Justice' (2010) 24(2) *Ethics & International Affairs* 191, 205–206. In fact, the notion of deterrence through accountability seems particularly misplaced in ICL because criminal law is built around a foundational belief in responsibility for wilful deviation from society's norms, and this cannot properly account for the fact that the ordinary perpetrator of mass atrocity crimes is 'normal' rather than deviant; see Mohamed (n 114) 1639.

[116] This fundamental dilemma was well captured in antiquity in Aeschylus' Agamemnon: 'Clytaemestra: . . . Why wasn't he the one/ you banished from the land in punishment/ for that foul act? Yet now you hear my case/ and all at once you are a ruthless judge./ Well, I warn you: threaten me all you want,/ and know that if you bring me down in a/ fair fight I am prepared to let you rule;/ But if by god's will it goes otherwise,/ you'll learn discretion, though you learn it late.' Aeschylus, 'Agamemnon' in Alan Shapiro and Peter Burian (eds) *The Oresteia* (Oxford University Press 2004) 94.

3. The legal nature of Security Council referrals

In the previous chapter, I demonstrated that the inclusion of the SC referral proved to be one of the most contentious issues during the preparatory work as well as at the Conference in Rome.[1] However, this debate concerned primarily the question of *what* role the SC should play with respect to the ICC and did not discuss the legal basis for any such role. Legal issues were raised as to whether the SC indeed possessed such powers, but this was soon overshadowed by political considerations and compromise. Whereas agreement on the text was reached during the negotiations in Rome, some questions remain open when one closely scrutinizes the underlying legal issues, particularly concerning the referral's legal qualification under international law.

This chapter thus analyzes the legal nature[2] of the SC referrals to the ICC. In the first part, a review of the literature will be conducted. I argue that existing scholarship has not yet offered a comprehensive theory that fully captures the SC referrals mechanism. Second, I clarify and respond to issues arising out of the principle of *pacta tertiis* to claim that action by the SC is necessary to provide a legal basis for the ICC to lawfully exercise jurisdiction. Third, the Relationship Agreement (RA) concluded between the UN and the ICC is analyzed to see whether it provides any clarifications of the legal relationship between the two institutions. Following an analysis of the judicial jurisdiction of the ICC, I conclude from these findings that the operation of SC referrals is best conceptualized as a conferral of powers from the SC to the ICC.

---

1 Christopher K. Hall, 'The First Two Sessions of the United Nations Preparatory Committee on the Establishment of an International Criminal Court' (1997) 91(1) *American Journal of International Law* 177, 181–82.

2 Black's Law Dictionary defines 'nature' as 'A fundamental quality that distinguishes one thing from another; the essence of something'; see *Black's Law Dictionary* (West Academic 2005) 867.

3.1 EXISTING SCHOLARSHIP AND CASE LAW

3.1.1 A Critical Review of Existing Scholarship

Article 13(b) of the Statute is the only provision dealing with the referral by the SC. It contains no detailed language of conditions or any particular mechanism for its operation.[3] Several interpretations regarding the relationship between the SC and the ICC have been put forward. These are distinguished by the extent of influence the SC may exercise regarding its scope. For example, Condorelli and Villalpando argue that the exercise of the SC's powers under art 13(b) is subject to certain conditions and limitations arising from the UN Charter but also the Statute and that, ultimately, these conditions and limitations are under the judicial control of the ICC itself.[4] Furthermore, Condorelli and Villalpando consider that

> the rules concerning the functioning of the Court and characterizing it as an independent judiciary body respectful of the principles of due process of law also find full application in case of referral of a situation by the Security Council; moreover, the Security Council cannot in any way modify those rules.[5]

The SC referrals' parameters and limitations are to be inferred 'from an interpretation of the Statute read as a whole and from the relevant provisions of the UN Charter'.[6]

In contrast, William Schabas argues that by 'triggering' the Court's jurisdiction, 'the Council must live within the parameters of the Rome Statute with respect to such matters as jurisdiction'.[7] According to this view, the act of referring implies the acceptance that investigation and prosecution will be conducted according to the Statute.[8] As a consequence, the SC could not extend

3 Luigi Condorelli and Santiago Villalpando, 'Referral and Deferral by the Security Council' in Antonio Cassese, Paola Gaeta and John R. Jones (eds), *The Rome Statute of the International Criminal Court* (Oxford University Press 2002) 629; William Schabas, *The International Criminal Court: A Commentary on the Rome Statute* (Oxford commentaries on international law, Oxford University Press 2010) 293.

4 Condorelli and Villalpando (n 3) 629. The question regarding judicial control, i.e. judicial review, will be addressed below.

5 Ibid. 629.

6 Ibid. See also Jennifer Trahan, 'The Relationship Between the International Criminal Court and the U.N. Security Council: Parameters and Best Practices' (2013) 24(4) *Criminal Law Forum* 417, 419.

7 Schabas (n 3) 301.

8 Ibid.

the ICC's jurisdiction, for example, beyond its temporal jurisdiction which is limited to crimes committed after the entry into force of the Statute.[9]

About the legal basis for the SC action, Condorelli and Villalpando identify the SC's power to create *ad hoc* international criminal tribunals under Chapter VII as applicable *mutatis mutandis* for the source for authority to refer cases to the ICC. They argue that

> under Article 39 of the Charter, the Security Council is entitled to 'decide what measures shall be taken in accordance with Articles 41 and 42, to maintain or restore international peace and security', and the referral to the ICC would fall squarely within its powers under Article 41 as constituting a measure 'not involving the use of armed force'.[10]

William Schabas equally finds the basis for such SC action in equating it to the now undisputed power of the SC to establish ad hoc tribunals.[11]

Upon closer inspection, several issues about the current state of research regarding the legal basis of SC referrals arise. First, the reasoning of the famous *Tadic* judgment that confirmed the legality of the establishment of the ad hoc tribunals applied *per analogiam* to the situation of a referral power of the SC ignores the fact that – as will be demonstrated in the next chapter – important legal differences exist between the establishment of ad hoc tribunals and the SC referral. These legal differences are decisive because the Appeals Chamber's reasoning relies on certain characteristics of the ad hoc tribunal for establishing the legality of their establishment which are not present in case of a SC referral.[12]

---

[9] Ibid. Here Schabas states: 'The SC cannot provide by resolution that the Court exercise jurisdiction prior to 1 July 2002, which is the start date of its temporal jurisdiction in accordance with article 11. Nor can it expand or otherwise alter the subject-matter jurisdiction of the Court defined in art. 5. It cannot authorize the prosecution of individuals for crimes committed under the age of eighteen, because this is prohibited by art 26. This logic may also extend to art 27(2), which removes the immunity of heads of state.' See also William Schabas, *Introduction to the International Criminal Court* (3rd edn, Cambridge University Press 2007) 169–70.

[10] Condorelli and Villalpando (n 3) 630.

[11] Schabas (n 9) 168. Sharing this view are Louise Arbour and Morten Bergsmo, 'Conspicuous Absence of Jurisdictional Overreach' in Herman von Hebel, J. G. Lammers and Jolien Schukking (eds), *Reflections on the International Criminal Court: Essays in Honour of Adriaan Bos* (T.M.C. Asser Press; Kluwer Law International 1999) 140. Another author views such referral power 'partly grounded' in the power of the SC to establish ad hoc tribunals without further elaboration: Deborah R. Verduzco, 'The Relationship between the ICC and the United Nations Security Council' in Carsten Stahn (ed), *The Law and Practice of the International Criminal Court* (Oxford University Press 2015) 32.

[12] See Chapter 4.1.

Another issue concerns the compatibility of the SC referral with the law of treaties. The ICC Statute's status as an international treaty means that it binds the contracting states only.[13] It is a general rule of international law, codified in art 34 of the Vienna Convention on the Law of Treaties (VCLT), that 'a treaty does not create either obligations or rights for a third state without its consent'.[14] The referral means that a state not party to the Rome Statute must be considered to be bound by the provisions of the Statute by virtue of the SC decision.[15] In other words, broadening the scope of the ICC's jurisdiction to include non-party states through a SC referral could undermine the law of treaties.[16] This view was prominently voiced by the Representative of India during the Rome Conference, stating that 'the power to bind non-States Parties to any international treaty is not a power given to the Council by the Charter'.[17] Contrary to this argument, some writers argue that while it would be difficult to construe the SC's powers under the Charter to bind a state to a treaty,[18] the SC referral does not, according to this view, make the Rome Statute binding

---

[13] Gennady M. Danilenko, 'ICC Statute and Third States' in Cassese (n 3) 1871; Alexandre Galand, 'Security Council Referrals to the International Criminal Court as Quasi-Legislative Acts' (2015) 19 *Max Planck Yearbook of United Nations Law* 142, 143–44.

[14] The general rule *pacta tertiis nec nocent nec prosunt* is supported, as the International Law Commission has observed, by 'almost universal agreement'; see International Law Commission, 'Report of the International Law Commission on the Work of its Eighteenth Session' (UN Doc A/6309/Rev.1. 1966) 226. On the general issue of the evolving erosion of the consent requirement in international law see e.g. Anne Peters, 'Global Constitutionalism Revisited' (2005) 11 *International Legal Theory* 39, 51; Nico Krisch, 'The Decay of Consent: International Law in an Age of Global Public Goods' (2014) 108(1) *American Journal of International Law* 1.

[15] Dapo Akande, 'The Legal Nature of Security Council Referrals to the ICC and its Impact on Al-Bashir's Immunities' (2009) 7(2) *Journal of International Criminal Justice* 333, 342; Michael Wood, 'The Law of Treaties and the UN Security Council: Some Reflections' in Enzo Cannizzaro (ed), *The Law of Treaties Beyond the Vienna Convention* (Oxford University Press 2011) 250; A. G. Kiyani, 'Al-Bashir & the ICC: The Problem of Head of State Immunity' (2013) 12(3) *Chinese Journal of International Law* 467, 481.

[16] See Dilip Lahiri, 'Explanation of Vote by Head of the Delegation of India on the Adoption of the International Criminal Court' (Rome Conference, 17 July 1998), available at www.un.org/icc/speeces/717ind.htm (accessed 11 November 2015). Contra this view see e.g. Arbour and Bergsmo (n 11) 140.

[17] Lahiri (n 16).

[18] Critically also Kiyani (n 15) 504–505. See however, Stefan Talmon, 'Security Council Treaty Action' (2009) 62(1) *Revue hellénique de droit international* 65. On this issue, see the detailed discussion below (quasi-legislative powers of the SC, Chapter 5.5.2).

upon states that have not ratified it, but only give effect to its provisions.[19] In a similar vein, Bardo Fassbender sees in the referral nothing more than establishing criminal jurisdiction, which does not necessarily have to be exercised through a subsidiary organ of the SC.[20]

The problem regarding the *pacta tertiis* principle is not easily dismissed. The distinction between being bound by the provisions of a treaty but not by the treaty itself appears to be artificial, particularly because the Statute asserts the right of the Court to determine its own jurisdiction and thus giving authority to it. This will be further addressed in section 3.2 of this chapter.

Avoiding such difficulties, some authors argue that the legal basis for the exercise of jurisdiction by the ICC is based on the universal jurisdiction and only 'triggered' by the SC in cases of non-party states.[21] The source of the jurisdiction of the ICC over situations in non-party states is – according to this view – not dependent on the SC acting under Chapter VII but upon the *jus cogens* nature of the crimes under the jurisdiction of the Court.[22]

---

[19] Wood (n 15) 250; Kiyani (n 15) 481. Similarly Akande (n 15) 341, who argues that 'a non-party to the Statute is bound by the Statute in the case of a referral in the sense that it is bound to accept the jurisdiction of the Court and legality of the Court's operation in accordance with its Statute'.

[20] Bardo Fassbender, 'Reflections on the International Legality of the Special Tribunal for Lebanon' (2007) 5 *Journal of International Criminal Justice* 1091, 1097. Similarly, Sarah Nouwen argues that '[j]ust as the Council has been considered to have the competence to establish international tribunals by resolution, so it has the power to refer matters to existing courts'; Sarah M. H. Nouwen, *Complementarity in the Line of Fire: The Catalysing Effect of the International Criminal Court in Uganda and Sudan* (Cambridge studies in law and society, Cambridge University Press 2013) 256–57.

[21] See the discussions in Roger O'Keefe, *International Criminal Law* (Oxford University Press 2015) 541; Leila N. Sadat, 'The International Criminal Court' in William Schabas (ed), *The Cambridge Companion to International Criminal Law* (Cambridge companions to law, Cambridge University Press 2016); Cherif M. Bassiouni, *The Legislative History of the International Criminal Court* (International and comparative criminal law series, Transnational Publishers 2005) 135; Cherif M. Bassiouni, 'Universal Jurisdiction for International Crimes: Historical Perspectives and Contemporary Practice' (2001) 42 *Virginia Journal of International Law* 81, 106. Similarly, some authors saw in the principle of universality the jurisdictional basis for the ad hoc tribunals, see e.g., Revised Report of the Working Group on the Draft Statute for an International Criminal Court, UN Doc A/CN.4/L.490 and Add.1 (1993) 72–73; Yoram Dinstein, 'The Universality Principle and War Crimes' in Michael Schmitt and Leslie Green (eds), *The Law of Armed Conflict: Into the Next Millennium* (Naval War College 1998) 17–37. See further Madeline Morris, 'High Crimes and Misconceptions: The ICC and Non-party States' (2001) 64 *Law and Contemporary Problems* 13, 35–36.

[22] Explaining the reasoning behind this, see e.g. Leila N. Sadat, *The International Criminal Court and the Transformation of International Law: Justice for the New Millennium* (International and comparative criminal law series, Transnational Publishers 2002) 270.

This argument that the ICC's lawful exercise of jurisdiction is independent from the acceptance of the states not party to the Rome Statute or the binding nature of SC decisions is difficult to support.[23] In this context the term 'universal jurisdiction' seems to be used in the sense that states parties to the ICC have delegated their powers to exercise universal jurisdiction to the ICC and the ICC is merely exercising this delegated universal jurisdiction, thus not requiring consent or any other legal source for such exercise of jurisdiction.[24] The main problem with this view is that not all crimes included in the Rome Statute give rise to universal jurisdiction, so it remains doubtful whether states that do not possess the right to exercise universal jurisdiction are nevertheless capable of delegating universal jurisdiction over these crimes to the ICC. Furthermore, the concept of universal jurisdiction would only allow for the exercise of adjudicative jurisdiction; it does not create any obligations to cooperate with the prosecution or give effect to decisions of the Court.[25] Also,

---

[23] Dan Sarooshi, 'The Peace and Justice Paradox: The International Criminal Court and the UN Security Council' in Dominic McGoldrick, Peter Rowe and Eric Donnelly (eds), *The Permanent International Criminal Court: Legal And Policy Issues* (Hart Publishing 2004) 98: 'The Security Council can, however, enhance considerably the jurisdictional reach of the ICC by using its power of referral in relation to situations involving non-States Parties. Such referrals would in effect allow the ICC to exercise its jurisdiction in relation to non-States Parties, a jurisdiction that would not exist but for the Security Council's referral'.

[24] William Schabas, *An Introduction to the International Criminal Court* (4th edn, Cambridge University Press 2011) 65. Similarly Michael P. Scharf, 'The ICC Jurisdiction over the Nationals of Non-party States: A Critique of the U.S. Position' (2004) 64 *Law and Contemporary Problems* 67, 72–75. Contra this view see e.g. Morris (n 21) 50–51; David J. Scheffer, 'Staying the Course with the International Criminal Court' (2001–2002) 35 *Cornell International Law Journal* 47, 65.

[25] Absent a permissive rule of international law. Adjudicative jurisdiction and enforcement jurisdiction are separate concepts and universal jurisdiction does not provide for the latter. This is illustrated by the Eichmann trial. Adolph Eichmann was kidnapped in Argentina by Israel and prosecuted in Jerusalem in 1961 for crimes against humanity and war crimes based on universal jurisdiction: *Attorney General of Israel v Eichmann*, 36 ILR 277, 299, 304 (Israel Supreme Court 1962). The SC rightfully condemned Israel for violating Argentina's territorial sovereignty for the abduction, but did not question the jurisdiction to try him; see UNSC Res 138 (23 June 1960) UN Doc S/RES/138. See also Roger O'Keefe, 'Universal Jurisdiction: Clarifying the Basic Concept' (2004) 2(3) *Journal of International Criminal Justice* 735, 736. For other authors some general confusion exists regarding the concept of universal jurisdiction. To clarify: '"Universal jurisdiction" is generally defined as "refers to the competence of a state under international law to criminalize and, should the occasion arise, prosecute conduct when no other internationally recognized prescriptive link – chief among them territoriality, nationality, passive personality and the protective principle – exists at the time of the alleged commission of the offence"'; see ibid.; Roger O'Keefe, 'The Grave Breaches Regime and Universal Jurisdiction' (2009) 7(4) *Journal of International*

the ICC was clearly not endowed with universal jurisdiction.[26] While such basis for the ICC's jurisdiction was proposed during the negotiations, it was eventually rejected.[27] And even if it had been adopted, it remains questionable whether it could lawfully be exercised.[28]

Roger O'Keefe acknowledges this problem and argues that because the SC is not bound by general international law, it may authorize the ICC to exercise universal jurisdiction beyond those crimes.[29] It is then, of course, the SC's powers that enable the ICC to exercise jurisdiction and not the universal jurisdiction that states have supposedly delegated to the ICC.

Criminal Justice 811. Similarly, Scharf argues that 'the delegation of jurisdiction to the ICC would be compatible with the non-prejudice principle since no right of the state of nationality of the accused is prejudiced by assignment of the case to an international criminal court'. Scharf (n 24) 75.

[26] Dapo Akande, 'The Jurisdiction of the ICC over Nationals of Non-Parties: Legal Basis and Limits' (2003) 1 *Journal of International Criminal Justice* 618, 623.

[27] The proposal (UN Doc A/AC 249/1998/DP 2.) was met with two objections, one based on the fact that universal jurisdiction is rarely exercised, and the other one doubting the legality to exercise the universal jurisdiction; see UN Doc A/CONF.183/SR.9, para 28 (US), para 37 (China). See also Michael A. Newton, 'How the International Criminal Court Threatens Treaty Norms' (2016) 49 *Vanderbilt Journal of Transnational Law* 371, 380. For a discussion of the variety proposals in favour of an 'inherent jurisdiction', see Schabas (n 3) 278–83; Newton (n 27) 383–84; see also Bartram Brown, 'Primacy or Complementarity: Reconciling the Jurisdiction of National Courts and International Criminal Tribunals' (1998) 23 *Yale Journal of International Law* 383, 417–28, discussing the advantages and disadvantages of such an approach.

[28] But see Werle, who argues that under international law this would be permissible, although not adopted in the Rome Statute: Gerhard Werle, *Völkerstrafrecht* (2nd edn, Mohr Siebeck 2007) 183. On the problems regarding universal jurisdiction see e.g. *Case Concerning the Arrest Warrant of 11 April 2000 (Democratic Republic of Congo v Belgium)* [2002] ICJ Rep 3; Separate Opinion of Judge ad hoc Bula-Bula, paras 9–14; Separate Opinion of President Guillaume, para 15. For a very critical view on the concept of universal jurisdiction see Luc Reydams, 'The Rise and Fall of Universal Jurisdiction' in William Schabas and Nadia Bernaz (eds), *Routledge Handbook of International Criminal Law* (Routledge handbooks, Routledge 2011) 350. For the views of governments regarding the concept of universal jurisdiction, see particularly UNGA, 'Report of the Secretary-General: The Scope and Application of the Principle of Universal Jurisdiction' (1 July 2015) UN Doc A/70/125. See also regarding the concern and criticism on the part of African states of the principle of universal jurisdiction, e.g. the creation and work of the African Union Commission on the Abuse of the Principles of Universal Jurisdiction.

[29] O'Keefe (n 21) 541.

3.1.2 The Chambers' View

The Chambers of the ICC themselves did not directly address these issues. In one case, the Pre-Trial Chamber I merely noted that

> article 12(2) [setting out as preconditions to the exercise of jurisdiction the consent of the territorial state or the state of the nationality of the accused] does not apply where a situation is referred to the Court by the Security Council acting under Chapter VII of the Charter, pursuant to article 13(b) of the Statute. Thus, the Court may, where a situation is referred to it by the Security Council, exercise jurisdiction over crimes committed in the territory of States which are not Party to the Statute and by nationals of States not Party to the Statute.[30]

Regarding the first SC referral, concerning the situation in Darfur, the Pre-Trial Chamber I held that

> by referring the Darfur situation to the Court, pursuant to article 13(b) of the Statute, the Security Council of the United Nations has also accepted that the investigation into the said situation as well as any prosecution arising therefrom, will take place in accordance with the statutory framework provided for in the Statute, the Elements of Crimes and the Rules as a whole.[31]

In another decision, the single judge found that

> [i]n respect of the question whether the Chamber has jurisdiction over the Situation in Darfur, Sudan, the Single Judge notes that the Situation in Darfur, Sudan was referred to the Prosecutor of the Court by the United Nations Security Council on 31 March 2005. On 1 June 2005, the Prosecutor initiated an investigation into the Situation in Darfur, Sudan. Therefore, pursuant to article 13(b) of the Statute, the Court may exercise its jurisdiction over crimes committed in Darfur, Sudan.[32]

However, the Court did not provide any further legal justification for its findings but appears to simply assume the SC's powers and its competences in this area.[33]

---

[30] *Prosecutor v Harun and Kushayb* (Decision on the Prosecution) ICC-02/05-01/07-1-Corr (27 April 2007), para 16.

[31] *Prosecutor v Omar Hassan Ahmad Al-Bashir* (Decision of the Pre-Trial Chamber I on the Prosecution's Application for a Warrant of Arrest against Omar Hassan Ahmad Al-Bashir) ICC-02/05-01/09 (4 March 2009) para 45.

[32] *Decision on the Applications for Participation in the Proceedings of Applicants a/0011/06 to a/0015/06, a/0021/07, a/0023/07 to a/0033/07 and a/0035/07 to a/0038/07* (Decision) ICC-02/05 (14 December 2007) para 6.

[33] It is also submitted here that, as a separate international institution, the ICC's pronouncement of the legal basis for the SC's actions vis-à-vis the ICC can only be

3.2 THE NEED FOR SC ACTION: THE *PACTA TERTIIS* PRINCIPLE

The Rome Statute explicitly recognizes the fact that it cannot bind third states. Article 4(2) provides that the 'Court may exercise its functions and powers, as provided in this Statute, on the territory of any state party and, by special agreement, on the territory of any other State'. This means that in principle 'any extension of the powers of the Court as regards third States must be based on a strict consensual basis'.[34] The obligations arising out of the Statute are therefore obligations only for states parties. This is of course in accordance with the well-established principle of international law reflected by art 34 of the VCLT (*pacta tertiis* principle).[35] It follows that the obligations to cooperate with the Court put forward in Part 9 of the Statute cannot as such impose obligations upon states not party to the treaty.[36]

In principle, as the legal order of an international organization, the Rome Statute of the ICC has the same status for third states as the legal order of any foreign state.[37] Madeline Morris even claims that 'by conferring upon the ICC jurisdiction over non-party nationals, the ICC Treaty would abrogate

---

understood as a subsidiary means to determine such legal basis, and does not by itself confirm its legality.

[34] Francesca Martines, 'Legal Status and Powers of the Court' in Cassese (n 3) 215, pointing out that 'the same would have been true if the Court had been endowed with jurisdiction without the existence of a link. In this case even in the presence of universal jurisdiction, the exercise of the powers and functions of the Court (as, for instance, the calling of witnesses) would in any case have been limited to the State Parties to the Statute.'

[35] Annalisa Ciampi, 'The Obligation to Cooperate' in Cassese (n 3) 1608–9. Article 34 VCLT (considered consonant with customary international law).

[36] O'Keefe (n 21) 563. The wide acceptance of the Rome Statute notwithstanding, *pacta tertiis nec nocent nec prosunt* remains the general rule and 'rights and obligations of third States stemming from treaties to which they are not parties remain exceptional'; Malgosia A. Fitzmaurice, 'Third Parties and the Law of Treaties' (2002) 6 *Max Planck Yearbook of United Nations Law* 37, 136; see also *Case Concerning the Factory at Chorzow (Germany v Poland) (Merits)* PCIJ Rep Series A No 17, 45; *Customs Regime between Germany and Austria* (Advisory Opinion) PCIJ Rep Series A/B No 41, 48. As Roger O'Keefe correctly points out, '[i]t is axiomatic that treaties are binding only on the states parties to them; O'Keefe, 'The Grave Breaches Regime and Universal Jurisdiction' (n 25) 811 fn 4 (with further references).

[37] Henry G. Schermers, 'The Legal Bases of International Organization Action' in René-Jean Dupuy (ed), *A Handbook on International Organizations* (2nd edn, Les livres de droit de l'Académie/ Académie de Droit International de La Haye, Nijhoff 1998) 405. Interestingly, the rhetoric of the preamble of the Statute points to the drafters' claim of being an organization that acts on behalf of the international community as a whole. For a critical analysis of this so-called 'we-talk' in international criminal law,

the pre-existing rights of non-parties which, in turn, would violate the law of treaties'.[38] In support she cites the ILC's official Commentaries on the Vienna Convention, which states that '[i]nternational tribunals have been firm in laying down that in principle treaties, whether bilateral or multilateral, neither impose obligations on States which are not parties *nor modify in any way their legal rights* without their consent'.[39] From this she argues that 'the right of a state to be free from the exercise of exorbitant enforcement jurisdiction over its nationals cannot be abrogated by a treaty to which it is not a party'.[40] However, as Dapo Akande correctly points out, states parties to the ICC have a right 'to create an international court endowed with the criminal jurisdiction ordinarily possessed by the parties'.[41] What they cannot of course delegate to the ICC is enforcement jurisdiction in the territory of another state. In other words, any enforcement measures with respect to non-party nationals in the territory of non-party states would violate that state's sovereignty under international law.[42]

Equally flowing from the ICC's status as established by a multilateral treaty, the Court's jurisdiction over crimes set forth in the Statute is, in principle, limited to state parties pursuant to art 12 of the Statute.[43] In fact, art 12, under the heading of 'preconditions for the exercise of jurisdiction' provides jurisdiction only in cases where the states could have acted individually on

---

see e.g. I. Tallgren, 'The Voice of the International: Who is Speaking?' (2015) 13(1) *Journal of International Criminal Justice* 135.

[38] Morris (n 21) 26–27. She also cites Arnold McNair, *The Law of Treaties* (Clarendon Press 1961) 321 ('A State which learns that a treaty concluded between two other States has for its object or probable consequence the impairment of its rights, whether enjoyed under customary international law or under a treaty with one of the contracting parties, is entitled at once to lodge a diplomatic protest with those parties and to apply to the International Court of Justice . . . for a declaration and . . . for interim measures of protection.').

[39] ILC, 'Report of the International Law Commission on the Work of its eighteenth Session' (4 May–19 July 1966) UN Doc A/CN.4/SER.A/1966/Add.1, 226. See also Roger O'Keefe, 'The United States and the ICC: The Force and Farce of the Legal Arguments' (2011) 24 *Cambridge Review of International Affairs* 343. Emphasis added.

[40] Morris (n 21) 27. Contra this view, see Dapo Akande, 'The Jurisdiction of the International Criminal Court over Nationals of Non-Parties: Legal Basis and Limits' (2003) 1 *Journal of International Criminal Justice* 618.

[41] Akande (n 26) 649.

[42] *The case of the SS 'Lotus'*, Judgment (7 September 1927) PCIJ Rep Series No 10, 18–19.

[43] Kenneth S. Gallant, 'The International Criminal Court in the System of States and International Organizations' (2003) 16(3) *Leiden Journal of International Law* 553, 580.

the basis of the territoriality principle or nationality principle.[44] Interestingly, this provision does not contain a reference to the SC referral. Furthermore, as discussed above, art 4(2) makes clear that the ICC does not assert powers over states not party to the Rome Statute.

However, the Statute does provide for the possibility to exercise its powers over non-party states under certain circumstances: in cases provided for *by special agreement*.[45] What this provision omits is any reference to the special situation concerning the assertion of the ICC to exercise jurisdiction in case of SC referrals. While the ICC Statute generally provides the Court with jurisdiction only in cases where the state concerned has consented to it (see art 12 Rome Statute), the possibility of a SC referral pursuant to art 13(b) clearly departs from this consent-based system and asserts jurisdiction over situations (in which crimes appear to have been committed) referred to it by the SC acting under Chapter VII.[46] This exercise of jurisdiction over situations in non-party states is problematic since it is not based on the consent or acceptance of the ICC by the state concerned.[47] It is these third states that are affected by a SC referral.[48] Therefore, unlike state party referrals or the Prosecutor acting

---

[44] Akande (n 26) 621–22; Scharf (n 24) 98; Danilenko (n 13) 1874.

[45] The same would have been true without such explicit reference, since the exercise of the powers and functions of the Court (as, for instance, the calling of witnesses) would in any case have been limited to the State Parties to the Statute; see Ralf Michaels, 'Recognition and Enforcement of Foreign Judgments' in Rüdiger Wolfrum (ed), *Max Planck Encyclopedia of Public International Law* (Oxford University Press 2009) 11; Martines (n 34) 215.

[46] The ICC Statute also asserts jurisdiction over situations in non-state parties in cases where the state has accepted the jurisdiction of the Court (see art 12(3)) and over nationals of third states when it appears that they committed crimes on territory of a state party. The latter constitutes of course a lawful exercises of criminal jurisdiction of states delegated to the ICC and thus does not pose any problems under the *pacta tertiis* principle.

[47] See e.g. *Prosecutor v Al-Bashir* (Decision on the Prosecutor's Request for a Finding of Non-Compliance Against the Republic of the Sudan) ICC-02/05-01/09 (9 March 2015) para 13; *Prosecutor v Hussein* (Decision on the Prosecutor's Request for a finding on non-compliance against the Republic of the Sudan) ICC-02/05-01/12 (26 June 2015) para 12. While the 'erosion' or 'decay' of consent may be witnessed in international law generally, it must be noted that the principle of *pacta tertiis nec nocent nec prosunt* remains the general rule and that rights and obligations of third states stemming from treaties to which they are not parties remain exceptional. See further Krisch (n 14); Fitzmaurice (n 36); Peters (n 14).

[48] Luigi Condorelli and Annalisa Ciampi, 'Comments on the Security Council Referral of the Situation in Darfur to the ICC' (2005) 3(3) *Journal of International Criminal Justice* 590, 593. While the Rome Statute also provides for the referral of a situation of a state party to the ICC by the SC, the present study concerns only SC referrals over non-state parties.

proprio motu, the SC referral endows the Court with jurisdiction which it otherwise would not possess, and imposes obligations on a state flowing from a treaty it has not consented to.[49] These concerns were indeed raised at the Conference in Rome,[50] but were not addressed further. The root cause of this is the linkage between the SC as a principal organ of the UN and a treaty body established by a certain number of states,[51] which results in blurring the actual legal basis of SC referrals.

In conclusion, without the binding nature of SC resolutions under Chapter VII, the ICC would not be authorized to exercise jurisdiction in non-party states.[52] It is true that, by itself, the decision to confer jurisdiction to an international tribunal does not necessarily require the state concerned to do anything.

---

[49] Trahan (n 6) 419. The jurisdictional authority in this case is similar to that of the SC establishment of the ICTY/ICTR; see Morris (n 21) 35–36. On the other hand, Bekou and Cryer as well as Condorelli and Clampi argue that states have passed on their universal jurisdiction to the ICC and this is exercised by virtue of the SC referral; see Condorelli and Ciampi (n 48) 593; Olympia Bekou and Robert Cryer, 'The International Criminal Court and Universal Jurisdiction: A Close Encounter?' (2007) 56(1) *International & Comparative Law Quarterly* 49. This is not entirely convincing since universal jurisdiction primarily concerns jurisdiction of domestic courts; see particularly Morris (n 21) 27–43. Generally O'Keefe, 'Universal Jurisdiction' (n 25); Bruce Broomhall, *International justice and the International Criminal Court: Between Sovereignty and the Rule of Law* (Oxford University Press 2004) 106.

[50] GA, 'Report of the Ad Hoc Committee on the Establishment of an International Criminal Court Fiftieth Session' (1996) UN Doc No 22 A/50/22, paras 120–21; Report of the Preparatory Committee, UN Doc A/51/22 (1996) paras 132–36. See further references in Morten Bergsmo, 'Occasional Remarks on Certain State Concerns about the Jurisdictional Reach of the International Criminal Court, and Their Possible Implications for the Relationship between the Court and the Security Council' (2000) 69 *Nordic Journal of International Law* 87, 93; Lionel Yee, 'The International Criminal Court and the Security Council' in Roy S. Lee (ed), *The International Criminal Court: The Making of the Rome Statute; Issues, Negotiations, Results* (Kluwer Law International 2002) 146.

[51] ILC, 'Report of the International Law Commission on the work of its forty-sixth session' (2 May–22 July 1994) UN Doc A/49/10, 44; see also the discussion surrounding the establishment of the Special Tribunal for Lebanon (STL), established by an 'Agreement' between the United Nations and the Lebanese Republic pursuant to Security Council Resolution 1664 (2006) of 29 March 2006; SC Res. 1757 (2007); the recent findings of its Appeals Chamber refrained from considering arguments challenging the legality of its establishments without giving any convincing arguments. This casts doubt on the predominant understanding of the powers of the UN SC in the field of international criminal law; see the Appeals Chamber of the Special Tribunal avoiding this question: Ayyash et al., *Decision on the Defence Appeals against the Trial Chamber's 'Decision on the Defence Challenges to the Jurisdiction and Legality of the Tribunal'*, STL-II-OIIPT/AC/AR90.1 (24 October 2012), paras 36–53.

[52] See further Akande, (n 15) 341. See mutatis mutandis e.g. Jochen A. Frowein and Nico Krisch, 'Chapter VII. Action with respect to Threats to the Peace, Breaches of the

However, a non-party state would then not have to accept the exercise of jurisdiction in its territory and would not be obliged to cooperate with and carry out the decisions of the ICC (including the Office of the Prosecutor).[53] For these reasons, it was necessary to rely on the powers of the SC to establish a lawful exercise of jurisdiction in case of SC referrals.

3.3 THE REFERRAL AND THE RELATIONSHIP AGREEMENT

Certain aspects of the SC referral and the legal relationship between the UN and the ICC are addressed in the RA concluded between the Assembly of States Parties of the ICC (ASP) and the UN.[54] The RA establishes a formal legal relationship between the two independent international organizations.[55] It does not, however, set any legal parameters regarding the SC referral, nor does it provide any clues as regards the legal nature of the referrals. It primarily addresses issues affecting cooperation and exchange of information between the two institutions.[56] Article 2, establishing the principles of this legal relationship, states

> 1. The United Nations recognizes the Court as an independent permanent judicial institution which, in accordance with articles 1 and 4 of the Statute, has international legal personality and such legal capacity as may be necessary for the exercise of its functions and the fulfilment of its purposes.
> 2. The Court recognizes the responsibilities of the United Nations under the Charter.
> 3. The United Nations and the Court respect each other's status and mandate.

Peace, and Acts of Aggression' in Bruno Simma and others (eds), *The Charter of the United Nations, A Commentary* (2nd edn, C.H. Beck 2002) 45.

[53] For this see the distinction made by Gallant of jurisdiction to prosecute individuals and jurisdiction over a state: Gallant (n 43) 580.

[54] Negotiated Relationship Between the International Criminal Court and the United Nations, ICC–UN, ICC-ASP/3/Res.1 (4 October 2004). Article 2 of the Rome Statute stipulates that the Court must be brought into relationship with the United Nations.

[55] Schabas (n 3) 63; Hans-Peter Kaul, 'Developments at the International Criminal Court: Construction Site for more Justice: The International Criminal Court after Two Years' (2005) 99 *American Journal of International Law* 370, 382.

[56] Georghios M. Pikis, *The Rome Statute for the International Criminal Court: Analysis of the Statute, the Rules of Procedure and Evidence, the Regulations of the Court and Supplementary Instruments* (Nijhoff 2010) 47.

From paragraphs 2 and 3 it follows that the RA does not seek to determine the specific legal bases or competences under the respective constituent treaties. Article 18 concerns the cooperation between the UN and the ICC prosecution and emphasizes that 'with due regard to its responsibilities and competence under the Charter of the United Nations and subject to its rules, the United Nations undertakes to cooperate with the Prosecutor'. From the wording 'subject to its rules' it clearly follows that the RA does not in any way seek to provide an additional legal basis for the exercise of powers that would otherwise not stem from the respective constitutive instruments. This is further supported by the rather soft language adopted in various provisions in the RA. For example, art 15, under the heading 'General provisions regarding cooperation between the United Nations and the Court', notes that '[w]ith due regard to its responsibilities and competence under the Charter and subject to its rules as defined under the applicable international law, the United Nations undertakes to cooperate with the Court.' It is therefore difficult to conclude that the RA intends to legally bind the SC to the provisions of the Statute or the other way around.

Another view – written before the conclusion of the RA – held that the SC could be legally bound by the provisions of the Statute through the RA. The argument is that from the mutual recognition of international personality, responsibilities and the mandate of the UN and the ICC (see art 2 RA), it is implied that 'UN organs are obliged to respect the principles established in the Statute'[57] because 'in terms of legal logic, it is self-evident that the Security Council could not be allowed to ignore the jurisdictional limits imposed by the ICC Statute'.[58] The reasons for this is that '[w]hen referring a situation to the Court, the Security Council is to be considered bound by those elements that constitute the intrinsic and essential features of the ICC as established in the Statute'.[59]

Whether the RA provides the legal basis for this obligation is doubtful for several additional reasons. First, this is contradicted by the preparatory work, in which most delegations regarded the SC referral as a simple recognition of the existing powers of the SC under the UN Charter and valuable for the effectiveness of the ICC and not as a limitation to it.[60] Second, the same line of

---

[57] Luigi Condorelli and Santiago Villalpando, 'Can the Security Council Extend the ICC's Jurisdiction?' in Cassese (n 3) 575.

[58] Ibid.

[59] Ibid.

[60] Philippe Kirsch and Darryl Robinson, 'Reaching Agreement at the Rome Conference' in Cassese (n 3) 82–83. In the discussion in the International Law Commission, members stressed that the referral option 'did not intend in any way to add to or increase the powers of the Council as defined in the Charter, as distinct from

argument could be used to argue that through the RA the ICC is bound by the UN Charter. Neither can be the case, of course, as the wording clearly indicates that no such hierarchy or subordination of one international organization to the other has been introduced.[61] In the relevant parts regarding the SC referral, the agreement merely instructs the Secretary-General of the UN to transmit the written decision of the SC to the Prosecutor along with the necessary documents and materials, and obligates the ICC to inform the SC pursuant to art 17(1). Hence, the RA merely defines rules regarding the communication between the two IOs and further extrapolates the various details of such cooperation.[62]

On a related note, the RA does not turn the ICC into a specialized agency of the UN system.[63] A proposal to include the possibility for the ICC to become a specialized agency under the UN Charter was rejected, because some states questioned whether this is an appropriate or even a relevant relationship between the two organizations.[64] No such language or reference to the relevant provision in the UN Charter regarding specialized agencies are made in the RA. Furthermore, becoming a specialized agency is also a matter of a UN decision and is reserved for organizations that have 'wide international responsibilities, as defined in their basic instruments, in economic, social, cultural, educational, health, and related fields'.[65] No such decision has been made.

Nor is the ICC a principle or subsidiary organ of the UN, since arts 1 and 4 of the Rome Statute, which are expressly acknowledged and recognized in the RA, establish the Court as an independent international institution with international legal personality.[66]

---

making available to it the jurisdiction mechanism created by the statute'. International Law Commission, 'Report of the Commission to the General Assembly on the work of its forty-sixth Session, 2 May–22 July 1994, Geneva', *Yearbook of the International Law Commission* vol 2 (United Nations 1997) 44.

61 In fact the preparatory work would have suggested the opposite: initially the ILC had envisioned a court that was perfectly subordinated to the SC and operating within the UN Charter; see Mahnoush H. Arsanjani, 'The Rome Statute of the International Criminal' (1999) 93 *American Journal of International Law* 22; William Schabas, 'United States Hostility to the International Criminal Court: It's All About the Security Council' (2004) 15 *European Journal of International Law* 701.

62 On the important practical cooperation between the two IOs, see Tamara Cummings-John, 'Cooperation Between the United Nations and the International Criminal Court' (2013) 10(1) *International Organizations Law Review* 223.

63 Gallant (n 43) 571.

64 See Report of the Preparatory Committee on the Establishment of an International Criminal Court (vol 1, Proceedings of the Preparatory Committee during March-April and August 1996) UN Doc A/51/22, 4, para 31.

65 Article 57 UN Charter.

66 Kiyani (n 15) 476.

In conclusion, the RA does not determine the legal basis for SC referrals or the legal nature of the referral to the ICC.

3.4 THE JUDICIAL JURISDICTION OF THE ICC AS AN INTERNATIONAL COURT

For parties to the Rome Statute, the jurisdiction[67] of the ICC[68] as an international court is explained on the basis of delegation of authority by states parties.[69] Under international law, it is within the sovereign right of a state to voluntarily designate an international court to exercise the jurisdiction over a crime committed on its territory by virtue of a multilateral treaty.[70] In such cases, jurisdiction of the ICC satisfies the classic logic of criminal justice and state sovereignty.[71] The delegation of criminal jurisdiction by states is also common legal practice.[72]

Relating to this delegation, there exist certain limits to an international court's jurisdiction. First, the outer limits of this delegation is determined by

---

[67] See generally on the meaning of 'jurisdiction' under international law, e.g. ILC, 'Preliminary Report on Immunity of State Officials from Foreign Criminal Jurisdiction' (5 May–6 June 2008 and 7 July–8 August 2008) UN Doc A/CN.4/601, para 44 (with further references).

[68] Articles 12, 13(a), 14, 98 Rome Statute.

[69] Akande (n 26); Michail Vagias, 'The Territorial Jurisdiction of the International Criminal Court – A Jurisdictional Rule of Reason for the ICC?' (2012) 59(1) *Netherlands International Law Review* 43, 44; Gerhard Werle, *Völkerstrafrecht* (3rd edn, Mohr Siebeck 2012) 94; Michael König, *Die völkerrechtliche Legitimation der Strafgewalt internationaler Strafjustiz* (Nomos 2003) 157ff; Yuval Shany, *Assessing the Effectiveness of International Courts* (Oxford University Press 2016) 69–70; Shlomit Wallerstein, 'Delegation of Powers and Authority in International Criminal Law' (2015) 9(1) *Criminal Law, Philosophy* 123, 134. This is also sometimes called 'derivative jurisdiction' granted by states when they ratify the Rome Statute; see Newton (n 27) 375.

[70] The importance for this basis of the exercise of sovereign powers by international organizations is exemplified by the very early notion found in the Declaration of the Rights of Man and Citizen that 'no body and no individual may exercise authority which does not emanate expressly from the nation'. See Dan Sarooshi, *International Organizations and their Exercise of Sovereign Powers* (Oxford monographs in international law, Oxford University Press 2007) 18; Claudia Fritsche, 'Security Council Resolution 1422: Peacekeeping and the International Criminal Court' in Jochen A. Frowein (ed), *Verhandeln für den Frieden: Negotiating for peace: liber amicorum Tono Eitel* (Beiträge zum ausländischen öffentlichen Recht und Völkerrecht vol 162, Springer 2003) 111; Bassiouni, *The Legislative History of the International Criminal Court* (n 21) 136.

[71] Ibid. 136.

[72] See further Wallerstein (n 69) 134.

the relevant constituent treaty (in the present case the Rome Statute), which forms, according to Yuval Shany's typology, the foundational jurisdiction of the court.[73] Second and following from the foundational jurisdiction, the specific jurisdiction refers to the power to have jurisdiction over any given case.[74] Thus, that outside this delegation, the ICC lacks jurisdiction and any attempt to adjudicate cases would be ultra vires.[75]

However, in case of a SC referral, the state concerned has not directly delegated its criminal jurisdiction to the ICC. Here, the ICC gains jurisdiction through a referral by the SC acting under Chapter VII of the UN Charter.[76] The SC decisions to refer a situation as provided for in art 13(b) of the Rome Statute is therefore a delegation of criminal jurisdiction by states with primary jurisdiction to the ICC.[77] And while states with primary jurisdiction over the situation addressed in the SC referral may in practice oppose a referral decision of the SC, art 25 of the Charter requires them to accept and give effect to it.[78]

In conclusion, the primary source for the jurisdictional authority of the ICC over situations in non-party states is *solely* the SC referral.[79] The exact scope of the jurisdiction that is conferred will be addressed in Chapter 5. Suffice it to note here that this will depend on the wording adopted in the SC referral, as the source of the delegation.[80] Thus, the scope of jurisdiction *ratione loci, ratione personae, ratione materiae, ratione temporis* of the ICC is determined primarily by the referral and limited only by restraints of the UN Charter itself

---

73 Shany (n 69) 69.

74 Ibid.

75 Ibid.

76 See for the similar situation regarding the ad hoc tribunals, Shany (n 69) 70 ('[I]n the case of some courts such as the two ad hoc international criminal tribunals, the mandate provider comprises another IGO (the UN Security Council) that delegates to international courts powers that were bestowed upon it by its own member states').

77 Sharing this view, Wallerstein (n 69) 135.

78 Wallerstein (n 69), 135; Akande (n 15) 341.

79 Ibid. 342.

80 To illustrate this, consider the analogous situation of the Dayton Peace Agreement, in which three states of the former Yugoslavia conferred powers on the SC to ensure implementation of the terms of the agreement (art 1(1)(a) of Annex 1A of the Agreement on the Military Aspects of the Peace Settlement between the Republic of Bosnia and Herzegovina, the Federation of Bosnia and Herzegovina, and the Republika Srpska). Sarooshi argues that since '[t]he SC adopted a resolution acting under Chapter VII . . . it is clear the SC was exercising its own powers and not a power conferred by the States parties to the Agreement. As such, the Council was not constrained "to do only what the Bosnian sides agreed to", since the authority of the Council did not derive from the Agreement but from its own powers under Chapter VII of the Charter which in the area of military enforcement action does not require the consent of a target State.' Sarooshi (n 70) 21–23.

and limitations which derive from peremptory norms (*jus cogens*).[81] These limitations are therefore analyzed in detail in Chapter 4. The scope of the jurisdiction is only secondarily governed by the Rome Statute.[82]

3.5 CONCLUSION: THE SC REFERRAL AS CONFERRAL OF POWERS

The careful analysis of the legal nature of SC referrals to the ICC shows that the SC referral is best conceptualized as a conferral of powers by the SC through a binding resolution under Chapter VII.[83] A precise definition of the concept of conferral of powers based on existing scholarship or case law is difficult. As noted by Dan Sarooshi, there is 'a considerable lack of clarity and constituent usage in the conceptual labels used to describe different types of conferrals by States of powers on international organizations'.[84] For example, the terms 'transfer', 'delegation' and 'authorization' are often used interchangeably by commentators as well as international and domestic courts referring to the same type of conferral of powers.[85] While Dan Sarooshi offers a coherent terminology in this regard,[86] the distinction between a delegation of

---

81 This is supported by an early commentator who wrote: 'whenever a matter is referred to the future ICC by the SC, the ICC would then act within the framework and on the basis of the resolution granting jurisdiction.' Andreas Zimmermann, 'The Creation of a Permanent International Criminal Court' in Jochen A. Frowein, Rüdiger Wolfrum and Christiane Philipp (eds), *Max Planck Yearbook of United Nations law* (Kluwer Law International 1998) 216; a more recent study confirms this view: Jakob Pichon, *Internationaler Strafgerichtshof und Sicherheitsrat der Vereinten Nationen: Zur Rolle des Sicherheitsrats bei der Verfolgung völkerrechtlicher Verbrechen durch den* IStGH (Max-Planck-Gesellschaft zur Förderung der Wissenschaften e.V 2011). Similarly Condorelli and Villalpando (n 3) 630. On the issue of *jus cogens* binding the SC, see below Chapter 4.5.5.

82 What this entails is discussed in Chapter 5.

83 Discussing how Sudanese president Al-Bashir's immunities under international law could be removed, one commentator lists the delegation of Chapter VII powers as one possible explanation of how a SC referral could bind a non-state party to the ICC to the Rome Statute, but rejects this reasoning because only UN member states, regional arrangements and UN organs are competent to receive Chapter VII powers from the SC, see Kiyani (n 15) 474.

84 Sarooshi (n 70) 28.

85 Dan Sarooshi, 'Conferrals by States of Powers on International Organizations: The Case of Agency' (2004) 74 *British Yearbook of International Law* 291, 295.

86 Sarooshi (n 70) 28–32. Regarding the delegation of powers, Sarooshi defines it as 'taking place whenever an organ of an international organization which possesses an express or implied power under its constituent instrument conveys the exercise of this power to some other entity. In many cases this will involve a delegation of competence which enables the delegate to carry out acts which would otherwise be unlawful.'

powers and a transfer of powers, for instance – albeit analytically undoubtedly useful[87] – does not necessarily always reflect the nuances and different forms of actual conferral of powers in practice.[88] This is particularly the case regarding the referral mechanism.

Dan Sarooshi paid particular attention to the conferral of powers by the SC, defined as 'delegation of Chapter VII powers'.[89] In these instances, however, the SC generally relied on specific provisions in the UN Charter, specifically art 98 for the Secretary-General, arts 42 and 48 for military action by member states (including action through regional arrangements) and arts 7 and 29 UN Charter for the creation of subsidiary organs.[90] The referral mechanism clearly does not fall within any of these categories.[91] And the term 'delegation' does not appear particularly apt as it is generally defined as 'the grant of authority to a person to act on behalf of one or more others, for agreed purposes'.[92] With

---

Dan Sarooshi, *The United Nations and the Development of Collective Security: The Delegation by the UN Security Council of its Chapter VII Powers* (Clarendon Press; Oxford University Press 1999) 4–5.

[87] Sharing this view, Jan Klabbers, *Advanced Introduction to the Law of International Organizations* (Edward Elgar 2015) 77.

[88] Ibid. See, for example, the case of a transfer of powers where control was still present; Daniela Obradovic, 'Repatriation of Powers in the European Community' (1997) *Common Market Law Review* 59.

[89] Sarooshi (n 86). See the criticism voiced by Bardo Fassbender regarding Sarooshi's concept of delegation of Chapter VII powers: Bardo Fassbender, 'Review Essay: Quis judicabit? The Security Council, Its Powers and Its Legal Control' (2000) 11(1) *European Journal of International Law* 219, 228, 230 ('However, the "delegation" the author describes is a phenomenon only resulting from his own perception of what the Security Council, without always saying so, in fact has done when including other UN organs or UN member states in the exercise of its powers under Chapter VII of the UN Charter. "Delegation" is an umbrella notion allowing the author to understand a number of seemingly unconnected occurrences and practices as part of a larger, and perhaps even coherent, picture, and to subject them to a consistent legal regime – albeit one at least in part of his own making . . . does [the SC] really consider the addressee of its recommendations or authorizations as a "delegate" as defined by the author, i.e. someone holding in principle the same powers as the Council itself? Perhaps we are faced not with a delegate but with a mandatory as an entity holding a specific mandate.').

[90] Nico Krisch, 'Introduction to Chapter VII: The General Framework' in Bruno Simma (ed), *The Charter of the United Nations: A Commentary* (3rd edn, Oxford University Press 2012) para 53.

[91] Kiyani (n 15) 475.

[92] Jonathan Law (ed), *A Dictionary of Law* (8th edn, Oxford University Press 2015).

referring a situation to the ICC, the SC is not granting the ICC the authority to act on its behalf.[93]

Hence, for the purposes of this analysis, I define the legal nature of the SC referral as the legal authorization of the (otherwise unlawful) exercise of jurisdiction by the ICC over situations in states not party to the Rome Statute.[94] This constitutes the conferral of powers from the SC to the ICC for it to exercise jurisdiction over individuals[95] in the state addressed in the referral and to impose obligations on the state concerned with regards to cooperation and compliance with the decisions and orders of its organs (including the Chambers and the Prosecutor, and in principle the obligations set out in Part 9 of the Rome Statute).

The reasons for this conceptualization of SC referrals are as follows. In principle, any exercise of powers by an international organization, including the ICC, must be based on some form of (indirect) conferral of powers by states.[96] It is the power conferred to the SC by UN member states that is being

---

[93] If it did, the question regarding responsibility could arise and it seems difficult to construe the SC referral as having the effect that the SC should be held responsible for acts of the ICC; in particular, the ICC acting on the referral should not be viewed as the 'conduct of an organ or agent of an international organization in the performance of functions of that organ or agent shall be considered an act of that organization under international law, whatever the position the organ or agent holds in respect of the organization' (art 6(1) of the Draft Articles on the Responsibility of International Organizations 2011, DARIO). An agent of an international organization is defined in art 2(d) DARIO as 'an official or other person or entity, other than an organ, who is charged by the organization with carrying out, or helping to carry out, one of its functions, and thus through whom the organization acts'. Neither applies to the relationship between the SC and the ICC.

[94] This definition seems to be covered by the (legal and social science) definition of international delegation adopted in an influential piece elsewhere, which defines it as 'a grant of authority by two or more states to an international body to make decisions or take actions', which also covers the further delegation (here called 'redelegation') since it also emanates from states, albeit indirectly; see Curtis A. Bradley and Judith G. Kelley, 'The Concept of International Delegation' (2008) 71 *Law and Contemporary Problems* 1, 3–5.

[95] This also includes the indirect delegation of powers in the sense of the courts' legal authority to adjudicate cases, as established in Chapter 3.4.

[96] See already the PCIJ, *Jurisdiction of the European Commission of the Danube between Galatz and Braila*, Advisory Opinion, [1927] PCIJ Series B, no 14, 64. ('organizations have the powers (competences) their members endow them with'). The ICJ specified that international organizations do not possess a general competence like states; see *Legality of the Threat or Use of Nuclear Weapons* (Advisory Opinion) [1996] ICJ Rep 226. See also Jan Klabbers, *An Introduction to International Organizations Law* (3rd edn, Cambridge University Press 2015) 160; Klabbers (n 87) 22–23; Henry G. Schermers and Niels Blokker, *International Institutional Law: Unity within Diversity* (5th rev edn, Martinus Nijhoff Publishers 2011) §209. It is important to note that this

used by the SC to (further) confer powers to the ICC.[97] For example, for the ICC to lawfully issue binding decisions on a third state, these must also find its basis in a conferral of powers.[98] This was elaborated on by the ICTY Appeals Chamber in the *Blaskic Subpoena* case:

> the obligation [on States] to lend cooperation and judicial assistance to the International Tribunal . . . is laid down in Article 29 and restated in paragraph 4 of Security Council resolution 827 (1993). Its binding force derives from the provisions of Chapter VII and Article 25 of the United Nations Charter and from the Security Council resolution adopted pursuant to those provisions. The exceptional legal basis of Article 29 [providing for the duty to cooperate with the tribunal and comply with any requests for assistance or orders issued by the Chambers] accounts for the novel and indeed unique power granted to the International Tribunal to issue orders to sovereign States (under customary international law, States, as a matter of principle, cannot be 'ordered' either by other States or by international bodies).[99]

In the case of the SC referral, the power stems from the further conferral of powers. This process is like the concept of redelegation, which is 'taking place whenever an organ of an international organization which possesses an express or implied power under its constituent instrument conveys the exercise

---

includes implied powers or the exercise of certain powers based on (accepted) subsequent practice. It is what Franck referred to writing that '[t]he legality of actions by any UN organ must be judged by reference to the Charter as a "constitution" of delegated powers'. See Thomas M. Franck, 'The "Powers of Appreciation": Who is the Ultimate Guardian of UN Legality?' (1992) 86 *American Journal of International Law* 519, 523. See also Sarooshi (n 86) 24–26.

[97] Similarly, ibid. (although using the term 'delegation of powers'). See also Akande (n 26) 628; Sarooshi (n 86) 25.

[98] The ICJ stated in the Nuclear Weapons Advisory Opinion: 'International institutional law doctrine is still at a very rudimentary stage. It generally states that international organizations may only adopt binding legal acts on the basis of a power – implied or explicitly attributed to them. It further holds that legal acts that do not remain within the confines of such powers are ultra vires and consequently invalid: a legal act which does not originate from an institutional power cannot come into existence'; see *Legality of the Threat or Use of Nuclear Weapons* (Advisory Opinion) [1996] ICJ Rep, 80–81. Generally, '[t]he most popular theoretical basis espoused (and in harmony with the broader functionalist logic) holds that the binding nature of acts of organizations can be explained on the basis of a delegation of powers. In this view, the member states, when consenting to be bound to the constitution of an organization, may or may not give that organization the power to create binding rules of law. If and when they do, they can be seen to have delegated some law-making powers to that particular organization.' Klabbers, *An introduction to International Organizations Law* (n 96) 160.

[99] *Prosecutor v Tihomir Blaskic*, Judgment on the Request of the Republic of Croatia for Review of the Decision of Trial Chamber II of 18 July 1997, T-95-14 (29 October 1997) para 26.

of this power to some other entity'.[100] In case of the SC referral, the SC as the principle organ of the UN in charge of international peace and security, and possessing a wide set of powers conferred to it by the member states under Chapter VII of the Charter, confers powers to the ICC in order for it to lawfully exercise jurisdiction.[101]

The conferral of powers by an organ of an international organization, such as the SC in the present case, raises difficult legal issues regarding the parameters and limits of such process.[102] In his seminal study of international organizations and their exercise of sovereign powers, Dan Sarooshi analyzes delegations of powers as a special instance of the conferral of powers. He finds that a general competence of an international organization to delegate powers without a specific authorization in the constituent instrument is limited to delegations within the organization.[103] This means for the present inquiry that for a delegation of powers from the SC to another separate IO to be lawful, a specific competence must be found in either express or implied terms in the UN Charter for the SC.[104] While Sarooshi has addressed the delegation by the SC of its Chapter VII powers,[105] his study did not address conferral of powers to other IOs. His focus was the delegations of powers to UN member states and regional arrangements (Chapter VIII).[106] Still, his study provides important insights into the legal issues that are also relevant for the present inquiry.

---

100 Sarooshi (n 86) 4–5.

101 As regards such delegation, Sarooshi notes that '[i]n many cases this will involve a delegation of competence which enables the delegate to carry out acts which would otherwise be unlawful'; ibid.

102 Rejecting the SC powers to do so, see Kiyani (n 15) 475.

103 Sarooshi (n 86) 18–19 (with further references).

104 Ibid. This also reiterates the argument regarding the important legal distinction between the establishment of ad hoc tribunals and the SC referral to the ICC.

105 Sarooshi (n 86).

106 Ibid.

4. The powers of the Security Council under the UN Charter

Article 13(b) of the Rome Statute requires that the SC resolution making the referral has to be adopted under Chapter VII of the Charter.[1] As established in the previous chapter, this provision does not affect the powers of the SC under the Charter:[2] a Chapter VII resolution is necessary as a matter of UN Charter law and general international law.[3] Only binding decisions under Chapter VII are capable of creating legal obligations for UN members that have not accepted the obligations arising out of the Rome Statute (either ad hoc or by becoming states parties). For these decisions to be binding, the SC's decisions must be in accordance with the Charter.[4] The question is therefore whether it is in accordance with the Charter for the SC to confer jurisdictional power to the ICC.

1 See Sharon A. Williams and William Schabas, 'Article 13' in Otto Triffterer and Kai Ambos (eds), *Commentary on the Rome Statute of the International Criminal Court: Observers' Notes, Article by Article* (2nd edn, C.H. Beck; Hart; Nomos 2008) 573; Luigi Condorelli and Santiago Villalpando, 'Referral and Deferral by the Security Council' in Antonio Cassese, Paola Gaeta and John R. Jones (eds), *The Rome Statute of the International Criminal Court* (Oxford University Press 2002) 630–33.

2 See however on the question of operability of SC measures vis-à-vis the ICC in Chapter 5.

3 *Prosecutor v Al-Bashir* (Decision on the Prosecutor's Request for a Finding of Non-Compliance Against the Republic of the Sudan) ICC-02/05-01/09 (9 March 2015) paras 14–15.

4 See Article 25 of the UN Charter. See also Stefan Talmon, 'Security Council Treaty Action' (2009) 62(1) *Revue hellénique de droit international* 65, 66. In its advisory opinion on Namibia the ICJ held that 'when the Security Council adopts a decision under article 25 in accordance with the Charter, it is for member States to comply with that decision . . . To hold otherwise would be to deprive this principal organ of its essential functions and powers under the Charter'; *Legal Consequences for States of the Continued Presence of South Africa in Namibia (South West Africa) notwithstanding Security Council Resolution 276 (1970)*, Advisory Opinion (ICJ, 21 June 1971) para 116. See also *Admission of a State to the United Nations*, Advisory Opinion, ICJ Rep 1948, 57, 64.

The general principle of law, *nemo dat quod non habet* (one cannot give what one does not possess) is applicable to the question of conferrals.[5] For a conferral of powers from the SC to the ICC to be lawful, the SC must either expressly or implicitly possess the power to confer authority under the UN Charter in the first place.[6] As pointed out, the powers of international organizations are in principle limited to such that have been conferred to them by states (including implied powers).[7] The SC may only confer powers it possesses.[8] These may include powers that the SC itself is unable to exercise. For example, it is now largely undisputed that the establishment of the ICTY and ICTR as subsidiary organs of the SC to determine individual criminal responsibility fall within the powers of the SC.[9] However, the SC referral is legally to be distinguished from

---

[5] For application of this principle in another area of international law, the acquisition of title to territory, see, for example, the *Island of Palmas case (or Miangas)* (Award) II RIAA 829, ICGJ 392 (PCA 1928) (4 April 1928) 842.

[6] In this sense Dan Sarooshi, *The United Nations and the Development of Collective Security: The Delegation by the UN Security Council of its Chapter VII Powers* (Clarendon Press; Oxford University Press 1999) 20. Under general international law, international organizations may not create their own powers but must find their legal basis in their constituent treaty or in another instrument of international law; see Henry G. Schermers and Niels Blokker, *International Institutional Law: Unity within Diversity* (5th rev. edn, Martinus Nijhoff Publishers 2011) §209.

[7] See further Dan Sarooshi, *International Organizations and their Exercise of Sovereign Powers* (Oxford University Press 2005).

[8] These include express powers as well as implied powers. Nico Krisch, 'Introduction to Chapter VII: The General Framework' in Bruno Simma (ed), *The Charter of the United Nations: A Commentary* (3rd edn, Oxford University Press 2012) para 54. For the doctrine of implied powers, see *Reparation For Injuries Case* (Advisory Opinion) [1949] ICJ Rep 174, 182.

[9] Krisch (n 8) paras 53–54. See also Jochen A. Frowein and Nico Krisch, 'Chapter VII. Action with respect to Threats to the Peace, Breaches of the Peace, and Acts of Aggression' in Bruno Simma and others (eds), *The Charter of the United Nations, A Commentary* (2nd edn, C.H. Beck 2002) para 33; Sarooshi (n 6) 92–98; William Schabas, *An Introduction to the International Criminal Court* (4th edn, Cambridge University Press 2011) 168. The Appeals Chamber of the ICTY itself expressly held: 'The establishment of the International Tribunal by the Security Council does not signify, however, that the Security Council has delegated to it some of its own functions or the exercise of some of its own powers. Nor does it mean, in reverse, that the Security Council was usurping for itself part of a judicial function which does not belong to it but to other organs of the United Nations according to the Charter. The Security Council has resorted to the establishment of a judicial organ in the form of an international criminal tribunal as an instrument for the exercise of its own principal function of maintenance of peace and security, i.e., as a measure contributing to the restoration and maintenance of peace in the former Yugoslavia.' The emphasis on the determination that the SC has not delegated some of its own functions or the exercise of some of its own powers should not be misconstrued to reject the notion that a delegation of power indeed took place. Instead the Appeals Chamber draws the distinction between powers

the SC's powers to establish the ad hoc tribunals, particularly because the ICC is no organ of the UN. This I will address in more detail below. Still, what the legality of the creation of the ad hoc tribunals does establish is the presumption that the SC indeed possesses the power to confer authority to judicial bodies to determine individual criminal responsibility.

4.1 DIFFERENCES BETWEEN THE REFERRAL AND THE AD HOC TRIBUNALS

4.1.1 Review of the Literature

As mentioned earlier, the justification for the SC's power to refer situations involving non-party states is widely equated with the power with which it established the ad hoc tribunals.[10] It is clear that the drafters viewed the ICC in some respects as a permanent version of the ad hoc tribunals.[11] The referral power (limited to SC acting under Chapter VII of the UN Charter) was in fact supported in the name of the ICC acting as a permanent version of the ad hoc tribunals.[12] The extremely costly ad hoc establishment would not be necessary anymore.[13] Legally, the power of the SC to establish ad hoc tribunals was soon confirmed in the authoritative judgment in *Tadic* and the legality of their establishment has not been seriously contested since.[14] Indeed, the judgment

---

and functions it can perform itself and those that require the establishment of judicial organs in order to fulfil its mandate under the Charter. This point is confirmed by the literature cited above.

10 See Chapter 3.1.

11 See 'Report of the Commission to the General Assembly on the work of its forty-sixth Session, (2 May–22 July 1994, Geneva)', *Yearbook of the International Law Commission* 1994, vol 2, part 2 (United Nations Publications 1997) 44; William Schabas, *The International Criminal Court: A Commentary on the Rome Statute* (Oxford commentaries on international law, Oxford University Press 2010) 294; Condorelli and Villalpando (n 1) 630.

12 Bruce Broomhall, *International Justice and the International Criminal Court: Between Sovereignty and the Rule of Law* (Oxford University Press 2004) 79.

13 On the high costs of the ad hoc tribunals, see David Wippman, 'The Costs of International Justice' (2006) 100 *American Journal of International Law* 861 (arguing that 'the price of international justice will remain high' but that is inherent to international criminal trials that cannot be compared to domestic trials and therefore that would also be true for trials before the ICC).

14 Decision on the Defence Motion for Interlocutory Appeal on Jurisdiction, *Tadic* (ICTY-IT-94-l-A), Appeals Chamber, 2 October 1995; Decision on the Defence Motion on Jurisdiction, *Kanyabashi* (ICTR-96-15-T), Trial Chamber 2, 18 June 1997; Decision on Preliminary Motions, *Milosevic* (ICTY-IT-99-37-PT), Trial Chamber, 8 November 2001; Schabas (n 11) 294; Antonio Cassese, 'The Legitimacy of International Criminal

provided important impetus for the creation of the ICC and as a result the SC's powers with regards to referrals were not seriously debated.[15]

Before looking at the important legal differences between the two instances, it is important to address the argument *a maiore ad minus*. This argument is adopted by some[16] inferring that if the SC has the power to establish ad hoc tribunals, then the 'mere' referral of jurisdiction to an existing court must be covered by such powers as well. However, after closer inspection it becomes clear that this argument is fallacious. It is fallacious because it presupposes that the SC referral is just a more limited measure compared to the establishment of the ICTY. However, whether this is actually the case is precisely the question.[17] I will return to this below.

Similarly, the argument *a fortiori* is problematic, because logically the argument *a fortiori* is not a logical inference but equally involves a value judgment about the similarity between the ad hoc tribunals and the SC referral.[18] An early commentator argued as follows:

> [a]fter the decision of the Appeals Chamber of the ICTY . . . in the case of Tadic and the decision of . . . Kanyabashi, no serious doubts seem to exist that the Security Council might within the framework of its competences under Chapter VII of the UN Charter, also establish ad hoc tribunals if the Council considers it to be necessary for the maintenance of international peace and security. A fortiori this must be also true where the Security Council was not to create a new ad hoc tribunal but instead where it would solely confer certain competences upon an already existing criminal tribunal provided that, however, in a given situation the requirements of Chapter VII of the Charter are indeed fulfilled.[19]

As will be seen, this equally sidesteps the important legal differences between establishing ad hoc tribunals and SC referrals.

Tribunals and the Current Prospects of International Criminal Justice' (2012) 25(02) *Leiden Journal of International Law* 491, 494.

15 In Commentary (1), the ILC suggested this, saying: 'This power may be exercised, for example, in circumstances where the Council might have authority to establish an ad hoc tribunal under Chapter VII of the Charter of the United Nations.' International Law Commission, 'Report of the International Law Commission on the work of its forty-sixth session' (Yearbook of the International Law Commission 1994, vol II(2)) 44.

16 See e.g. Andreas Zimmermann, 'The Creation of a Permanent International Criminal Court' in Jochen A. Frowein, Rüdiger Wolfrum and Christiane Philipp (eds), *Max Planck Yearbook of United Nations law* (Kluwer Law International 1998) 216.

17 On the fallacious logic of such arguments see Egon Schneider, *Logik für Juristen* (4th edn, Verlag Vahlen 1995) 147–50.

18 See on this ibid. 144–46.

19 A. Zimmermann (n 16) 216.

Indeed, the differences of the legality of the establishment ad hoc tribunals compared to that of the SC referral were also raised in the preparatory work of the ILC. There, opinions were divided regarding the significance of the precedent-setting character of the establishment of the ad hoc tribunals for the ICC.[20] It was argued that almost all the features of the ICTY (as well as those of the ICTR) concerning the election of judges, the jurisdiction of the tribunals and the requirements of state cooperation were *unlike* the provisions of the proposed ICC.[21]

interesting

4.1.2 The Relevant Legal Differences

Broadly speaking, there are three main differences to be considered in turn, all related to the ad hoc tribunal's status as a subsidiary organ of the UN. This was also the departure for the justification of the legality of the establishment of the ICTY by the Appeals Chamber in *Tadic*.[22]

From the outset an important clarification must be made. The value of *Tadic* for questions relating to the powers of the SC under Chapter VII must not be overstated. First, under general international law, and especially under UN law, the ICTY cannot determine the legality of a SC resolution.[23] Indeed, no court, be it international, regional or domestic, not even the International Court of Justice (ICJ) has the competence to pronounce on the legality of SC decisions with binding force.[24] In fact, while the ICJ has indeed ruled on the legality of SC decisions in various older cases (always affirming its legality),[25]

---

[20] See ILC, 'Report of the International Law Commission on the work of its forty-sixth session, 2 May–22 July 1994, Official Records of the General Assembly, Forty-ninth session, Supplement No. 10', para 47; Adriaan Bos, 'The Experience of the Preparatory Committee' in Mauro Politi and Giuseppe Nesi (eds), *The Rome Statute of the International Criminal Court: A Challenge to Impunity* (Ashgate 2001) 17.

[21] Bos (n 20) 23.

[22] *Tadic Case* (Decision on the Defence Motion for Interlocutory Appeal on Jurisdiction) ICTY-IT-94-l-A (2 October 1995) para 38.

[23] It is important to clarify that the ICTY only indirectly reviewed the legality of its establishment; see e.g. Susan Lamb, 'Legal Limits to United Nations Security Council Powers' in Guy S Goodwin-Gill (ed), *The Reality of International Law: Essays in Honour of Ian Brownlie* (repr. Clarendon 2003) 364.

[24] Antonios Tzanakopoulos, *The Solange Argument as a Justification for Disobeying the Security Council in the Kadi Judgments* (2013) (*forthcoming* in M. Avbelj, F. Fontanelli and G. Martinico (eds), *Kadi on Trial: A Multifaceted Analysis of the Kadi Judgement* (Routledge 2014) 121.

[25] As August Reinisch correctly points out: 'What is sometimes overlooked is the fact that the Court had done exactly that in a number of older cases. The ICJ did not refrain from deciding on the lawfulness of the establishment of the UN Administrative Tribunal, nor on the legality of UN peacekeeping, nor on the lawfulness of the UN reso-

this must not be confused with a binding determination of its legality under international law, since the ICJ lacks the competence to exercise direct control over SC measures with a view to annul them. Instead, it may be regarded as merely an opinion about the legality by a court,[26] which – in the case of the ICJ – undeniably carries a lot of authority for the determination of rules of international law according to art 38(1)(d) ICJ Statute. But it is clear that any such finding as such has no direct legal consequences in international law.[27] The ICTY Appeals Chamber's finding in *Tadic* is a very strong argument, and its importance is not questioned here. However, for the purpose of this study, a closer look is important for the conceptualization of the SC referral. In any event, how much weight for the determination of legality of a SC measure not directly at issue (such as the SC's referral powers) should then be given to a decision of a subsidiary organ whose very own legality was questioned?[28]

Regardless of whether or not one accepts the premise that in fact the SC has the power to establish ad hoc tribunals, either conclusion does not directly bear on the question of whether the SC enjoys a competence to refer a situation of a non-state party to the Rome Statute to the jurisdiction of the Court, for the following important reasons.

4.1.2.1 SC referral goes beyond mere law enforcement

The first main difference between the establishment of the ad hoc tribunals and the SC referral lies in the fact that when establishing the tribunals, the Council stressed that it merely ensured compliance with international humanitarian

lutions terminating South Africa's League of Nations mandate over South-West Africa. Surely, by concluding that all of these acts of political organs of the UN had been within the (implied) powers of such organs, the ICJ avoided open confrontation. Nevertheless, it clearly affirmed its own jurisdiction to decide such matters. The question, of course, remains: what would be the consequence of a judicial finding that certain acts exceeded the General Assembly's or the Security Council's powers?' See August Reinisch, 'Should Judges Second-Guess the UN Security Council?' (2009) 6(1) *International Organizations Law Review* 257, 259 (with further references).

26 Georg Schwarzenberger, *International Law as Applied by International Courts and Tribunals* (vol 1, Stevens & Sons 1957) 30–31.

27 See A. Zammit Borda, 'A Formal Approach to Article 38(1)(d) of the ICJ Statute from the Perspective of the International Criminal Courts and Tribunals' (2013) 24(2) *European Journal of International Law* 649. See also Reinisch (n 25) 259.

28 Indeed, one Judge of the ICTY Appeal's Chamber took the view in her dissenting opinion in the *Tadic* case that the review of the SC measure was 'worthless both in fact and in law' pointing out that there was no express power granted to the ICTY to do so and further that it did not have the expertise to determine the appropriateness of the SC actions; see *Tadic Case* (Decision on the Defence Motion for Interlocutory Appeal on Jurisdiction) ICTY-IT-94-l-A (2 October 1995) (Separate and Dissenting Opinion of Judge Li, paras 2–4).

law acting to some degree as a law enforcement organ of the international community.[29] Indeed, establishing these criminal tribunals, the SC stressed that merely existing law would be applied and no new law created because the SC is not a legislative body and would not possess the powers to do so.[30] The enforcement of international law may be regarded as a necessary means of maintaining international peace and security.[31] Following this logic, the SC referral seems to be a convenient and appropriate means for just that. Through the possibility of a SC referral, acting under Chapter VII of the UN Charter, the ICC could in principle enjoy universal jurisdiction by virtue of a SC acting in the interest of international criminal justice.[32] However, the difference lies in the fact that the legal regime of the ICC was established by a separate multilateral treaty that creates its own legal obligations to which the state, where a situation is referred to the ICC, has not consented to.[33] These obligations go beyond the mere enforcement of international humanitarian law. Therefore, it is questionable whether the SC referral really is merely a less invasive measure compared to the establishment of the ad hoc tribunals.

4.1.2.2 The referral does not turn the ICC into a subsidiary organ of the SC

Another important distinction concerns the tribunal's and the ICC's respective relationship with the UN. In the case of the ICTY/ICTR, it was the subsidiary organs of the SC themselves (the establishment of the ad hoc tribunals, conceived as subsidiary organs, rested on art 29 UN Charter)[34] which exercised

---

[29] As A. Paulus put it, '[s]ince the SC is not empowered to legislate in a technical sense, ICTY is limited to the application of existing international criminal law'; Andreas L. Paulus, 'Article 29' in Simma (n 8) para 69. See also Frowein and Krisch (n 9) para 18.

[30] See, in particular, SC Res. 827 (1993), and the Report of the *UN Secretary-General*, UN Doc. S/25704, 3 May 1993. Ibid. para 19. See also Michael Wood, 'The Interpretation of Security Council Resolutions' (1998) 2 *Max Planck Yearbook of United Nations Law* 73, 78; Daphna Shraga and Ralph Zacklin, 'The International Criminal Tribunal for the Former Yugoslavia' (1994) 5 *European Journal of International Law* 360, 363ff.

[31] Nicolas Angelet, 'International Law Limits to the Security Council' in Vera Gowlland-Debbas (ed), *United Nations Sanctions and International Law* (The Graduate Institute of International Studies, Kluwer Law International 2001) 79.

[32] Mauro Politi, 'The Rome Statute of the ICC: Rays of Light and Some Shadows' in Politi (n 20) 13. It must be noted however, that in this case the ICC still functions on the basis of the complementarity principle (see art 17 Rome Statute) and it therefore remains doubtful whether this need might not arise under such circumstances; ibid.

[33] This will be discussed in more detail below.

[34] Sarooshi (n 6) 95; Paola Gaeta, 'Does President Al-Bashir Enjoy Immunity from Arrest?' (2009) 7(2) *Journal of International Criminal Justice* 315, 330.

public authority immediately over persons.[35] In contrast, the ICC is based on a multilateral treaty, separate from the UN system, and therefore not a subsidiary organ of the UN.[36] Thus, the ICC is a separate international organization established by the Rome Statute which exercises this public authority over individuals.[37] With the referral of situations of non-party states, the SC establishes international criminal jurisdiction over individuals[38] in a state *not* party to the treaty governing this jurisdiction.[39] This is an important difference because that is where the legal basis of the SC's powers are founded. As Sarooshi demonstrated,

> The International Criminal Tribunals are UN subsidiary organs established by the SC to exercise judicial functions which the Council itself does not possess the competence to exercise. The SC does not possess the competence to determine individual cases of criminal liability. As such, the Council has not delegated to the Tribunals the performance of its own functions but rather those powers that are necessary for the exercise of their designated judicial functions. The exercise of these functions by the Tribunals does not detract, however, from the legal position, that as UN subsidiary organs they are an integral part of the United Nations. The Council

---

35 Frowein and Krisch (n 9) para 45 ('Without any need for action by a State (except for the mere factual surrender of persons to the international tribunals). With respect to the criminal tribunals, this reflects the substantive obligations individuals incur under international criminal law.').

36 A. G. Kiyani, 'Al-Bashir & the ICC: The Problem of Head of State Immunity' (2013) 12(3) *Chinese Journal of International Law* 467, 476; Ruth Mackenzie and others, *Manual on International Courts and Tribunals* (2nd edn, International courts and tribunals, Oxford University Press 2010) 159.

37 For the issue of *jus puniendi* in ICL, see e.g. Kai Ambos, 'Punishment without a Sovereign? The Ius Puniendi Issue of International Criminal Law: A First Contribution towards a Consistent Theory of International Criminal Law' (2013) 33(2) *Oxford Journal of Legal Studies* 293. On the exercise of public authority over individuals by international courts and tribunals see also Armin von Bogdandy and Ingo Venzke, *In wessen Namen?: Internationale Gerichte in Zeiten globalen Regierens* (Suhrkamp Taschenbuch Wissenschaft vol 2088, 1. Aufl, Suhrkamp 2014) 96–103.

38 Richard Goldstone, 'International Criminal Court and Ad Hoc Tribunals' in Sam Daws and Thomas G. Weiss (eds), *The Oxford Handbook on the United Nations* (Oxford University Press 2009) 465. The conferral of compulsory jurisdiction over individuals is not a novel concept; see Cherif M. Bassiouni, 'The Need for an International Criminal Court in the New International World Order' (1992) 25(2) *Vanderbilt Journal of Transnational Law* 151, 165 (with further references). While the ICC's jurisdiction is called merely 'complementary' (art 17 Rome Statute) to the States jurisdiction, one must not forget that it is the Court which decides on a potential admissibility challenge (art 19 Rome Statute); see on this Sarah M. H. Nouwen, *Complementarity in the Line of Fire: The Catalysing Effect of the International Criminal Court in Uganda and Sudan* (Cambridge studies in law and society, Cambridge University Press 2013) 34–110.

39 For the general problem of the *jus puniendi* issue of ICL see e.g. Ambos (n 37) 294.

has established the Tribunals as a measure that is necessary for the restoration and maintenance of international peace and security.[40]

In light of this, the ICC cannot be viewed as a subsidiary organ even in the case of a referral by the SC, since the preconditions for a lawful establishment are clearly not met.[41] The ICC is not established by the SC and it is also not under the authority and control of the SC.[42] For example, while the ad hoc tribunals were established as independent judicial entities, the SC, as part of its authority and control that a principal organ possesses over its subsidiary, could change the statute of the tribunals and thus change the scope of the tribunal's jurisdiction.[43] It is clear that the SC does not have the power to alter the Rome Statute of the ICC. Furthermore, as I will develop in more detail below, the SC referral does not constitute a simple delegation of power from a principal organ (the SC) to a subsidiary organ (ICC) – meaning that the conferral of powers in case of a SC referral poses a whole set of different legal questions.

4.1.2.3 Different sources of authority

With regards to the ICC, authority and control is exercised, unlike with the ad hoc tribunals, by the ASP and not by the SC.[44] The ASP is the main political body overseeing the operations of the ICC.[45] It is authorized to consider and determine the budget for the Court (art 112(2)(d) Rome Statute), and is competent to modify the jurisdiction and structure of the ICC through amendments to the Statute and other constitutive instruments.[46] Its mandate also includes providing 'management oversight to the Presidency, the Prosecutor and the

---

[40] Danesh Sarooshi, 'The Powers of the United Nations International Criminal Tribunals' in Jochen A. Frowein, Rüdiger Wolfrum and Christiane Philipp (eds), *Max Planck Yearbook of United Nations Law* (Kluwer Law International 1998) 143–44.

[41] Sarooshi (n 6) 119–41.

[42] Sarooshi also identifies a third precondition before an entity can be lawfully considered a UN subsidiary organ that it is not violating the delimitation of the Charter powers between the principal organs; ibid.

[43] Cf ibid. 103–104.

[44] Similarly Kiyani (n 36) 477.

[45] The ASP acts in its own right and through its subsidiary bodies such as the Committee on Budget and Finance. It convenes once a year, but its responsibilities are assured on a continuous basis through its permanent Secretariat and Bureau; see arts 112(2)(c) and 112(3) Rome Statute. While the ASP is not listed as one of the 'organs' of the Court in Art 34, and is treated separately from the Court for the purpose of financing in art 115, this is only due to the insulation of the political from the judicial function of the ICC as an international organization. Similarly see Rosalyn Higgins and others, *Oppenheim's International Law: United Nations* (vol 1, Oxford University Press 2017) 1343 FN 297.

[46] Articles 9, 51, 121–22 Rome Statute.

Registrar regarding the administration of the Court'[47] and the election and removal from office of senior office holders.[48] Finally, the ASP has the general power to 'perform any other function consistent with this Statute or the Rules of Procedure and Evidence'.[49]

To illustrate these powers of the ASP, it is useful to consider the recent amendments to the Rules of Procedure and Evidence concluded at an ASP session in November 2013, where only member states have a vote.[50] This is a crucial difference, since in fact, if one was to put much weight on provisions of the Rome Statute, in particular its limitations on the powers of the SC, the ASP does have the authority to amend the Rome Statute including those concerning the ICC's jurisdiction (art 121 Rome Statute), entirely irrespective of the powers of the SC or the UN Charter.[51]

4.1.2.4 Justifying the formalistic approach

One might dismiss these arguments as overly formalistic, since the object and purpose of establishing an ad hoc tribunal and the referral of a case to an already existing permanent tribunal appear to align. While that may be so in theory, one must view such referrals as effectively conferring jurisdictional authority over a situation in a UN member state, to a court established by a multilateral treaty. Through it, the SC provides all further authority to this separate institution (the ICC and its organs) without retaining any control for the SC (except for the possibility of a deferral pursuant to art 16 of the Statute and possibly through a termination of the referral[52]), because it is the court itself that determines its own jurisdiction and the ASP that possesses ultimate authority over the ICC and the cases concerned, even though the situation state is not part thereof. To illustrate this further, consider, for instance, the role of the ASP in the election of judges and the fact that only nationals of state parties may be elected as judges.[53]

---

47 Article 112(2)(b) Rome Statute.

48 Articles 36, 42(4), 43(4), 46(2) Rome Statute.

49 Article 112(2)(g) Rome Statute.

50 Twelfth Session of the Assembly of States Parties to the Rome Statute of the International Criminal Court; for resolutions see https://asp.icc-cpi.int/en_menus/asp/sessions/documentation/12th-session/Pages/default.aspx (accessed 30 March 2018).

51 Luigi Condorelli and Santiago Villalpando, 'Can the Security Council Extend the ICC's Jurisdiction?' in Cassese (n 1) 573.

52 See below section 4.5.4.

53 Article 36 Rome Statute.

4.1.2.5 Conclusion

The competence of the SC for excursions into the field of administration of justice should not be taken for granted.[54] Even accepting the premise that the SC has the power under the Charter to establish ad hoc tribunals,[55] one must still deal with the problem that, in fact, the grounds for a potential competence in the case of a SC referral are very different from those invoked by the SC regarding the ad hoc tribunals.[56] Taken seriously, the Appeals Chamber in *Tadic* held that the SC is not '*legibus solutus*' since 'neither the text nor the spirit of the Charter conceives of the Security Council as unbound by law'.[57] This means that the competences for the referral must be found elsewhere. Therefore, a thorough analysis must be conducted to establish the legal basis and limits for the operation of the SC referral in such cases. To this I will now turn.

4.2 THE POWER TO CONFER POWERS

Generally, a further conferral of powers takes place when an international organization, that derives its powers from a conferral of powers from its member states, itself further confers powers to another entity. A special form of such conferral of powers is the *delegation* of powers. A delegation of powers in the law of international organizations can be defined as 'taking place

---

[54] Tono Eitel, 'The UN Security Council and its Future Contribution in the Field of International Law: What may we expect?' in Jochen A. Frowein and Rüdiger Wolfrum (eds), *Max Planck Yearbook of United Nations Law* (Kluwer Law International 2000) 69. In this contribution he also comments: 'the Council . . . was meant to become a Holy Alliance of Oligarchs whose decisions would be taken in consequence of a multilateral parallelogram of forces . . . What we now have is a sort of Pantheon with the U.S. as the mightiest, not yet almighty head god surrounded by the four other Veto-Powers as equal immortals who then together allow 10 mortals to sit at their table for two years (Art. 23). This Mount Olympus suffers from deficiencies and disappointments, from thwarted good intentions and unexpected frustrations, from intrigues and power play, sometimes building up to a small palace rebellion, but never to a really revolutionary upheaval.' Ibid. 54.

[55] At the meeting at which Res 827, which created the tribunal, was adopted, numerous state representatives complained that the establishment of the Tribunal exclusively through a resolution of the Security Council left unresolved a number of legal issues relating to the powers and competences attributed to the Council by the Charter, especially problems of overlapping competences between the Council and the General Assembly as to the Tribunal's financing, see UNSC Verbatim Record (25 May 1993) UN Doc S/PV.3217.

[56] Sharing this view Condorelli and Villalpando (n 51) 577.

[57] *Tadic Case* (Decision on the Defence Motion for Interlocutory Appeal on Jurisdiction) ICTY-IT-94-1-A (2 October 1995).

whenever an organ of an international organization which possesses an express or implied power under its constituent instrument conveys the exercise of this power to some other entity'.[58] According to Dan Sarooshi, this will in many cases also 'involve a delegation of competence which enables the delegate to carry out acts which would otherwise be unlawful'.[59] The same seems true for the SC referral as it also enables the ICC to exercise jurisdiction in situations where this would otherwise be unlawful.

There exists a wealth of accepted practice regarding delegation of powers as defined by Sarooshi. The World Health Organization and other UN implementing agencies, for example, often delegate various in-country tasks by subcontracting with various non-governmental organizations or even with private, for-profit organizations.[60] Such redelegation (because it further delegates) may also entail the creation of new bodies that emanate from the original international body, as was the case when the SC created the ad hoc tribunals.[61] Redelegation is not confined to issues of particular substance and may occur even in sensitive areas, as illustrated by the UN's redelegation of peacekeeping activities to regional organizations such as NATO or specific member states.[62] This lends support for the view that the SC is in principle not barred under the UN Charter to confer powers to an entity outside the UN system.

The key issue is under what conditions and on what grounds the SC, itself an entity to which states conferred powers (arts 24 and 25 UN Charter),[63] may (further) confer powers to a separate entity, such as the ICC. First, there is in principle the limitation stemming from the maxim *delegatus non potest delegare*: the delegate may not delegate further. Second, on what grounds does the SC possess the authority to further delegate?[64]

Dan Sarooshi established that the maxim called non-delegation doctrine is applicable to the SC for three reasons. First, the doctrine is applicable because it is a general principle of law for the purposes of art 38(1)(c) of the Statute of

---

58 Sarooshi (n 6) 4–5.

59 Ibid. 5.

60 Curtis A. Bradley and Judith G. Kelley, 'The Concept of International Delegation' (2008) 71 *Law and Contemporary Problems* 1, 17.

61 Ibid.

62 UNSC Res 1244 (10 June 1999) UN Doc S/RES/1244 (authorizing NATO to deploy forces in Kosovo to maintain security). See Bradley and Kelley (n 60) 17. See further on these delegations to regional arrangements or member states Sarooshi (n 6).

63 Krisch (n 8) 1256.

64 This could be called the authority of redelegation. It permits the international body to further delegate authority to another entity; Bradley and Kelley (n 60) 17; Dan Sarooshi, 'The Essentially Contested Nature of the Concept of Sovereignty: Implications for the Exercise by International Organizations of Delegated Powers of Government' (2004) 25 *Michigan Journal Of International Law* 1107, 1125–26.

the ICJ and as such is applicable to the UN and thus to the SC:[65] the doctrine is applied in some form to delegations of governmental power in a variety of states which represent both common and civil law systems.[66] Second, the fundamental object and purpose of the maxim is applicable to the SC. Finally, accountability for the exercise of certain powers – which is also an important reason for the existence of the maxim – is also applicable to the SC.[67]

According to Sarooshi, the application of the non-delegation doctrine entails four main effects on the general competence of the SC to confer powers. First, the Council is prohibited from delegating certain Chapter VII powers. Second, a discretionary power can only be delegated when the SC retains such a degree of authority and control over its delegate that it can change the decision of its delegate at any time.[68] Third, when powers are being delegated, the limitations

---

65 Cf ibid. 1125–34.

66 Compare the analogous general principle of public and administrative law present in various domestic systems of government. See, for example, the legal position in the following states – Austria: art 18 of the Austrian Constitution (last amended 8 June 2016); see also Ludwig K. Adamovich and others, *Allgemeine Lehren des Verwaltungsrechts* (Verlag Österreich 2009) 37; Canada: see the case of *Gavin v The Queen*, 23 ILR 154 (Supreme Court PEI 1956); France: see art 38 of the 1958 French Constitution (last amended 23 July 2008), see Conseil Constitutionnel, available at http://www.conseil-constitutionnel.fr/conseil-constitutionnel/francais/la-constitution/la-constitution-du-4-octobre-1958/texte-integral-de-la-constitution-du-4-octobre-1958-en-vigueur.5074.html (accessed 24 June 2016); Germany: see arts 80 and 129 of the German Basic Law of 23 May 1949 (last amended 23 December 2014); see also Uwe Kischel, 'Delegation of Legislative Power to Agencies: A Comparative Analysis of United States and German Law' (1994) 46(2) *Administrative Law Review* 213; India: *Jatindra Nath Gupta v Province of Bihar* [1949] FLJ 225; see also C. H. Alexandrowicz-Alexander, 'Delegation of Legislative Power in India' (1954) 3(1) *The American Journal of Comparative Law* 72; Ireland: Irish High Court case of *The State (at the Prosecution of Brendan Devine) v Larkin and Others*, 70 ILR 110, 113-114 (High Ct. 1975)(Ir.); United Kingdom: *Jackson and others v Attorney General* [2005] UKHL 56, see also J. F. Northey, 'Sub-Delegated Legislation and Delegatus Non Potest Delegare' (1953) 6 *Res Judicatae* 294; USA: see e.g. US Supreme Court in *National Cable Television Assn v United States*, 415 US 336, 342 (1974); see also *Industrial Dept. v American Petroleum Inst*, 448 US 607, 675 (1980); *American Textile Mfrs v Donavan*, 452 US 490, 543 (1981), and see Kischel (this note, above); Sarooshi (n 64) 1125–34; Sarooshi (n 7) 157.

67 Sarooshi (n 6) 24–26, with further references and arguments for such conclusion.

68 This is, however, subject to the *sui generis* exception in the case of UN subsidiary organs exercising functions which the Council does not itself possess; see on this the debate concerning the establishment of the ad hoc tribunals; see also Paulus (n 29) para 12.

on the exercise of the power must be imposed on the delegate.[69] Fourth, the terms of a delegation of Chapter VII powers are to be construed narrowly.[70]

This conclusion warrants a closer look at the limits on the conferral of powers under the UN Charter. Limits on SC concerning the conferral of powers are not expressly provided for in the UN Charter. Hence, they must be deduced from 'general principles and from the object and purpose of the SC's delegation authority'.[71]

Because of its particular institutional design, the Charter endows the SC with wide-ranging discretionary powers.[72] Generally, these discretionary powers may not be delegated to another entity such as the ICC, unless the SC clearly circumscribes the delegated powers and supervises their exercise.[73] Consequently, the general delegation of the competence to determine a threat to the peace or to decide upon the measures to be used to restore the peace would be inadmissible, and any delegation of discretionary powers should be construed narrowly.[74] In any event, the entity endowed with delegated powers is subject to their limits.[75]

4.2.1 Conditions for a Lawful Conferral of Powers to the ICC

Three conditions must be met for the lawful conferral of powers by the SC to member states, and Sarooshi demonstrates that the same is applicable to the question of delegation of powers by the SC to regional arrangements.[76] Since the delegation of powers is one specific form of the conferral of powers, there is no reason apparent why the following general principles should not apply *mutatis mutandis* to the conferral of powers in case of SC referrals insofar they share the same characteristics.

The first condition sets out a certain minimum degree of clarity in the resolution which delegates the power.[77] In other words, the objective for which the power is being delegated must be unequivocally specified. The same must be true for a conferral of powers because it authorizes the exercise of jurisdiction for a specified purpose that must be clear for the recipient of that power. In

---

69 This issue will be addressed in Chapter 5.

70 Sarooshi (n 6) 46.

71 Frowein and Krisch (n 9) para 33.

72 Ibid.

73 Ibid.

74 Sarooshi (n 6) 32–46.

75 Frowein and Krisch (n 9) para 33. But see Sarooshi (n 6) 57–59 (with respect to the role of the Secretary-General of the UN).

76 '[T]he legal points in play are in substance the same as those relating to a delegation to individual Members', Sarooshi (n 6) 247. See also Sarooshi (n 64) 1134–38.

77 Sarooshi (n 6) 157.

case of the SC referral, this is not posing any problems. The SC referral is clearly meant to achieve the objective of conferring powers to the ICC to bring perpetrators of international crimes to justice and through that contributes to the restoration or maintenance of international peace and security.[78]

The second condition for the lawful delegation of powers is that some form of supervision is exercised by the SC over the way in which the delegated powers are being exercised.[79] However, here the *sui generis* exception applies for the powers of judicial bodies that the SC cannot itself exercise. As the ICJ pointed out in the *Awards Opinion*,[80] principal organs may go beyond the delegation of the exercise of their own competences to a subsidiary organ if authorized to do so by a substantive provision of the Charter.[81] In this case, the ICJ also held that the subsidiary organ will ultimately remain subordinate to its creator, in that the latter can abolish the subsidiary organ or amend the terms under which it is to function.[82] However, the SC must at least possess the substantive competence to adopt measures in the area concerned (i.e. they must relate to the maintenance of peace and security). One of these measures may be the establishment of a tribunal or another judicial mechanism.[83] Whether such substantive authorization for the SC referral is found in the Charter will be addressed in the following section. Suffice it to note here that the situation of a SC referral is in this aspect similar to the establishment of the ad hoc tribunals, that are also then independently issuing decisions and orders, and making judicial findings that the SC must accept.

The third requirement for a lawful delegation is that the SC must impose an obligation to report the way in which the powers are being exercised.[84] In practice, it is clear that states also viewed that necessary for the SC referral.

---

[78] In the Darfur referral, the resolution referenced the report of the International Commission of Inquiry on violations of international humanitarian law and human rights law in Darfur (S/2005/60) in its preamble in which the justification for suggesting the involvement of the court was clearly articulated; see Report of the International Commission of Inquiry on Darfur to the Secretary-General Pursuant to Security Council resolution 1564 (2004) UN Doc S/2005/60 (18 September 2004) para 571. In the referral of the situation in Libya it stressed in the preamble of S/RES/1970 (2011) 'the need to hold to account those responsible for attacks, including by forces under their control, on civilians'. See further in Chapter 6.

[79] Sarooshi (n 6) 157.

[80] *Effect of Awards Case* (Advisory Opinion) [1954] ICJ Rep 47, paras 46ff.

[81] Erika de Wet, *The Chapter VII Powers of the United Nations Security Council* (Hart Publishing 2004) 339.

[82] Ibid.

[83] Paulus (n 68) 12.

[84] Sarooshi (n 6) 157.

Here the RA provides for such requirement and in reality the SC imposes such an obligation in the respective resolution.[85]

All these conditions have been recognized by the SC itself, as well as by UN member states.[86] Agreement on this is also reflected by the accepted practice of the SC to delegate Chapter VII powers to member states.[87] The same must apply *mutatis mutandis* to conferral of powers. Like the delegation of powers, the conferral of powers – as a characteristic of power – has an implicit coercive or forceful element that demands compliance with a decision.[88] This is why the SC referral is adopted as a coercive measure under Chapter VII and is therefore similar to a delegation of powers and constitutes not just authority or competence.[89] Therefore, the following section will deal with the legal basis under Chapter VII and then proceeds by looking at the limits to the SC's powers under the Charter.

4.3 CHAPTER VII POWERS OF THE SC

Pursuant to art 24(1) UN Charter, the SC is charged with the primary responsibility for international peace and security:[90]

> In order to ensure prompt and effective action by the United Nations, its Members confer on the Security Council primary responsibility for the maintenance of international peace and security, and agree that in carrying out its duties under this responsibility the Security Council acts on their behalf.

Article 24(1) represents a delegation of international 'police' power by states to the SC.[91] Accordingly, in the exercise of its Chapter VII powers the SC is responsible to UN member states.[92]

---

[85] Article 17(1) Relationship Agreement; Security Council Res 1593 (2005) para 8; Security Council Res 1970 (2011) para 7.

[86] Sarooshi (n 6) 154–55.

[87] Ibid. 167–246.

[88] Ibid. 5.

[89] Ibid.

[90] de Wet (n 81) 1.

[91] As Sarooshi correctly points out, states did possess a policing power prior to the Charter, and that even if this view is not accepted, art 24(1) of the Charter could be viewed as a delegation of a policing power from the international community, i.e. the vast majority of states at any particular period in time to the SC (when accepting the premise that the 'powers which can be exercised by the collective totality of sovereign States is greater than the sum of the individual powers of these States'); see Sarooshi (n 6) 26–31; 29 (with further references).

[92] Ibid. 26–31, with further references.

In discharging its duties, the SC may adopt coercive measures under Chapter VII, which by virtue of art 25 UN Charter bind all UN members.[93] According to art 103 UN Charter, the obligations stemming from binding SC resolutions adopted under Chapter VII enjoy primacy over any other international agreement.[94] This means that only *binding* decisions of the SC enjoy this primacy over other obligations under international law (such as those stemming from the Rome Statute). For these reasons, the present study is concerned only with the analysis of such binding decisions.[95] While the SC may also adopt recommendations, these would not legally bind the member states and therefore have no bearing on the research question of this study.[96]

To look at the competences of the SC vis-à-vis the ICC, a thorough analysis must be conducted regarding the pertinent articles in the UN Charter. This is because the SC, as any other organ of an international organization, enjoys powers only insofar as they are conferred on it by or implied in the constituent instrument of the organization.[97] Thus, the range of powers of the SC under Chapter VII of the Charter is determined by arts 39 to 42, and any discretionary power of the SC must be derived from these specific authorizations and cannot be presumed.[98]

In order to adopt a binding Chapter VII resolution, the SC must make an art 39 determination that a particular situation constitutes a threat to, or breach of, the peace or act of aggression.[99] This links the peace and security mandate of the SC to the justice mandate of the ICC.[100] What this means is that the SC

---

93 The question of whether UNSC measures under Chapter VII also binds other subjects of international law, such as international organizations or non-state actors, will be discussed below.

94 Article 103 UN Charter reads: 'In the event of a conflict between the obligations of the Members of the United Nations under the present Charter and their obligations under any other international agreement, their obligations under the present Charter shall prevail'.

95 For a decision to be binding, the SC must act in accordance with the Charter; see Article 25 UN Charter. The specific limits are addressed in Chapter 5.5 below.

96 For the customary international law rules that bind international organizations, see e.g. Schermers and Blokker (n 6) 1339; Ignaz Seidl-Hohenveldern and Gerhard Loibl, *Das Recht der internationalen Organisationen einschliesslich der supranationalen Gemeinschaften* (6th edn, Academia iuris, C. Heymann 1996) para 1512.

97 Anne Peters, 'Article 25' in Simma (n 8) para 90.

98 Krisch (n 8) 1256.

99 Judge Weeramantry in the *Lockerbie* case (Order) [1992] ICJ Reports 66, 176.

100 See also Sarooshi who views this link as a potentially serious impediment to the independent functioning of the ICC. Dan Sarooshi, 'The Peace and Justice Paradox: The International Criminal Court and the UN Security Council' in Dominic McGoldrick, Peter Rowe and Eric Donnelly (eds), *The Permanent International Criminal Court: Legal And Policy Issues* (Hart Publishing 2004) 100.

must determine that the commission of international crimes constitutes a threat to, or breach of, the peace or act of aggression, either in themselves or as part of a broader situation, and that a referral to the ICC is necessary.

4.4 ARTICLE 39 OF THE UN CHARTER

Pursuant to art 39, the 'Security Council shall determine the existence of any threat to the peace, breach of the peace, or act of aggression and shall make recommendations, or decide what measures shall be taken in accordance with Articles 41 and 42, to maintain or restore international peace and security'.[101] Article 39 has been viewed as concentrating the 'most important powers of the Security Council',[102] since it defines the main prerequisites for the application of the provisions regulating the adoption of enforcement measures in cases of threats to the peace, breaches of the peace or acts of aggression.[103]

Careful reading of this provision establishes two important qualifications for actions under Chapter VII. First, the SC must – when adopting coercive measures – determine the existence of either a threat or breach of the peace or act of aggression.[104] Second, measures taken in accordance with arts 41 and 42 must be adopted in order to maintain or restore international peace and security.[105]

It is controversial whether the determination of a threat to the peace, breach of the peace or an act of aggression itself must be expressly made. Whereas it has been asserted that of the few material standards contained in the Charter, these should not be disregarded by reference to mere formalities,[106] it is generally accepted that a resolution does not need to contain an express reference to art 39.[107] This follows from the UN Charter itself, as

---

[101] Article 39 UN Charter.

[102] US Secretary of State, 'Report of the President on the Results of the San Francisco Conference' (1945) 90–91, available at https://catalog.hathitrust.org/Record/011394708 (accessed 12 May 2016).

[103] Nico Krisch, 'Article 39' in Simma (n 8) para 3; Jochen A. Frowein and Nico Krisch, 'Article 39' in Simma (n 9) 1.

[104] Ibid. para 26; David Schweigman, *The Authority of the Security Council under Chapter VII of the UN Charter: Legal Limits and the Role of the International Court of Justice* (Studies and materials on the settlement of international disputes v. 8, Kluwer Law International 2001) 34; Frederic L. Kirgis, 'The Security Council's First Fifty Years' (1995) 89 *American Journal of International Law* 506, 512.

[105] Article 39 UN Charter.

[106] Frowein and Krisch (n 103) para 26. Similarly, Krisch (n 103) para 45.

[107] Ibid. para 47; Frowein and Krisch (n 103) 27; Schweigman (n 104) 157; Michael E. Kurth, *Das Verhältnis des Internationalen Strafgerichtshofes zum UN-Sicherheitsrat: Unter besonderer Berücksichtigung von Sicherheitsratsresolution 1422 (2002)* (Nomos 2006) 16; Jakob Pichon, *Internationaler Strafgerichtshof und Sicherheitsrat der Vereinten Nationen: Zur Rolle des Sicherheitsrats bei der Verfolgung völkerrech-*

> [i]n setting forth the powers of the Council, [the UN Charter] nowhere provides that the Council should, when making use of those powers, cite the source of its authority. In other words, the Council is entirely free to take formal action, under any provision of the UN Charter . . . that vests it with powers, without citing that provision.[108]

This view is confirmed by the *travaux préparatoires*[109] because the committee dealing with the issue even decided 'to leave to the Council the entire decision as to what constitutes a threat to the peace, a breach of the peace or an act of aggression'.[110]

Recent institutional practice, which at times only contains implicit determinations of the prerequisites of art 39 in its resolutions, supports this conclusion.[111] For example, the SC did not expressly determine a threat to the peace in its Res 1970 (2011) in which it was acting upon Chapter VII, adopting coercive measures against Libya (including an arms embargo and travel bans for listed individuals), which contained the referral of the situation to the ICC.[112] This practice appears to be accepted by states.[113] This of course finds an explanation in the politically delicate consequences of such a determination and should therefore be understood within the context of the situation, and every hint in the text pointing to an implicit determination should be picked up.[114]

---

tlicher Verbrechen durch den IStGH (Max-Planck-Gesellschaft zur Förderung der Wissenschaften e.V 2011) 122.

[108] Roberto Lavalle, 'The "Acting under Chapter VII" Clause in Security Council Resolutions under Article 41 of the United Nations Charter: A Misconceived and Harmful Way of Invoking Authority' in Benedetto Conforti and others (eds), *The Italian Yearbook of International Law: 2009* (vol XIX, Martinus Nijhoff 2010) 234.

[109] Proposals to restrict the discretion of the Security Council were rejected in order to leave the SC with great freedom in its decision to determine a threat to the peace, breach of the peace, or an act of aggression; see Krisch (n 103) para 3; Frowein and Krisch (n 103) para 2.

[110] Report of Paul-Boncour (Rapporteur), 'on Chapter VIII Section B' (10 June 1945) UN Doc 881 III/3/46, 502-514, available at http://www.derechos.org/peace/dia/doc/dia31.html (accessed 24 June 2016).

[111] S/RES/1448 (2002) (9 December 2002) (terminating sanctions against UNITA); S/RES/1506 (2003) (12 September 2003 (terminating sanctions against Libya); S/RES/1837 (2008) (29 September 2008); S/RES/1476 (2003) (24 April 2003); S/RES/1490 (2003) (3 July 2003) (both concerning Iraq); S/RES/1160 (1998) (31 March 1998); most recently Res 1970 (2011). See also Patrik Johansson, 'The Humdrum Use of Ultimate Authority: Defining and Analysing Chapter VII Resolutions' (2009) 78 *Nordic Journal of International Law* 309, 311.

[112] UN Security Council Res 1970 (2011).

[113] Critical Pichon (n 107) 123–24.

[114] On the other hand, the lack of an art 39 determination may be healed by subsequent resolutions. This was the case of Res S/RES/1160 (1998) of March 31 1998 deciding on a weapons embargo against the Federal Republic of Yugoslavia

The UN Charter does not per se limit the reasons on which the SC can base an art 39 determination.[115] In fact the SC has over time decided that a threat to peace and security exists in a number of cases with differing causes that have included human rights violations,[116] large-scale human suffering occurring within a state[117] and the restoration of democracy in a state.[118] The SC enjoys a broad political discretion to make an art 39 determination, and as such the only barrier to the SC making such a determination is the lack of political will on the part of its members.[119]

It follows that the commission of international crimes that the SC wishes to be subjected to the jurisdiction of the ICC forms grounds for the SC to make an art 39 determination. Doing so, the SC determines that the commission of these international crimes such as genocide, crimes against humanity, war crimes and the crime of aggression constitute a threat to, or breach of, the peace or an act of aggression (either in themselves or as part of a broader situation), and

---

regarding the situation in Kosovo, which did not include an art 39 determination, but was then considered as being healed by subsequent Res 1199 (1998) which did contain such determination; see Vera Gowlland-Debbas (ed), *United Nations Sanctions and International Law* (The Graduate Institute of International Studies, Kluwer Law International 2001) 290; Pichon (n 107) 123–24.

[115] Krisch (n 103) para 6. See also Dan Sarooshi, 'Conferrals by States of Powers on International Organizations: The Case of Agency' (2004) 74 *British Yearbook of International Law* 291, 103; Benedetto Conforti and Carlo Focarelli, *The Law and Practice of the United Nations* (Legal aspects of international organization vol 53, 4th edn, Martinus Nijhoff Publishers 2010) 205; Michael Wood, 'The United Nations Security Council and International Law: The Security Council's Powers and their Limits' [2006] Lauterpacht Memorial Lectures 2006, paras 12–13, available at http://www.lcil.cam.ac.uk/sites/default/files/LCIL/documents/lectures/2006_hersch_lecture_2.pdf (accessed 12 May 2016).

[116] See e.g. UNSC Res 688 (5 April 1991) UN Doc S/RES/688; UNSC Res 794 (3 December 1992) UN Doc S/RES/794; UNSC Res 929 (22 June 1994) UN Doc S/RES/929; UNSC Res 1078 (9 November 1996) UN Doc S/RES/1078; UNSC Res 1593 (31 March 2005) UN Doc S/RES/1593; see also Krisch (n 103) para 25–27; Dan Sarooshi, 'The United Nations Collective Security System and the Establishment of Peace' (2000) 53(1) *Current Legal Problems* 621, 627.

[117] For example, UNSC Res 1308 (17 July 2000) UN Doc S/RES/1308.

[118] See e.g. UNSC Res 841 (16 June 1993) UN Doc S/RES/841; UNSC Res 917 (6 May 1994) UN Doc S/RES/917; UNSC Res 940 (31 July 1994) UN Doc S/RES/940; see generally the Presidential Note of the SC stating that '[t]he non-military sources of instability in the economic, social, humanitarian and ecological fields have become threats to peace and security', UNSC Presidential Note (31 January 1992) UN Doc S/23500. See also Sarooshi (n 116) 628–32.

[119] Sarooshi (n 115) 103.

that because of this, a referral to the ICC is necessary.[120] It is important to note that art 39 empowers but does not oblige the SC to act under Chapter VII.[121]

In conclusion, if the SC seeks to invoke the binding powers of arts 41 and 42 to enforce its decisions, the plain language of the Charter dictates that it must make a determination (implicit) of a threat to the peace, breach of the peace or an act of aggression. Only then may the SC employ a broad array of powers, including the use of force and coercive measures,[122] making such determination 'a caveat which bestows upon the Security Council a power of appreciation not easily subject to control'.[123]

4.4.1 Threat to the Peace

Generally, the SC enjoys broad discretionary powers with regards to determining what constitutes a threat to the peace.[124] It was only in 1960, however, that the SC acknowledged that systematic violations of human rights and fundamental freedoms and the general absence of the rule of law could constitute a threat to international peace and security.[125] After the end of the Cold War, the SC has greatly broadened this concept of 'threat to the peace' and has recognized that besides systematic violations of human rights, flood of refugees and internal armed conflicts may constitute a threat to the peace.[126]

With a view to crimes under the jurisdiction of the ICC, the SC has considered violations of international humanitarian law as threats to the peace (and considered prosecution of such violations on the international level necessary

---

[120] Sarooshi (n 100) 100.

[121] Krisch (n 103) para 5.

[122] Jared Schott, 'Chapter VII as Exception: Security Council Action and the Regulative Ideal of Emergency' (2007) 6 *Northwestern Journal of International Human Rights* 24, 29.

[123] Mariano J. Aznar-Gomes, 'A Decade of Human Rights Protection by the UN Security Council: A Sketch of Deregulation' (2002) 13(1) *European Journal of International Law* 223, 234.

[124] Krisch (n 103) para 4; Frowein and Krisch (n 103) para 4 (with further references). See also Michael Wood, 'The United Nations Security Council and International Law: The Legal Framework of the Security Council' (2006) Lauterpacht Memorial Lectures 2006, para 25, available at http://www.lcil.cam.ac.uk/sites/default/files/LCIL/documents/lectures/2006_hersch_lecture_1.pdf (accessed 12 May 2016).

[125] See e.g. UNSC Res 217 (20 November 1965) UN Doe S/RES/217; UNSC Res 221 (9 April 1966) UN Doc S/RES/221. See also Bruno S. Ugarte and Jared Genser, 'Evolution of the Security Council's Engagement on Human Rights' in Jared Genser and Bruno S. Ugarte (eds), *The United Nations Security Council in the Age of Human Rights* (Cambridge University Press 2014) 5.

[126] Pichon (n 107) 125; Malcolm N. Shaw, *International Law* (7th edn, Cambridge University Press 2014) 898; Krisch (n 103) para 19.

to maintain international peace and security).[127] On this basis the SC established the ad hoc tribunals ICTY and ICTR. Proponents of such tribunals argued that the SC had already viewed the violations of international humanitarian law as a threat to international peace and security, creating the option to take binding enforcement measures under Chapter VII.[128] In response, the SC asked member states to collect information on such violations[129] and established a Commission of Experts, charged with examining and analyzing that information,[130] which determined in its interim report that in fact grave breaches and other violations had occurred.[131] In fact, the SC has repeatedly adopted measures under Chapter VII to prevent atrocities by governments against their own people.[132]

In fact, the SC has made such determination in the case of Darfur[133] and in Libya,[134] referring these situations to the ICC. In Darfur, for instance, it is argued that investigations and prosecutions of crimes perpetrated in that country before an independent, impartial and fair institution is a means of removing serious obstacles to national reconciliation and the restoration of peaceful relations in Darfur, thus contributing to international peace and security.[135] Such a broad understanding of what can constitute a 'threat to peace' allows the SC to approach each particular case with differing levels of formal

---

[127] See UNSC Res 808 (22 February 1993) UN Doc S/RES/808; UNSC Res 955 (8 November 1994) UN Doc S/RES/955. See also Kenneth Manusama, *The United Nations Security Council in the Post-Cold War Era: Applying the Principle of Legality* (Martinus Nijhoff Publishers 2006) 159.

[128] UNSC Verbatim Record (22 February 1993) UN Doc S/PV.3175, 11–13.

[129] For the ICTY: UNSC Res 771 (13 August 1992) UN Doc S/RES/771; UNSC Res 780 (6 October 1992) UN Doc S/RES/780; with respect to the ICTR: UNSC Res 935 (1 July 1994) UN Doc S/RES/935.

[130] UNSC Res 780 (6 October 1992) UN Doc S/RES/780, para 2.

[131] Report of the Secretary-General on the Situation in Rwanda (31 May 1994) UN Doc S/1994/640.

[132] UNSC Res 1593 (31 March 2005) UN Doc S/RES/1593; UNSC Res 1973 (17 March 2011) UN Doc S/RES/1973; UNSC Res 1975 (30 March 2011) UN Doc S/RES/1975 (on Côte d'Ivoire). Critical about this practice due to its redefinition of threats to domestic peace and security as international threats, which in turns destabilizes international law and 'encourages the imperial tendencies of the Security Council'; see Ian Hurd, 'The Selectively Expansive UN Security Council: Domestic Threats to Peace and Security' (2012) *American Society of International Law Proceedings* 9, 11–12.

[133] UNSC Res 1593 (31 March 2005) UN Doc S/RES/1593.

[134] In the case of Libya the SC only implicitly determined a threat to the peace in Res 1970 (2011). In the subsequent resolution following the referral, the SC determined a threat to the peace in Res 1973 (2011).

[135] Luigi Condorelli and Annalisa Ciampi, 'Comments on the Security Council Referral of the Situation in Darfur to the ICC' (2005) 3(3) *Journal of International Criminal Justice* 590, 592.

and material 'intensity', leaving room for an ad hoc approach in each particular case.[136]

However, this broad interpretation of a 'threat to the peace' has also been met with criticism.[137] Suffice it to note here that such an approach is another instance of a general practice of deregulation of the entire process of Chapter VII measures due to the fact that, as expressed by Jean Combacau in a deliberate truism, 'une menace pour la paix au sens de l'article 39 est une situation dont l'organe compétent pour déclencher une action des sanctions déclare qu'elle menace effectivement la paix.'[138]

As a result, situations where international crimes have been committed may constitute a threat of the peace under art 39 UN Charter, thus enabling the SC to act under Chapter VII of the UN Charter, should the SC so determine.

4.4.2 Breach of the Peace

Typically, a breach of the peace refers to the use of armed force between armed units of two states.[139] It is not relevant whether the hostilities end quickly because of the defeat of one side.[140] For instance, the SC regarded the invasion of Argentina of the Falkland/Malvinas Islands as a breach of the peace, although at the time of the adoption of the resolution no further resistance took place on the islands: the United Kingdom, however, was planning their recapture.[141] Furthermore, a breach of the peace exists if armed force is applied by or against an effective independent de facto regime which is not recognized as a state, as such a regime equally enjoys the protection of the prohibition on the use of force. Accordingly, the SC determined a breach of the peace after North Korean troops had attacked South Korea in 1950,[142] and the opposite view, based on the civil war character of the hostilities, did not prevail.[143]

In fact, internal armed conflicts may constitute breaches of the peace once it is accepted that these might pose threats to the peace regardless of any ensuing

---

[136] Aznar-Gomes (n 123) 233–34.

[137] Hurd (n 132).

[138] Jean Combacau, *Le Pouvoir de sanction de l'O.N.U.: étude théorique de la coercition non militaire* (Pedone 1974) 100; Aznar-Gomes (n 123) 233.

[139] Krisch (n 103) para 41; Frowein and Krisch (n 103) para 11; Conforti and Focarelli (n 115) 206.

[140] Krisch (n 103) para 41; Frowein and Krisch (n 103) para 11.

[141] Krisch (n 103) para 40; Frowein and Krisch (n 103) para 11.

[142] UNSC Res 82 (25 June 1950) UN Doc S/RES/82. See on this Hanspeter Neuhold, *The Law of International Conflict: Force, Intervention and Peaceful Dispute Settlement* (Collected courses of the Xiamen Academy of International Law, vol 5, Brill Nijhoff 2016) 53.

[143] Frowein and Krisch (n 103) para 11.

risk of an international war. If the prospect of a destabilization of the respective country, of human rights violations and of dire humanitarian consequences is considered as the cause of a threat to the peace, a breach of the peace occurs when these consequences manifest. In practice, however, the SC has not yet termed such a situation a 'breach' but has confined itself to determining 'threats to the peace'.[144]

As a result, grave breaches of international humanitarian law during an internal armed conflict appear not to constitute a breach of the peace in the practice of the SC but rather a threat to the peace.

4.4.3 Act of Aggression

At the San Francisco Conference, a definition of the term 'aggression' was deliberately avoided.[145] Generally, in public international law, it is widely established that, as the House of Lords stated in the *Jones* case, 'waging aggressive war is a crime under existing international law'.[146] The nature of the crime of aggression was famously described in the International Military Tribunal in Nuremberg, which termed 'crimes against peace' the 'supreme international crime differing only from other war crimes in that it contains within itself the accumulated evil of the whole'.[147] Because of its direct link to *jus ad bellum*, it is deeply (more than in the other crimes of the Rome Statute) embedded in peace maintenance.[148]

An act of aggression is limited to the use of armed force.[149] Thus, economic and/or political coercion (applying a teleological interpretation of art 2(4)

---

144 Krisch (n 103) para 40; Frowein and Krisch (n 103) para 12.

145 Conforti and Focarelli (n 115) 206.

146 *R v Jones and others* (2006) UKHL 16, (2006) All ER 741, paras 19 (Lord Bingham), 59 (Lord Hoffmann), 99 (Lord Mance). See also e.g. Andreas L. Paulus, 'Second Thoughts on the Crime of Aggression' (2010) 20(4) *European Journal of International Law* 1117, 1118.

147 *France et al. v Göring et al.*, (1947) 41 AJIL 172, 186. See also Schabas (n 11) 109.

148 Carsten Stahn, 'The "End", the "Beginning of the End" or the "End of the Beginning"? Introducing Debates and Voices on the Definition of "Aggression"'; (2010) 23(4) *Leiden Journal of International Law* 875, 875–76.

149 Declaration on the Principles of International Law concerning Friendly Relations and Cooperation among States in accordance with the Charter of the United Nations, General Assembly Res 2625 (XXV) of 24 October 1970; see also de Wet (n 81) 145–46. Economic and/or political coercion are thus not acts of aggression, a notion that is confirmed by the Friendly Relations Declaration (Declaration on the Principles of International Law concerning Friendly Relations and Cooperation among States in accordance with the Charter of the United Nations, General Assembly Res 2625 (XXV) of 24 October 1970).

of the Charter) cannot be characterized as an act of aggression. This notion of an act of aggression is confirmed by the Friendly Relations Declaration (FRD).[150] Meant as a guide to the SC, the GA adopted a definition of an act of aggression in Res 3314 (XXIX),[151] also called the 'Definition of Aggression Resolution'.[152]

At the review conference of the ICC in Kampala in March 2010, the ASP adopted an amendment for the crime of aggression pursuant to art 5(2) Rome Statute, containing a definition of the crime of aggression based on this GA resolution.[153] As opposed to the other core crimes contained in art 5 of the Statute, there is no element of immediacy or directness involved,[154] and only when state aggression exists can the individual commit the crime of aggression.[155]

The determination of an act of aggression by the SC is a political finding and not a judicial one. It is thus problematic that such a determination could be given weight in judicial proceedings as has been proposed with respect to the ICC.[156] While it is necessary to ensure that the ICC's work does not adversely affect the exercise of the SC's Chapter VII powers, the recognition of the binding force of a SC determination in criminal proceedings would neglect the political role of the SC as well as the necessary independence of the ICC.[157] Thus, whereas an act of aggression results in state responsibility, the crime of aggression is a crime entailing individual criminal accountability under the Rome Statute. The determination of an act of aggression does not, however, preclude the ICC to independently investigate whether a crime of aggression has been committed. It is important to note that the SC's primary responsibility regarding the maintenance of international peace and security is not exclusive.[158]

---

[150] FRD (n 149). See also de Wet (n 81) 145–46.

[151] General Assembly Res 3314 (XXIX) of 14 December 1974.

[152] Frowein and Krisch (n 103) para 14; Conforti and Focarelli (n 115) 206.

[153] Amendment to Article 8 of the Rome Statute of the International Criminal Court Kampala (10 June 2010) Assembly of States Parties Res RC/Res.5.

[154] Matthias Schuster, 'The Rome Statute and the Crime of Aggression: A Gordian Knot in Search of a Sword' (2003) 14(1) *Criminal Law Forum* 1, 22.

[155] Ibid. 36. See also, Proceedings of the Preparatory Commission, at Its Ninth Session (8–19 April 2002), UN Doc PCNICC/2002/L.1/Rev.1, 23.

[156] Zimmermann (n 16) 202–204.

[157] Frowein and Krisch (n 103) 13–15.

[158] Michael J. Glennon, 'The Blank-Prose Crime of Aggression' (2010) 35 *Yale Journal of International Law* 71, 104–105; Yengejeh, S., 'Reflections on the Role of the Security Council in Determining an Act of Aggression' in M. Politi and G. Nesi (eds) *The International Criminal Court and the Crime of Aggression* (2004) 76. See e.g. Uniting for Peace Resolution, United Nations General Assembly Res 377 UN Doc A/RES/377(V) (3 November 1950); *Nicaragua Case (Military and Paramilitary*

4.5 ARTICLE 41 UN CHARTER AND THE REFERRAL

Article 41 of the UN Charter lays out the substantive competence for the SC referral. This provision provides the legal basis for all non-military enforcement measures. According to the wording of the provision, the SC can decide which measures should be taken in order to implement its decisions.[159] It gives several examples of non-military enforcement measures, but, according to the wording and the history of the provision, this list is not exhaustive.[160] Thus, while many of the measures listed in art 41 have in fact been adopted, the SC has also employed such atypical measures as legal determinations,[161] the creation of international criminal tribunals[162] or the establishment of interim administrations of certain territories.[163] In leaving open the range of possible measures, art 41 allows for such a broad interpretation. It empowers the SC to take any measure short of the use of force it deems useful for the maintenance of international peace and security, as long as it remains within the general framework of its Chapter VII powers.[164]

Regarding the SC referral, the SC could decide that the referral is an appropriate measure to restore or maintain international peace and security. This determination raises the question of whether ICC prosecution may constitute a suitable means to achieve international peace. It has been argued that, in principle, the answer is positive in reference to the practice of the SC, particularly the establishment of the ICTY/ICTR.[165] In practice, however, political motivations based on the specific situation at stake could bring the SC to decide not to seize the Court, even when it appears that crimes within its jurisdiction have

---

Activities in and against Nicaragua, Nicaragua v United States of America) Jurisdiction and Admissibility [1984] ICJ Rep 392.

[159] Nico Krisch, 'Article 41' in Simma (n 8) paras 12–13.

[160] Krisch (n 159) paras 12–13; Jochen A. Frowein and Nico Krisch, 'Article 41' in Simma (n 9) 14.

[161] UNSC Res 276 (30 January 1970) UN Doc S/RES/276.

[162] UNSC Res 827 (25 May 1993) UN Doc S/RES/827 (ICTY); UNSC Res 955 (8 November 1994) UN Doc S/RES/955.

[163] UNSC Res 745 (28 February 1992) UN Doc S/RES/745 (Cambodia); UNSC Res 814 (26 March 1993) UN Doc S/RES/814 (Somalia); UNSC Res 1031 (15 December 1995) UN Doc S/RES/1031 (Bosnia-Herzegovina). Krisch (n 159) paras 12; Frowein and Krisch (n 160) 14.

[164] Krisch (n 159) paras 12–13; Frowein and Krisch (n 160) 14.

[165] The conviction of the States Parties at the Rome Conference that the prosecution of international crimes contribute to international peace and security (in the preamble of the Rome Statute) is also referenced as a reason for the appropriateness of such measures; see e.g. Condorelli and Villalpando (n 1) 631–32.

been committed.[166] Once again, the SC's discretionary power under Chapter VII remains untouched by the Statute.[167]

It has been established in the previous section that a situation in which crimes under the Statute of the ICC have been committed may constitute a threat to the peace, thus opening the door for Chapter VII measures of the SC, including a referral to the ICC. The following section now addresses the question of whether a referral to the ICC indeed falls within the SC's powers as a measure under Chapter VII of the UN Charter.

Due to the special nature of SC referrals to the ICC,[168] the starting point for this analysis must be the division of the forms of jurisdiction that is conferred to the ICC by virtue of a SC referral. As elaborated below,[169] the referral is in its nature legislative (in that it creates new obligations for the state addressed in the referral),[170] and (from the perspective of the Rome Statute) seeks to confer jurisdiction over a situation in a non-state party to the Rome Statute to the Court.[171] The subsequent analysis will therefore proceed with this distinction in mind, analyzing each form of jurisdiction separately with respect to the SC powers under Chapter VII of the Charter.

The analysis therefore requires a closer look at art 41 of the UN Charter, which is the legal basis for binding measures under Chapter VII of the Charter not involving the use of force.[172] After laying out the general parameters of art 41, the SC's (quasi-)legislative, (quasi-)judicial and enforcement powers are assessed and analyzed. Finally, the rest of this chapter addresses the SC's power to terminate the referral and considers whether there is an obligation to terminate it under certain circumstances.

4.5.1 Article 41 UN Charter

The adoption of Chapter VII enforcement action constitutes an exception to the principle stated in art 2(7) of the Charter, according to which the UN is not authorized 'to intervene in matters which are essentially within the domestic

---

166 Ibid.

167 Ibid.

168 See Chapter 3.

169 Chapter 4.5 and 4.6.

170 This is of course not uncontested, but for a similar discussion relating to the question of whether the Rome Statute is binding on individuals, see M. Milanovic, 'Is the Rome Statute Binding on Individuals? (And Why We Should Care)' (2011) 9(1) *Journal of International Criminal Justice* 25.

171 For an overview of the various forms of jurisdiction in international criminal law, see e.g. Robert Cryer and others, *An Introduction to International Criminal Law and Procedure* (3rd edn, Cambridge University Press 2014) 49ff (with further references).

172 See below.

jurisdiction of any state'.[173] For the analysis of the SC referral as a measure under Chapter VII, art 41 of the UN Charter is the starting point,[174] since it deals with the SC's binding measures short of armed force (the use of force is regulated in art 42 of the Charter).[175] Article 41 reads:

> The Security Council may decide what measures not involving the use of armed force are to be employed to give effect to its decisions, and it may call upon the Members of the United Nations to apply such measures. These may include complete or partial interruption of economic relations and of rail, sea, air, postal, telegraphic, radio, and other means of communication, and the severance of diplomatic relations.[176]

The wording of art 41 thus clearly indicates that measures listed therein are non-exhaustive.[177] This is also supported by the *travaux préparatoires* of the UN Charter, in which '[a]greement was finally reached on an illustrative, non-exhaustive enumeration'.[178] Accordingly, the SC enjoys a certain discretion in that regard and is therefore not limited to the measures explicitly mentioned in art 41.[179]

Having established the broad nature of art 41, the question is then whether a SC referral to the ICC falls within the scope of art 41. Before looking at this issue, it is important to note that there is agreement that enforcement measures are not necessarily limited to measures against those states from which the threat to the peace (or breach of the peace or an act of aggression) originates.[180] This is important for freeing the SC from extensive fact-finding in each case before acting (regarding the commission of international crimes, for example), which would prevent it from acting quickly and thus possibly compromise its efficiency.[181] It also means that enforcement measures generally, and the SC referral in particular, are not directed at states or entities that violated international (humanitarian) law.[182] Although the situation causing a threat

---

173 Shaw (n 126) 898; Krisch (n 8) 1257.

174 The nature and scope of the provisional measures pursuant to Article 40 are not addressed here, since these lack binding force and are thus not capable of transferring jurisdictional authority over a situation in a state not party to the Rome Statute to the ICC, see Chapter 3.

175 See further Frowein and Krisch (n 160) para 11.

176 Article 41 of the UN Charter.

177 'These [the measures not involving the use of armed force] *may* include' (emphasis added); see also Frowein and Krisch (n 160) para 14.

178 Ibid. para 3, with further references.

179 Ibid.

180 de Wet (n 81) 183.

181 Ibid.

182 Ibid. with further references.

to peace will often entail an illegal act, the upholding of international law is not the SC's primary concern.[183] In fact, the purpose of enforcement actions provided for in art 41 is to maintain or restore international peace and security, which is not necessarily identical with enforcing the law.[184] Most importantly this also means that the SC referral as a measure under Chapter VII is without prejudice for the investigation of the Prosecutor of the ICC and the findings of the Chambers.

This need for efficient enforcement action further implies that the SC enjoys a wide discretion in deciding how to make use of its Chapter VII powers. On the one hand, the SC is not obliged to adopt *any* enforcement measures after having determined that an art 39 situation exists, as art 41 (along with arts 40 and 42) is merely of a permissive nature.[185] On the other hand, if the SC does decide to resort to enforcement measures, it is not obliged to exhaust the mechanisms for the peaceful settlement of disputes provided for in Chapter VI, before adopting coercive measures under Chapter VII.[186] Once it has made a determination in terms of art 39, it can immediately resort to the measures provided for in art 41 of the Charter.[187]

For the SC referral to the ICC it thus follows that once the SC has made a determination under art 39, it does not have to wait for a commission of inquiry (or any other fact-finding mission)[188] to report on crimes under the Rome Statute being committed on the territory of a state, before it can take action referring a situation to the ICC.[189]

However, even within the broad confines of Chapter VII, the SC is not 'unbound by law', as the Appeals Chamber of the ICTY so famously stated.[190] At the same time it was the ICTY Appeals Chamber that held that the estab-

---

[183] Ibid.

[184] Hans Kelsen, *The Law of the United Nations: A Critical Analysis of its Fundamental Problems: with supplement* (F.A. Praeger 1951) 294.

[185] de Wet (n 81) 184.

[186] Ibid.

[187] Ibid.

[188] The SC has however done so in the case of Darfur (see Chapter 7.2.). In the second SC referral concerning Libya, the SC referred the situation to the ICC before a commission of inquiry into the violations of international human rights law issued its report (the SC referral was adopted on 26 February 2011 and the International Commission of Inquiry was established by a Resolution of the Human Rights Council on 25 February 2011); see UNHRC Res S-15/1 (25 February 2011) UN Doc A/HRC/S-15/1; Report of the International Commission of Inquiry to investigate all alleged violations of international human rights law in the Libyan Arab Jamahiriya (1 June 2011) UN Doc A/HRC/17/44.

[189] For the practice of the SC in that regard, see Chapter 6 below.

[190] *Tadic Case* (Decision on the Defence Motion for Interlocutory Appeal on Jurisdiction) ICTY-IT-94-1-A (2 October 1995) para 28.

lishment of the international tribunal fell squarely within the powers of the SC under art 41 of the UN Charter and was consequently legal.[191] This is now widely recognized by scholarship.[192] However, as established above, this conclusion does not apply to the SC referral by analogy and the referral must therefore be carefully and separately analyzed.

From the outset, in view of the broad discretion the SC enjoys under art 41, the argument that the SC is bound by the principle of proportionality[193] requiring a rational and proportional link between the means and the end pursued[194] is not convincing.[195] If the principle of proportionality were to be applied, the SC would be forced to exhaust all non-binding or non-military enforcement measures before authorizing the use of force. As was indicated above, this would not be reconcilable with the flexibility that the SC needs to fulfil its function of maintaining international peace and security, which requires quick and efficient action. Furthermore, it also does not pay due consideration to the interest of the world community in preventing war, or the uncertainty as to how those states or entities subjected to enforcement measures will react.[196]

Thus, art 41 allows for a broad interpretation leaving open a range of possible measures. It empowers the SC to take any measure short of the use of force it deems useful for the maintenance of international peace and security as long as it remains within the general framework of Chapter VII powers.[197]

---

[191] Cassese (n 14) 494; Dapo Akande, 'The Jurisdiction of the ICC over Nationals of Non-Parties: Legal Basis and Limits' (2003) 1 *Journal of International Criminal Justice* 618, 628. In addition, faced with the objection that the setting-up of the international tribunal was unlawful as being contrary to the general principle whereby courts must be 'established by law', the Appeals Chamber held that this objection as well was to be dismissed: indeed, the tribunal had 'been established in accordance with the appropriate procedures under the United Nations Charter and provide[d] all the necessary safeguards of a fair trial'; see *Tadic Case* (Decision on the Defence Motion for Interlocutory Appeal on Jurisdiction) ICTY-IT-94-l-A (2 October 1995) para 47.

[192] Cassese (n 14) 494; Reinisch (n 25) 264.

[193] On the concept of proportionality in international law, see Emily Crawford, 'Proportionality' [2011] *Max Planck Encyclopedia of Public International Law*.

[194] See e.g. Talmon (n 4) 68. Apparently also Stefan Talmon, 'Security Council Treaty Action', 62 *Revue Hellenique de Droit International* (2009) 65–116, at 68; apparently also Frowein and Krisch (n 160) paras 23–24. On the 'watered down' concept of proportionality applying to SC action, see Angelet (n 31) 73; de Wet (n 81) 185.

[195] Sharing this view e.g. de Wet (n 81) 185; Michael Wood, 'The Law of Treaties and the UN Security Council: Some Reflections' in Enzo Cannizzaro (ed), *The Law of Treaties Beyond the Vienna Convention* (Oxford University Press 2011) 247.

[196] de Wet (n 81) 185.

[197] Krisch (n 103) para 12; Frowein and Krisch (n 160) para 14.

Before turning to the limits of the Chapter VII powers of the SC, it is important to distinguish the different aspects of a SC referral as they relate to the Chapter VII powers. The first aspect is the quasi-legislative nature of the SC referral, since it is creating legal obligations for the situation state(s) concerned. Second, the referral may be considered as quasi-judicial/adjudicative in nature, since it hands over judicial authority for a situation in a third state to the ICC.[198]

4.5.2 The Powers of the SC and Quasi-Legislative Measures

Generally stated, by providing the SC with the power to adopt binding measures under Chapter VII, the Charter authorizes the SC to create new obligations for states and thus to act, to a certain degree, as a legislator.[199] In other words, the SC can regulate state behaviour worldwide and for extended periods of time through its Chapter VII measures, and although this constitutes legislation in form, it is, in principle, confined to specific situations and preliminary effects; it ends when the threat to the peace that has given rise to the measures fades. Thus, such law creation might in substance be regarded as analogous to executive regulations rather than to true legislation.[200]

However, SC referrals involving non-party states are going beyond such executive regulations in two important ways. First, the SC – when referring – seeks to impose obligations on the third state on whose territory the crimes that have allegedly been committed.[201] Such practice has been termed 'treaty action' and is legislative in nature, because it effectively binds a third state to the provisions of a treaty that it did not consent to.[202] Second, the referral could be viewed as seeking to legislate the crimes as included in the Statute for the Court to apply against individuals of that state's jurisdiction (because the jurisdiction of the ICC is arguably substantive in nature).[203] Thus, when looking at the powers of the SC under art 41 of the Charter, these issues of the legislative

---

198 For the question of judicial independence, see Chapter 6.1.1.8.

199 Angelet (n 31) 80.

200 Krisch (n 103) para 33; Frowein and Krisch (n 160) 21.

201 According to Michael Wood, the referral does not bind the third state to the Rome Statute, but only imposes its provisions of that treaty and is therefore not to be considered ultra vires; Wood (n 195) 251. Similarly Akande, who considers that by virtue of the SC referral the third state 'is bound to accept the jurisdiction of the Court and legality of the Court's operation in accordance with its Statute'; Dapo Akande, 'The Legal Nature of Security Council Referrals to the ICC and its Impact on Al-Bashir's Immunities' (2009) 7(2) *Journal of International Criminal Justice* 333, 341.

202 Talmon (n 4).

203 See Chapter 4.5.2.2.

nature of SC referrals with respect to third states and the SC referral legislating the crimes under the Statute – although related – must be dealt with separately.

4.5.2.1 SC referral as SC treaty action

Scholarship has recognized that the SC legislates with respect to different fields.[204] For example, SC Res 827 (1993) which installed the ICTY, SC Res 955 (1994) setting up the ICTR[205] and SC Res 1373 (2001) on the Financing of Terrorism[206] and SC Res 1540 (2004) regarding obligations against the proliferation of nuclear, chemical and biological weapons are referenced as legislation by the SC.[207] Also SC Res 1422 and 1487 were deemed legislative in nature.[208] A more recent example of legislative action by the SC is Res 2178 (2014) on foreign terrorist fighters.[209]

---

[204] Keith Harper, 'Does the United Nations Security Council have the Competence to Act as Court and Legislature?' (1994) 27 *New York University Journal of International Law & Politics* 103; Paul C. Szasz, 'The Security Council Starts Legislating' (2002) 96(4) *The American Journal of International Law* 901; Stefan Talmon, 'The Security Council as World Legislature' (2005) 99 *American Journal of International Law* 175; Anne Peters, 'Global Constitutionalism Revisited' (2005) 11 *International Legal Theory* 39, 51; Björn Elberling, 'The *Ultra Vires* Character of Legislative Action by the Security Council' (2005) 2 *International Organizations Law Review* 337. In the field of climate change this was also considered; see e.g. Nico Krisch, 'The Decay of Consent: International Law in an Age of Global Public Goods' (2014) 108(1) *American Journal of International Law* 1, 18–19. A recent empirical study points to the fact that the SC adopted legislative resolutions before the end of the Cold War; see Rossana Deplano, *The Strategic Use of International Law by the United Nations Security Council: An Empirical Study* (Springer briefs in law 2015) 15–19. Critical of this classification as legislative, see Alexander Orakhelashvili, *Peremptory Norms in International Law* (Oxford University Press 2008) 61.

[205] Martti Koskenniemi, 'The Police in the Temple Order, Justice and the UN: A Dialectical View' (1995) 6 *European Journal of International Law* 325, 326; Sebastian Heselhaus, 'Resolution 1422 (2002) des Sicherheitsrates zur Begrenzung der Tätigkeit des Internationalen Strafgerichtshof' (2002) 62 *Zeitschrift für ausländisches öffentliches Recht und Völkerrecht*, 921.

[206] Jurij D Aston, 'Die Bekämpfung abstrakter Gefahren für den Weltfrieden durch legislative Maßnahmen des Sicherheitsrats – Resolution 1373 (2001) im Kontext' (2002) 62 *Zeitschrift für ausländisches öffentliches Recht und Völkerrecht* 257.

[207] Peters (n 204) 51.

[208] See e.g. Talmon (n 204) 177–78; Andreas Zimmermann and Björn Elberling, 'Grenzen der Legislativbefugnisse des Sicherheitsrats: Resolution 1540 und abstrakte Bedrohungen des Weltfriedens' (2004) *Vereinte Nationen* 71, 72–73; Matthew Happold, 'Security Council Resolution 1373 and the Constitution of the United Nations' (2003) 16(3) *Leiden Journal of International Law* 593, 609. See on these two resolutions further Chapter 7.1.

[209] José E Alvarez, *The Impact of International Organizations on International Law* (Collected courses of the Xiamen Academy of International Law volume 7, Brill Nijhoff 2017) 125.

Such legislative action has been met with criticism, as it was considered to go beyond the SC's powers.[210] This practice points to the erosion of the consent requirement in international law.[211] From the perspective of national autonomy, democracy and sovereign equality, such criticism raised the issue that anything other than a consent-like criterion would be dictatorial.[212] While such legislative practice arguably constitutes a departure from the original spirit of the UN Charter,[213] it appears to be the SC's continued practice, which found some acceptance by states[214] and in scholarship alike.[215]

In regard to ICL, scholarship widely recognizes that the establishment of the international criminal tribunals, vested with the power to prosecute individuals, fell within the SC powers under art 41.[216] As established above, the criminal jurisdiction of such international tribunals was, however, exercised through subsidiary organs of the SC by virtue of art 29 of the Charter,[217] as has been prominently the case with the ad hoc tribunals for the former Yugoslavia (ICTY) and Rwanda (ICTR).[218] As this study has demonstrated, these prec-

---

210 N. Jain, 'A Separate Law for Peacekeepers: The Clash between the Security Council and the International Criminal Court' (2005) 16(2) *European Journal of International Law* 239; Elberling (n 204). In response to such criticism Johnstone proposes to enhance the legitimacy of such SC decisions by creating a more deliberative process of decision-making; see Ian Johnstone, 'Legislation and Adjudication in the UN Security Council: Bringing down the Deliberative Deficit' (2008) 102(2) *American Journal of International Law* 275.

211 Peters (n 204) 51–52; 58ff; Krisch (n 204) 5.

212 Krisch (n 204) 5; Jan Klabbers, 'Law-Making and Constitutionalism' in Jan Klabbers, Anne Peters and Geir Ulfstein (eds), *The Constitutionalization of International Law* (Oxford University Press 2009) 114.

213 For the view that the SC is not entitled to create general legal rules directly, Andreas Stein, *Der Sicherheitsrat der Vereinten Nationen und die Rule of Law: Auslegung und Rechtsfortbildung des Begriffs der Friedensbedrohung bei humanitären Interventionen auf der Grundlage des Kapitels VII der Charta der Vereinten Nationen* (Veröffentlichungen aus dem Institut für Internationale Angelegenheiten der Universität Hamburg vol 23, Nomos 1999); Kurth (n 107) 68.

214 Frowein and Krisch (n 9) para 23; Wood paras 23–26.

215 It did so in its response of the terrorist attacks against the United States of September 2001, including enacting many of the provisions contained in earlier conventions against terrorism (SC Res 1373); Frowein and Krisch (n 9) para 22; Peters (n 204) 51; Wood (n 124) paras 23–26. See also Rosand, who called SC Res 1373 and 1540 a 'triumph of pragmatism; see Eric Rosand, 'The Security Council As "Global Legislator": Ultra Vires or Ultra Innovative?' (2004) 28(3) *Fordham International Law Journal* 542, 546. See however a cautious stance on legislation by the Security Council with respect to climate change; see Krisch (n 204) 18–19.

216 Cassese (n 14) 494; Goldstone (n 38) 465.

217 Sarooshi (n 40) 143; Sarooshi (n 6) 95.

218 Bardo Fassbender, 'Reflections on the International Legality of the Special Tribunal for Lebanon' (2007) 5 *Journal of International Criminal Justice* 1091, 1097. For an interesting account of this practice of the SC, see Koskenniemi (n 205).

edents do not preclude the question whether a SC referral is also intra vires. Thus, it follows from the conclusions of the previous chapter regarding the legal nature of the referral that the SC referral is legislative in nature and thus constitutes treaty action, because it imposes general obligations turning a non-state party into the legally similar positions as states parties.

SC treaty action is defined as an action amending, altering, modifying, rewriting or interpreting existing treaties, or interfering in any other way in the ordinary treaty-making and treaty-reviewing processes.[219] As demonstrated above, the SC referral – in effect – binds the third state to a separate multilateral treaty that is the Rome Statute.[220] While disagreement exists as to whether the referral indeed binds the third state to the Rome Statute directly, or only imposes the provisions of that treaty,[221] it certainly does constitute SC treaty action in that it seeks to impose obligations stemming from a multilateral treaty on a third state.

However, such imposition of provisions of a treaty on a third party by SC resolution is not novel. Regarding the SC referral of the situation in Darfur, Sir Michael Wood points out that

> [o]nce again, we see the Council referring to the provisions of a treaty, rather than the treaty itself . . . Sudan had signed but not ratified the Rome Statute, but the Council nevertheless imposed upon it obligations to cooperate at least as comprehensive as those it would have if it had been a party.[222]

This distinction between imposing provisions of a treaty in lieu of imposing the treaty directly appears to represent continued practice of the SC. Sir Michael Wood elaborates:

Artificial distinction?

> Perhaps the clearest case of the distinction is to be found in resolution 1718 [in which] the Council demanded that the DPRK . . . shall act strictly in accordance with the obligations applicable to parties under the Treaty on the Non-Proliferation of Nuclear Weapons and the terms and conditions of its IAEA Safeguards Agreement, which had also ceased to be in force . . . An example where the Council imposed upon states the terms of a treaty, this time without any mention the treaty itself is resolution 1373, required all states to comply with provisions corresponding to those in the International Convention for the Suppression of Terrorist Financing of 1999 [which was not in force that time].[223]

---

219 See generally e.g. Talmon (n 4). See also Michael Wood's critique of Talmon (n 195).

220 Kiyani (n 36) 482.

221 For a discussion see ibid. Characterizing the referral as only imposing the provisions of the statute, see Wood, (n 195) 251. For the opposing view, see Talmon (n 4).

222 Wood (n 195) 250.

223 Ibid.

The latest example of SC treaty action particularly regarding international criminal tribunals is the establishment of the STL, which provides guidance for this problem. In SC Res 1757 (2007) the SC determined a threat to the peace and provided the following in its operative part:

> 1. Decides, acting under Chapter VII of the Charter of the United Nations, that:
> (a) The provisions of the annexed document, including its attachment, on the establishment of a Special Tribunal for Lebanon shall enter into force on 10 June 2007, unless the Government of Lebanon has provided notification under Article 19 (1) of the annexed document before that date.

Here, the SC annexed the 'Agreement between the United Nations and the Lebanese Republic on the establishment of a Special Tribunal for Lebanon' to the SC resolution. Without Lebanon having expressed its consent to the Agreement in accordance with its constitutional law and procedure, the STL was established. One commentator argued that this should not be interpreted as substituting the missing ratification of the Agreement by Lebanon with a decision of the SC under Chapter VII.[224] Instead, the SC 'established the STL by making the provisions of the agreement negotiated with Lebanon an integral part of a resolution adopted under Chapter VII'.[225] As a result, the STL was established not as a treaty-based institution but as an independent international tribunal under the authority of the UN.[226] Due to the absence of a treaty between the UN and Lebanon, the provisions of the Agreement are binding instructions addressed to the Lebanese Republic and other states, if applicable.[227]

The precedent of the establishment of the STL along with the above mentioned precedents confirms the view that the SC does not have the power to unilaterally impose on a member state a treaty obligation in the form of a treaty directly.[228] The wording of the Charter does not contemplate such a power

---

224 Fassbender (n 218) 1100.

225 Ibid.

226 Ibid.

227 According to Bardo Fassbender, 'This applies also to Article 5 of the Agreement according to which 49% of the expenses of the Tribunal shall be borne by the Government of Lebanon, a provision which is reasonable considering the fact that the Tribunal not only serves the purpose of maintaining international peace but also that of promoting domestic peace and justice by enforcing the Lebanese Criminal Code.' Ibid.

228 This view was also taken by several members of the Security Council in the meeting of the Council of 30 May 2007; see UNSC Verbatim Record (30 May 2007) UN Doc S/PV.5685. The representative of South Africa, stated that 'we also do not believe that the Council has the right to bypass the procedures required by the Lebanese Constitution for the entry into force of an agreement with the United Nations'; ibid. 4. The representative of China issued a statement that 'China believes that by invoking

and it cannot be justified as an implied power because Chapter VII offers all coercive powers to perform its function.[229] The type of measure the UN Charter provides is that of specific decisions by the SC to deal with a particular situation as evidenced by arts 27(3), 39 and 41 of the Charter. This result is confirmed by the very nature of a 'treaty', be it in national or international law, private or public law. According to universally recognized principles of law, a treaty is an agreement based on the concurrent consent of two or more parties to be bound by the terms of the treaty.[230] In practice, it is an open question whether the SC can oblige a state to become party to a treaty. As Sir Michael Wood correctly observes: 'This has remained a largely theoretical question, since – perhaps out of respect for the principle of consent that underlies the law of treaties – the Council has refrained from doing this. But it is difficult to see that it would necessarily be acting ultra vires if it did.'[231]

As a result, preference must be given to the interpretation which is most in accordance with public international law, UN law and general principles of law. Accordingly, the view is confirmed that the SC referral cannot be substituting the missing ratification of the Rome Statute by the state concerned. The important difference is that the SC arguably does not have the power to legislate a treaty. The SC does, however, enjoy the powers due to the quasi-jurisdictional means at its disposal under art 41 to impose the provisions of a treaty temporarily as long as this is necessary for the maintenance of international peace and security. This means that in the case of a SC referral, the state subject to the referral is not made a treaty party to the Rome Statute through a SC decision under Chapter VII substituting consent to the treaty. Instead, the state concerned is bound by the provisions of the treaty insofar as expressly or implicitly provided for in the SC referral decision, and bound to

---

Chapter VII of the Charter, the resolution will override Lebanon's legislative organs by arbitrarily deciding on the date of the entry into force of the draft statute. This move will give rise to a series of political and legal problems . . . and create a precedent of Security Council interference in the domestic affairs and legislative independence of a sovereign State. Such actions are likely to undermine the authority of the Council'; ibid. The representative of the Russian Federation, said that 'the Russian Federation made a number of constructive proposals that could have considerably improved the text. The draft should have focused on the implementation, under a Council decision, of the agreement between the United Nations and Lebanon, not on the entry into force of the agreement'; ibid. 5.

[229] *Reparation for Injuries Case* (Advisory Opinion) [1949] ICJ Rep 174, 182.

[230] Cf arts 2(1)(a), 11 of the VCLT, and of the Vienna Convention on the Law of Treaties between States and International Organizations or between International Organizations, respectively.

[231] Wood (n 195) 252.

accept the exercise of jurisdiction as provided for expressly or implicitly in the SC referral decision.[232]

4.5.2.2 Legislation of crimes under the jurisdiction of the ICC?

The referral does not only impose obligations contained in the Rome Statute on third states, but it also appears to legislate the crimes included in the Statute by making it binding on the individuals of that state's jurisdiction. In this respect, it has been argued that within the broad powers granted by Chapter VII of the Charter, the SC is not obliged to limit such criminal jurisdiction to serious violations of international humanitarian law, as it has done so far with regards to the ICTY or the ICTR.[233]

Such obligations could be viewed as legislative in nature. The referral arguably seeks to create jurisdiction over the crimes under the Statute, including those going beyond the elements of crimes as recognized by customary international law.[234] It seeks not just to extend the jurisdiction to adjudicate crimes under customary international law to the ICC but also with respect to crimes going beyond that.[235] It is clear from the provisions of the Statute that the ICC Statute disclaims an intent to define substantive ICL, for purposes other than the operation of the ICC under the Statute.[236] Article 10 Rome Statute clearly states: 'Nothing in this Part [Part 2: Jurisdiction, Admissibility and Applicable Law] shall be interpreted as limiting or prejudicing in any way existing or developing rules of international law for purposes other than this Statute.'[237] This means that the definitions adopted in the Rome Statute do not preclude the question of whether they indeed match customary international law.

It is interesting to note that in fact, academics and politicians alike refused to accept the ILC's proposition not to define crimes in the proposed Statute of

---

[232] The question of what legal effects such a decision has on the ICC (particularly in case the SC adopts a referral decision specifying in it obligations that are not compatible with the Rome Statute) will be addressed below in Chapters 5 and 7.

[233] Fassbender (n 218) 1097.

[234] See Chapter 5.1.3; Rogier Bartels, 'Dealing with the Principle of Proportionality in Armed Conflict in Retrospect: The Application of the Principle in International Criminal Trials' (2013) 46 *Israel Law Review* 271, 313–14. José Alvarez called it 'innovative definitions of crimes against humanity and war crimes'; José Alvarez, *International Organizations as Law-makers* (Oxford University Press 2005) 300.

[235] See Chapter 5.1.3.

[236] Kenneth S. Gallant, 'The International Criminal Court in the System of States and International Organizations' (2003) 16(3) *Leiden Journal of International Law* 553, 577. For a comprehensive account, see Milanovic (n 170).

[237] See also art 22(3) stipulating that '[t]his article shall not affect the characterization of any conduct as criminal under international law independently of this Statute'.

the permanent ICC at a very early stage.[238] Rather, it was referred to existing instruments,[239] because '[m]any felt that prosecutions in the proposed Court would run afoul of the *nullum crimen, nulla poena, sine lege* principle if crimes were not sufficiently defined in advance'.[240]

A similar problem arose with respect to the qualification of the Nuremberg trials. It was arguably a rather theoretical debate there whether the substantive criminal law applied during the Nuremberg trials matched customary international law,[241] or only law among the parties to the London Agreement and the Nuremberg Charter.[242]

This distinction now becomes relevant in the case of referrals, because some elements of the crimes in the Rome Statute seem to partially depart from present customary international law.[243] In fact, it has been pointed out that

> states with military forces that operate abroad will fear that soldiers and their commanders, including the highest political authorities responsible for military activities, will be dragged in front of an international court for war crimes prosecution and will, at a minimum, be inconvenienced and embarrassed. Indeed, because the definitions of international crimes are so vague, soldiers and officials might find themselves punished for activities that they consider legal and routine.[244]

---

[238] Leila N. Sadat, *The International Criminal Court and the Transformation of International Law: Justice for the New Millennium* (International and comparative criminal law series, Transnational Publishers 2002) 265–66 (with further references).

[239] Ibid.

[240] Ibid.

[241] Gallant (n 236) 577.

[242] See e.g. Leila N. Sadat and S. R. Carden, 'The New International Criminal Court: An Uneasy Revolution' (2000) 88 *Georgetown Law Journal* 381, 423; Gallant (n 236) 477.

[243] Regarding crimes against humanity, some elements appear to be new or differ from existing sources; Herman von Hebel and Darryl Robinson, 'Crimes within the Jurisdiction of the Court' in Roy S. Lee (ed), *The International Criminal Court: The Making of the Rome Statute; issues, negotiations, results* (Kluwer Law International 2002) 92; Roy S. K. Lee, 'States' Responses: Issues and Solutions' in Roy S. K. Lee (ed), *States' Responses to Issues Arising from the ICC statute: Constitutional, Sovereignty, judicial Cooperation and Criminal Law* (International and comparative criminal law series, Transnational Publishers 2005) 26. See also Hassan Jallow who sees considerable expansion of international criminal law particularly regarding crimes against humanity and war crimes; Hassan B. Jallow, 'International Criminal Justice: Reflections on the Past and the Future' (2010) 36(2) *Commonwealth Law Bulletin* 269, 275.

[244] Eric A. Posner and John C. Yoo, 'Judicial Independence in International Tribunals' (2005) 93(1) *California Law Review* 1, 69.

This ambiguity regarding the state of customary crimes under international law is further evidenced by the fact that the drafters viewed it necessary to include arts 10 and 22(3) into the Statute.[245]

The definitions of crimes against humanity and war crimes are problematic. First, no international treaty defines crimes against humanity. The Preparatory Committee of the future ICC did not reach consensus regarding the exact definition of crimes against humanity.[246] Hence, art 7 defining crimes against humanity for the Rome Statute may thus be regarded as creating an autonomous regime.[247] Another issue concerns the Rome Statute's definition of war crimes, since the definitions regarding non-international armed conflict arguably departs from accepted international custom.[248] It is clear, however, that in cases where the state in question is bound by international treaties applicable, their application by the ICC does not pose issues of legality. The operation of such differences in the scope of jurisdiction *ratione materae* is ensured by art 10 (reference to customary international law) in connection with arts 21 (applicable law) and 19 (determination of jurisdiction) of the Rome Statute.

It is beyond the scope of this study to analyze the state of crimes against humanity and war crimes under customary international law.[249] However, it is important to raise this issue.[250]

---

245 See below Chapter 5.1.3.

246 Zimmermann (n 16) 172.

247 Lee (n 243) 26.

248 An elaborate study of this issue is beyond the scope of this study but see n 249 below. See also Rogier Bartels, 'Legitimacy and ICC Jurisdiction Following Security Council Referrals: Conduct on the Territory of Non-Party States and the Legality Principle' in Nobuo Hayashi and Cecilia Bailliet (eds), *The Legitimacy of International Criminal Tribunals* (Cambridge University Press 2017) 141–78.

249 For the state of customary international law in the field of international humanitarian law, the International Committee of the Red Cross study concluded that most provisions of the Geneva Convention were customary international law, see Jean-Marie Henckaerts, 'Study on Customary International Humanitarian Law: A Contribution to the Understanding and Respect for the Rule of Law in Armed Conflict' (2008) 87(857) *International Review of the Red Cross* 187. See, however, the critique voiced by representatives of the United States government, John B. Bellinger and William J. Haynes, 'A US government Response to the International Committee of the Red Cross study Customary International Humanitarian Law' (2007) 89(866) *International Review of the Red Cross* 443.

250 Sharing this view regarding a SC request to the Court to exercise jurisdiction over acts that did not constitute crimes in international law at the time of their commission, see Condorelli and Villalpando (n 51) 580. On the other hand, several domestic legal systems permit retrospective application of crimes against humanity and war crimes; see e.g. art 5(4) of the Latvian Criminal Code; art 5(4) of the Estonian Criminal Code; similarly, both the Albanian (art 29) and Polish (art 42(1)). Constitutions provide an exception for international crimes in their formulation of the legality principle in

The limitation for the SC to establish criminal jurisdiction only over crimes recognized as customary international law has an important precedent in the ad hoc tribunals. The Secretary-General argued that 'the application of the principle nullum crimen sine lege requires that the [ICTY] should apply rules of international humanitarian law which are beyond doubt part of customary law so that the problem of adherence of some but not all States to specific conventions does not arise'.[251] On this basis, state practice has accepted the establishment and practice of the tribunals.[252] It did not accept the SC's power to directly bind individuals to ICL created by it. And the quasi-legislative practice of the SC that might have been accepted in practice likewise did not bind individuals but imposed obligations on states to prevent (and criminalize) certain conduct. As a result, the SC is arguably not empowered to legislate in this technical sense,[253] and thus criminalization of conduct beyond customary international law at the time of its commission appears problematic.[254]

From the foregoing remarks it follows that, of the two possible interpretations (of whether ICC jurisdiction in case of SC referrals is jurisdictional or substantive in nature), the interpretation which is most in accordance with public international law, UN law and general principles of law and is construed

---

national law. Similarly, some constitutional courts have upheld the retrospective application of criminal norms without breaching the *nulllum crimen sine lege.* For instance, the Hungarian Constitutional Court, referring to arts 15(2) and 7(2) of the Convention, held that criminal legislation incorporating legal norms on war crimes and crimes against humanity could be retroactively applied. In the same manner, in Slovenia, the Constitutional Court affirmed that the prohibition of retroactive effects of penal law does not apply for acts or omissions which at the time they were committed were considered criminal offences in accordance with the general legal principles recognized by all nations. See Hungary, Constitutional Court, Decision no. 53/1993, On War Crimes and Crimes against Humanity, 13 October 1993. See Slovenia, Constitutional Court, U-I-248/96, 30 September 1998 and Slovenia, Constitutional Court, U-I-6/93, 13 January 1994. See further Triestino Mariniello, 'The "Nuremberg Clause" and Beyond: Legality Principle and Sources of International Criminal Law in the European Court's Jurisprudence' (2013) 82(2) *Nordic Journal of International Law* 221, 224.

[251] UN Doc S/25704 (3 May 1993) para 34.

[252] Paulus (n 29) para 69; Frowein and Krisch (n 160) para 19; Rosand (n 215) 564. For a critique of the judicial law making in international criminal law through 'gap-filling' by invoking general principles of law in the practice of international courts and tribunals, see Neha Jain, 'Judicial Lawmaking and General Principles of Law in International Criminal Law' (2016) 57(1) *Harvard Journal of International Law* 111.

[253] Paulus (n 29) para 69. See also Wood (n 30) 78.

[254] Krisch (n 159) para 28. It must be noted, however, that the ICTY in *Tadic* held that 'it is open to the Security Council . . . to adopt definitions of crimes in the Statute which deviate from customary international law'; see *Tadic Case* (Decision on the Defence Motion for Interlocutory Appeal on Jurisdiction) ICTY-IT-94-1-A (2 October 1995) para 296.

narrowly must be preferred.[255] Accordingly, it is suggested that the ICC's jurisdiction in case of a SC referral of a situation in a non-state party must be presumed to be limited to crimes as recognized by customary international law or other pre-existing treaties in force in the state concerned.[256]

An additional issue arises in cases (as the SC has done in practice) where the SC refers a situation over a non-state party to the ICC referring to conduct that occurred before the date of the referral. In such situations the SC is not merely legislating but would run counter the principle of non-retroactive application of criminal law. In such situations there has been no prior consent by the relevant state to be bound by the ICC Statute and to the ICC exercising jurisdiction over its nationals, or over other individuals perpetrating crimes on its territory. The ICC Statute would thus be applied 'retroactively' to nationals (or individuals on the territory) of non-party states.[257] The SC must not retroactively apply criminal law. The STL has gone so far as to claim 'that it is warranted to hold that by now [the principle of non-retroactivity] has the status of a peremptory norm (jus cogens)'.[258] Theodor Meron also claims that the rule against retroactivity has reached the status of *jus cogens* and Kenneth Gallant recognizes that at least it is beginning to emerge as such a norm.[259] Because the SC is bound by *jus cogens* norms,[260] it follows that the SC is barred from retroactively applying criminal law.[261]

In conclusion, it should not be presumed that SC wishes to legislate ICL that goes beyond crimes as recognized by customary international law. It shall be

---

[255] Arriving at a similar conclusion see Paola Gaeta, who argues that in the case of a SC referral, provisions that in principle are only applicable to states parties because they depart from customary international law do not apply; see Gaeta (n 34).

[256] Similarly viewing the SC in that sense as a rule enforcer, see e.g. Deborah R. Verduzco, 'The Relationship between the ICC and the United Nations Security Council' in Carsten Stahn (ed), *The Law and Practice of the International Criminal Court* (Oxford University Press 2015) 35.

[257] Bartels (n 234) 311.

[258] Unnamed Defendant, Appeals Chamber, Interlocutory Decision on the Applicable Law: Terrorism, Conspiracy, Homicide, Perpetration, Cumulative Charging, STL, STL-11-01/I, 16 February 2011, para 76; see also *Maktouf and Demjanovic v Bosnia and Herzegovina* (Judgment) ECtHR Application Nos 2312/08 and 34179/08 (19 July 2013) [Concurring Opinion of Judge Pinto de Albuquerque, joined by Judge Vainie] para 45.

[259] Theodor Meron, *War Crimes Law Comes of Age: Essays* (Oxford University Press 1999) 244; Kenneth S. Gallant, *The Principle of Legality in International and Comparative Criminal Law* (Cambridge University Press 2009) 316.

[260] On this see Chapter 4.5.

[261] Concurring Pichon (n 107) 28; similarly Christian Tomuschat, 'Ein Internationaler Strafgerichtshof als Element einer Weltfriedensordnung' (1994) 49(61–70) *Europa-Archiv*, 65.

noted in this respect that the SC implicitly found itself to be bound by the principle of legality when it insisted that when establishing the ad hoc tribunals, it did not create new law but was merely applying existing law.[262] How this conclusion relates to the legal consequences of a SC referral for the exercise of jurisdiction by the ICC will be addressed in Chapter 5 below, along with the issue of the principle of legality in practice in the context of SC referrals with retroactive jurisdiction.

4.5.3 The Powers of the SC and Quasi-Judicial Measures

Measures under Chapter VII are in principle limited to preliminary measures,[263] excluding the imposition of specific terms of settlement by the SC.[264] This also flows from the UN Charter system of voluntary submission of states to third-party settlement.[265] It is therefore difficult to reconcile the tendency of the SC to assume quasi-judicial authority by means of Chapter VII measures.[266] It has to be recognized, however, that the quasi-judicial function is often related to the SC acting as law enforcer.[267] The SC has had to determine the violation of a norm in order to enforce the law. For example, during the war in Bosnia, the SC stressed that the practice of 'ethnic cleansing' by the Bosnian Serbs constituted a violation of international humanitarian law.[268]

Here the distinction between the SC referral and the establishment of the ad hoc tribunals is particularly important. Whereas the SC exercised judicial authority indirectly through the ad hoc tribunals, the SC referral is only confer-

---

[262] See Chapter 4.1.2.1. The Trial Chamber of the ICTY stressed in *Tadic* that 'It is not irrelevant that what the Security Council has enacted under Chapter VII is the creation of a tribunal whose jurisdiction is expressly confined to the prosecution of breaches of international humanitarian law that are beyond any doubt part of customary law'; *Prosecutor v Tadic*, Case No IT-94-1-T (10 August 1995) para 19. It must be noted, however, that the ICTY in *Tadic* held that 'it is open to the Security Council . . . to adopt definitions of crimes in the Statute which deviate from customary international law'; see *Tadic Case* (Decision on the Defence Motion for Interlocutory Appeal on Jurisdiction) ICTY-IT-94-l-A (2 October 1995) para 296. For a critical view, see Krisch (n 159) para 28.

[263] Frowein and Krisch (n 9) para 31.

[264] Ibid. para 20.

[265] Ibid. See also Article 40 UN Charter which provides that '[s]uch provisional measures shall be without prejudice to the rights, claims, or position of the parties concerned'.

[266] Indeed, as Lamb points out, the establishment of a judicial body (ICTY) constituted an unprecedented response to a threat to international peace and security; see Lamb (n 23) 376.

[267] Frowein and Krisch (n 9) para 19.

[268] UNSC Res 940 (31 July 1994) UN Doc S/RES/940.

ring jurisdictional authority to the ICC and not exercising this authority either directly or indirectly. Thus, SC referrals are only to a very limited extent to be considered judicial measures because the referral itself is without prejudice of criminal accountability of individuals. Such interpretation of the SC referral is also supported by systemic considerations. It is held that even a legal determination by the SC should be interpreted as only preliminary in nature without making a final determination.[269]

However, in many instances the SC obviously sought a final determination of the legal question, and while these measures did not remain entirely free from criticism, they appear to have been accepted by a majority of states.[270] Still, scholarship established that quasi-judicial determinations should remain exceptional and should be confined to cases where they are indispensable for the exercise of the police function of the SC.[271] Therefore, their effects should be limited to a particular situation. In addition, they should conform to the general standards for judicial findings, and thus meet the respective procedural requirements and respect the substantive law in place.[272] In contrast, no legal difficulties arise when legal determinations possess no binding character since they might then be characterized as recommendations of terms of settlement, which the SC is authorized to make under art 37 of the Charter.[273]

Furthermore, the SC does not have the power to determine individual criminal responsibility.[274] Thus, in case of SC referrals as well as in the analogous situation of the ad hoc tribunals,[275] the SC is not itself exercising these judicial functions but delegates such powers. The RA and the explicit provision in the Rome Statute makes it clear that the referral itself merely grants the ICC jurisdiction, but does not in any way attempt to prejudice the findings of the ICC as to whether or not crimes were committed and by whom. It also follows that a SC determination of an individual's criminal responsibility would be ultra vires and the ICC would not be bound by such a decision.[276]

In conclusion, the SC referral is better understood as an enforcement measure. Law enforcement is a common part of SC action.[277] Although the violation of international law is no condition for action under Chapter VII, enforcement measures are often taken explicitly in order to make states respect

---

[269] Frowein and Krisch (n 9) para 20.
[270] Ibid.
[271] Ibid. Similarly Manusama (n 127) 191–92.
[272] de Wet (n 81) 345.
[273] Frowein and Krisch (n 9) para 20.
[274] de Wet (n 81) 343.
[275] Ibid. 342.
[276] Since this would constitute a violation of a *jus cogens* norm, see ibid. 345–46.
[277] Frowein and Krisch (n 9) para 18.

specific legal norms, thus constituting a form of countermeasures to breaches of international law.[278] In the case of SC referrals, the SC seeks to enforce compliance with international humanitarian law as it did when establishing international criminal tribunals for the former Yugoslavia and Rwanda.[279] Similarly, some authority for the powers of the SC to refer jurisdiction to a court outside the UN system can be found in the *Lockerbie* case.[280] Here the SC decided that 'the trial of the two persons charged with the bombing of Pan Am flight 103 [be brought] before a Scottish court sitting in the Netherlands',[281] and that 'all States shall cooperate to this end, and in particular that the Libyan Government shall ensure the appearance in the Netherlands of the two accused for the purpose of the trial.'[282] Thus, the SC, although not limited to this function, has to some degree established itself as a law enforcement organ of the international community in the area of peace and security.[283]

only IHL?

4.5.4 The Termination of SC Referrals

In the general practice of the SC, problems have arisen with respect to the termination of Chapter VII measures. They are usually enacted for an unlimited period of time, and their termination would require a positive decision by the SC that is subject to the veto of the permanent members.[284] This so-called 'reverse veto' has created problems of legitimacy, since the measures stay in force even if they are no longer supported by the entire SC, and evasion becomes easier when this is the case.[285]

St what?

The question arises whether the SC has a duty to terminate a SC referral once the basis for the determination of a threat to the peace ceases to exist. One commentator concludes that a duty exists for the SC to terminate Chapter VII measures once a threat to the peace ceases to exist.[286] This is because the legal basis for Chapter VII measures is, as has been established above, the determination of a threat to the peace. If a threat to the peace ceases to exist, the grounds for the adoption of Chapter VII measures equally cease to exist.

---

278 Ibid. para 18.

279 de Wet (n 81) 347.

280 Nouwen (n 38) 256–57. Further on the *Lockerbie* case see Michael Plachta, 'The Lockerbie Case: The Role of the Security Council in Enforcing the Principle Aut Dedere Aut Judicare' (2001) 12(1) *European Journal of International Law* 125.

281 Security Council Res 1192 UN Doc S/RES/1192 (1998) para 2.

282 SC Res 1192, para 4.

283 Frowein and Krisch (n 9) para 18.

284 Krisch (n 8) para 63.

285 Ibid.

286 Pichon (n 107) 135–38.

This approach seems hardly supported by institutional practice. It is again the SC, due to its broad discretionary powers, that will determine if these conditions for its determination of a threat to the peace still exist. This is in line with the continued practice of the SC to terminate sanctions against states once it believes the objective of the sanctions has been met.[287] The SC has also introduced time-limited measures that required renewal, or has requested the Secretary-General to make such determination as to the objectives, where the measures then end automatically.[288]

Whether the SC is authorized to terminate the referral is a different question. In principle, following from the established practice, nothing appears to

[287] Security Council Committee established pursuant to Resolution 1572 (2004) concerning Côte d'Ivoire (terminated pursuant to Resolution 2283 (2016) of 28 April 2016); Security Council Committee established pursuant to Resolution 1737 (2006) concerning the Iranian nuclear issue (terminated pursuant to Resolution 2231 (2015) of 20 July 2015); Security Council Committee established pursuant to Resolution 1132 (1997) concerning Sierra Leone (terminated pursuant to Resolution 1940 (2010) of 29 September 2010); Security Council Committee established pursuant to Resolution 918 (1994) concerning Rwanda (terminated pursuant to Resolution 1823 (2008) of 10 July 2008); Security Council Committee established pursuant to Resolution 1343 (2001) concerning Liberia (terminated pursuant to Resolution 1521 (2003) of 22 December 2003, see 1521 Committee link in the column on the left); Security Council Committee established pursuant to Resolution 1298 (2000) concerning the situation between Eritrea and Ethiopia (terminated in pursuance of Presidential Statement S/PRST/2001/14 of 15 May 2001); Security Council Committee established pursuant to Resolution 1160 (1998) (terminated pursuant to Resolution 1367 (2001) of 10 September 2001); Security Council Committee established pursuant to Resolution 985 (1995) concerning Liberia (terminated pursuant to Resolution 1343 (2001) of 7 March 2001, see 1521 Committee link in the column on the left); Security Council Committee established pursuant to Resolution 864 (1993) concerning the situation in Angola (Monitoring Mechanism on Sanctions against UNITA) (terminated pursuant to Resolution 1448 (2002) of 9 December 2002); Security Council Committee established pursuant to Resolution 841 (1993) concerning Haiti (terminated pursuant to Resolution 944 of 29 September 1994); Security Council Committee established pursuant to Resolution 724 (1991) concerning Yugoslavia (terminated pursuant to Resolution 1074 of 1 October 1996); Security Council Committee established pursuant to Resolution 748 (1992) concerning the Libyan Arab Jamahiriya (terminated pursuant to Resolution 1506 (2003) of 12 September 2003); Security Council Committee established by Resolution 661 (1990) concerning the situation between Iraq and Kuwait (terminated pursuant to Resolution 1483 (2003) of 22 May); Security Council Committee established by Resolution 421 (1977) concerning the question of South Africa (terminated pursuant to Resolution 919 of 26 May 1994); Security Council Committee established in pursuance of Resolution 253 (1968) (terminated pursuant to Resolution 460 of 21 December 1979).

[288] Frowein and Krisch (n 9) 38.

limit the SC's powers to terminate the SC referral.[289] The termination of a SC referral resolution removes the legal basis for the exercise of jurisdiction of the ICC in non-party states and the ICC is thus barred from continuing to exercise it (absent another legal source for a lawful exercise of jurisdiction).[290] In practice, the SC has not terminated or otherwise limited the prospective scope of referrals, the legal qualification of which is addressed below.[291]

4.5.5 Limits for the SC under Chapter VII

It is a truism that 'what the Council says *is* the law'.[292] By virtue of Chapter VII of the UN Charter, the SC enjoys greater powers than any other international organ in history.[293] Questions to the limits of the SC's discretionary powers address whether there are such limits, and if so, what are those limits and what body, if other than the SC itself, is competent to say what they are?[294]

It is not the purpose of this section to determine in abstract terms the legal limits to SC action under Chapter VII. Suffice it to note that in any case, as an organ of an international organization established by treaty, the SC is subject to the constitutional limitations under its constituent treaty, i.e. the UN Charter.[295]

---

289 Pichon (n 107) 134. In relation to the power of the SC to dissolve the ad hoc tribunals see also Paulus (n 68) para 59.

290 Contra this view but without giving reasons why the ICC would still be authorized to exercise jurisdiction once the SC has terminated the delegation of powers, see Condorelli and Villalpando (n 1) 642–44.

291 Chapter 5.1.4.

292 Allan Pellet, 'Conclusions' in Brigitte Stern (ed) *Les aspects juridiques de la crise et de la guerre du Golfe* (Montchrestien 1991) 490 (translation by the author, emphasis in the original). For the political justification for such broad powers see Reisman, who correctly points out that '[t]he design of a realistic international security system cannot ignore how power is actually distributed'. W. M. Reisman, 'The Constitutional Crisis in the United Nations' in René-Jean Dupuy (ed), *Le développement du rôle du Conseil de sécurité: Peace-keeping and peace-building* (Martinus Nijhoff 1993) 420.

293 Krisch (n 8) 1239.

294 *Questions of Interpretation and Application of the 1971 Montreal Convention Arising from the Aerial Incident at Lockerbie* (Request for the indication of Provisional Measures) [1992] ICJ Rep 114, 142 (14 April 1992) (separate opinion of Judge Shahabuddeen). For an overview of the discussion of these questions see Gordon Joy, 'The Sword of Damocles: Revisiting the Question of Whether the United Nations Security Council is Bound by International Law' (2012) 12(9) *Chicago Journal of International Law* 605.

295 Michael Bothe, 'Les limites des pouvoirs du conseil de sécurité' in Dupuy (n 292) 69; August Reinisch, 'Developing Human Rights and Humanitarian Law Accountability of the Security Council for the Imposition of Economic Sanctions' (2001) 95 *American Journal of International Law* 851, 858; Wood (n 115) para 3; Higgins (n 45) 421. The political nature of its decision is not grounds to argue that the

Indeed, the ICJ noted in the *Admissions* case that '[t]he political character of an organ cannot release it from the observance of the treaty provisions established by the Charter when they constitute limitations on its powers and criteria for its judgment'.[296] In the same vein, the Appeals Chamber of the ICTY famously stated that the SC is not *legibus solutus* (unbound by law).[297] It is also generally accepted that in accordance with art 25 of the Charter, resolutions of the SC are only binding when adopted 'in accordance with the Charter'.[298] This also follows from the law of international organizations because the SC enjoys powers only insofar as they are conferred on it by or implied in the UN Charter.[299] As the grantors, members have the power to 'determine that the grantee has exceeded its authority and ultimately to withdraw the authority which has been granted'.[300] Thus, the range of powers of the SC under Chapter VII of the Charter is determined by arts 39 to 42; any discretionary power of the SC must be derived from these specific authorizations and cannot be presumed.[301]

Furthermore, art 24(2) UN Charter stipulates that '[i]n discharging these duties the Security Council shall act in accordance with the Purposes and Principles of the United Nations'. It follows from this wording that the SC

SC is not subject to the ultra vires doctrine; see Derek Bowett, 'The Impact of Security Council Decisions on Dispute Settlement Procedures' (1994) 5 *European Journal of International Law* 89, 95.

[296] *Conditions of Admission of a State to Membership in the United Nations* (Advisory Opinion) [1948] ICJ Rep 57, 64.

[297] *Tadic Case* (Decision on the Defence Motion for Interlocutory Appeal on Jurisdiction) ICTY-IT-94-l-A (2 October 1995) para 28 (emphasis in the original).

[298] On the various interpretations of this phrase, see Peters (n 97) 807; Jean-Pierre Cot, *La Charte des Nations Unies: Commentaire article par article* (3rd edn, Economica 2005) 916–17. See also *Legal Consequences for States of the Continued Presence of South Africa in Namibia (South West Africa) notwithstanding Security Council Resolution 276 (1970)* (Advisory Opinion) [1971] ICJ Rep 16, para 113 (dissenting opinion judge Fitzmaurice).

[299] Pursuant to art 24(1) of the Charter, 'its Members confer on the Security Council primary responsibility for the maintenance of international peace and security'. The wording suggests that the SC's powers stem from the UN Member States.

[300] Aziz T. Saliba, 'Is the Security Council Legibus Solutus?: An Analysis of the Legal Restraints of the UNSC' (2012) 20(2) *Journal of International Law and Practice* 401, 406.

[301] Krisch (n 8) 1256. See, however, on the argument that as the main executive organ of the UN, the SC was deliberately liberated from any legal constraints, Reinisch (n 295) 855. For the argument of the 'devil's advocate' see Oosthuizen, who arrives at the conclusion that '[t]he SC's powers are nowhere curtailed by an implicit or explicit reference to international law'. Gabriël H. Oosthuizen, 'Playing the Devil's Advocate: the United Nations Security Council is Unbound by Law' (1999) 12(3) *Leiden Journal of International Law* 549, 563.

is bound by the Purposes and Principles of the Charter.[302] However, it seems difficult to deduce concrete limits from these provisions, especially in the field of international criminal justice. Arguably these Purposes and Principles establish flexible guidelines for SC action.[303] The scope of the Charter's Purposes and Principles primarily laid down in art 1 does not provide for any 'tangible constraint'.[304] The wording of art 1 is more appropriate for political objectives rather than for legally binding obligations.[305]

What is clear is that the SC does not possess the power to determine authoritatively its own range of powers.[306] While it is true that every organ must, in the first instance, determine its own jurisdiction, such a determination is binding only if supported by the member states in general.[307] In this vein, the generally approved report of a sub-committee of the Committee on Legal Questions at San Francisco stated that '[i]t is to be understood . . . that if an interpretation made by any organ of the Organization . . . is not generally acceptable it will be without binding force'.[308]

This is not to say that the practice of the organs is not an important element of treaty interpretation,[309] but such practice only represents a binding determination of the content of the Charter if supported by state practice in general.[310]

---

302 Krisch (n 8) 1257.

303 Rüdiger Wolfrum, 'Article 1' in Simma (n 9) para 4.

304 Saliba (n 300) 406.

305 Wolfrum (n 303) para 4. See also W. Michael Reisman who correctly pointed out in 1993 that '[s]ome contemporary jurists, inspired by Professor Derrida, could certainly deconstruct "implied" restraints from the Charter but in that genre of interpretation, modality is message. The results often say far more about the interpreter's yearnings and interpretive creativity than about the intentions of the drafters or the contemporary expectations of the relevant parties or the community. Hard substantive and procedural standards for review of Chapter VII actions are difficult to pinpoint in the Charter. Their very absence, in a context in which so much power is assigned to the Council, is telling. A judicial review function, viewed from the formal Charter régime, seems quite hollow'; Reisman (n 292) 414. For the view that the Principles are legally binding, see Saliba (n 300) 407.

306 Krisch (n 8) 1256.

307 Ibid.

308 UNCIO Doc 750 IV/2/B/1.

309 *Namibia Case* (n 672) 22.

310 Oscar Schachter, 'The Quasi-Judicial Role of the Security Council and the General Assembly' (1964) 58(4) *American Journal of International Law* 960, 962; Schweigman (n 104) 207; Jan Klabbers, *An Introduction to International Organizations Law* (3rd edn, Cambridge University Press 2015) 87, pointing out that traditionally interpretation of treaties was subject to subsequent practice of parties to those treaties, whereas one can identify a shift from this traditional rule of interpretation towards considering the practice of the organs of international organizations as the relevant practice, as is evidenced in the *Certain Expenses Case* (Advisory Opinion) [1962]

In other words, the UN member states are – in this sense – the final arbiter for the determination of the legality of SC measures.[311] From the general acceptance of the SC referrals one might deduce that the power of the SC to refer a situation involving non-party states has been accepted by states.[312]

4.6 CONCLUSION: CONCRETE LIMITATIONS FOR THE SC REFERRAL

In conclusion, it is possible to establish several practical limits to the SC referral power based on its intuitional practice and the constitutional limits from the UN Charter. First, the SC is bound by peremptory norms of international law, *jus cogens*.[313] *Jus cogens* binds not only states but all subjects of international law, including international organizations.[314] These norms pose limits even to Chapter VII powers of the SC since no international treaty, including the UN Charter, could derogate from them, and arts 53 and 64 of the VCLT indeed indicate such a result.[315]

Recently, the ICJ's decision in *Germany v Italy* has arguably called into question the conventional wisdom regarding the effect of *jus cogens* norms.[316] For the SC referral, suffice it to note that the ICJ's decision – that the *jus*

ICJ Rep 151 and subsequently in the *Legal Consequences for States of the Continued Presence of South Africa in Namibia (South West Africa) notwithstanding Security Council Resolution 276 (1970)* (Advisory Opinion) [1970] ICJ Rep 1971, 16.

311 In this sense also Antonios Tzanakopoulos, *Disobeying the Security Council: Countermeasures against Wrongful Sanctions* (Oxford University Press 2011) 112–13. Furthermore, legal defects of acts of international organizations might be cured by operation of acquiescence or acceptance of Member States, thus giving Member States the possibility to determine, indirectly, the legality of SC measures; see Klabbers (n 310) 186. It is also worth noting that the conduct of states in connection with the activities of international organizations may be evidence of customary international law; see Michael Wood, 'International Organizations and Customary International Law' (2015) 48(3) *Vanderbilt Journal of Transnational Law* 609, 614–16.

312 See Chapter 6.

313 Wood (n 115) para 6.

314 See Chittharanjan F. Amerasinghe, *Principles of the Institutional Law of International Organizations* (2nd edn, Cambridge University Press 2005) 214; Simon Chesterman, *The UN Security Council and the Rule of Law: The Role of the Security Council in Strengthening a Rules-based International System: Final Report and Recommendations from the Austrian Initiative, 2004–2008* (United Nations 2008) para 29. See also Case T-306/01, *Yusuf and Al Barakaat v Council* [2005] ECR II-33533; Case T-315/01, *Kadi v Council* [2005] ECR II-3649; Klabbers (n 310) 183, 185.

315 Frowein and Krisch (n 9) para 29; Orakhelashvili (n 204) 63.

316 *Germany v Italy* (Judgment) [2012] ICJ Rep 99. See also Jure Vidmar, 'Rethinking jus cogens after Germany v. Italy: Back to Article 53?' (2013) 60(1) *Netherlands International Law Review* 1; Lorna McGregor, 'State Immunity and

cogens nature of international crimes does not preclude the applicability of state immunity – would arguably apply *mutatis mutandis* to personal immunities of heads of states.[317]

A second limitation is the principle of legality. The SC is therefore barred from retroactive application of ICL and it should not be presumed that its measures are intended to legislate ICL, due to constitutional limitations confining SC action to enforcement measures. In other words, the SC actions in international criminal justice are presumed to only enforce international criminal law which was in force at the time of the commission of the crime.

Finally, the SC is in principle limited to enforcement action and cannot directly legislate a treaty text such as the Rome Statute. Again, such measures would go far beyond the recognized limits of the SC to enforcement measures. And while the violation of international law is no condition for action under Chapter VII, enforcement measures are often taken explicitly to make states respect specific legal norms, thus constituting a form of countermeasures to breaches of international law.[318]

Human Rights: Is There a Future after Germany v. Italy?' (2013) 11(1) *Journal of International Criminal Justice* 125.

[317] See Chapter 5.1.5 further on this.

[318] This is not to say that this precludes any future accepted subsequent practice of an organ that might change this assessment; see Sarooshi (n 6) 24–26.

5. The ICC's exercise of the powers conferred by the Security Council

The previous chapter dealt with the question of how far-reaching are the powers of the SC vis-à-vis the ICC. A different but closely related question is what legal consequences SC measures have on the ICC. This is because the ICC as a separate international organization cannot act beyond its constituent treaty.[1] The incorporation of art 13(b) into the Rome Statute was important not because it gives or determines the powers of the SC but because without it, the ICC as an international organization would have no constitutional basis upon which to legally ground its actions to carry out the SC referral.[2] Hence, the question of what the SC is competent to do under its constituent treaty, the

[1] On the general point see also Judge Lauterpacht in the Voting Procedure case stating (with respect to the UN) that 'in the case of the United Nations, whether the action is taken in pursuance of the objects of [the] organization, or in pursuance of a function accepted under some extraneous instrument such as a treaty. Such function must in any case lie within the orbit of its competence as laid down in the Charter. For the organization cannot accept the fulfilment of a task which lies outside the scope of its functions as determined by its constitution . . . It cannot override a seemingly mandatory provision of the Charter by the device of accepting a task conferred by a treaty. It might otherwise be possible to alter, through extraneous treaties, the character of the Organization in an important aspect of its activity'. *South-West Africa-Voting Procedure* case, Advisory Opinion (7 June 1955) *ICJ Reports* (1955) 67, 109 (Separate Opinion of Judge Lauterpacht). Regarding the SC referral see Paola Gaeta, 'Does President Al-Bashir Enjoy Immunity from Arrest?' (2009) 7(2) *Journal of International Criminal Justice* 315, 324.

[2] These phenomena can also be witnessed in the case law of the Court of Justice of the European Union (and its predecessor, the European Court of Justice) in the famous *Kadi* jurisprudence; see Case C–402/05 P and C–415/05, P. *Kadi and Al Barakaat International Foundation v Council and Commission* [2008] ECR I–6351. While one might understand this as the continuity of the old struggle in the history of ideas between monist and dualist theories of international and domestic law, this seems to only explain part of it. Namely it can be witnessed that courts and other organs of states are reluctant to give effect to international law, when the constitutional basis on which these same courts are established does not explicitly or implicitly grant them the power to implement international law, which is not in conformity with other domestic law and does not explicitly provide for a pre-emptory clause overruling domestic provisions. See on this Gabriel M. Lentner, 'Kadi II before the ECJ – UN Targeted Sanctions and the European Legal Order' (2013) 6 *European Law Reporter* 202.

UN Charter, is different from the question of what the ICC is competent to do under its constituent treaty, the Rome Statute, and whether and to what extent the ICC can act upon the authority that the SC is giving the Court through a resolution referring a situation over a non-state party to the ICC.

In addressing these issues, two sets of legal consequences are distinguished in this chapter. First, the legal consequence of a SC referral that is intra vires is considered. This must be further distinguished by intra vires SC referrals that are in accordance with the Rome Statute, and other intra vires SC referrals deviating from the Rome Statute. Second, the legal consequences of a SC referral that is ultra vires is considered. I will then turn to the related question of the possibility of judicial review of SC referrals by the ICC. The final section will analyze the distinct issues raised by the crime of aggression.

5.1 SC ACTING INTRA VIRES AND IN ACCORDANCE WITH THE STATUTE

5.1.1 General Remarks

A referral in accordance with the Statute should not pose too many difficult legal issues. However, the practice of the SC suggests that it does not explicitly state which provisions of the Rome Statute shall apply nor does it make any other express reference to the applicability of the Rome Statute. In this context it is important to be reminded that the SC is a political, not a legal body, and its members are not necessarily legally minded.[3]

From the outset, it must be emphasized that a SC referral to the ICC is assumed to be in accordance with the Statute, unless a deviation from the provisions of the Statute can be deduced from the SC resolution including the referral.[4] This follows from the general rule that statements of governments must be construed as 'producing and intending to produce effects in accordance with existing law and not in violation of it'.[5] This applies, at least in prin-

[3] Roberto Lavalle, 'The "Acting under Chapter VII" Clause in Security Council Resolutions under Article 41 of the United Nations Charter: A Misconceived and Harmful Way of Invoking Authority' in Benedetto Conforti and others (eds), *The Italian Yearbook of International Law: 2009* (vol XIX, Martinus Nijhoff 2010) 235.

[4] Akande correctly points out that a SC referral must be understood as implicitly adopting the regime of the Statute into the relevant SC resolutions; Dapo Akande, 'The Effect of Security Council Resolutions and Domestic Proceedings on State Obligations to Cooperate with the ICC' (2012) 10(2) *Journal of International Criminal Justice* 299, 309.

[5] *Case concerning the Right of Passage over Indian Territory (Preliminary Objections) (Portugal v. India)* ICJ Rep 1957, 142 referenced also in ILC, 'Report of the Study Group of the ILC on Fragmentation of International Law: Difficulties Arising

ciple, also to the interpretation of SC resolutions. Thus, a strong presumption against conflict exists and calls for techniques of harmonious interpretation to be used so that the conflict does not materialize in a genuine one.[6] Hence the presumption that unless it explicitly and clearly states the contrary, the SC intended to refer a situation in accordance with the Statute.

In practice the SC adopts no detailed language in its resolution providing for the referral.[7] In various decisions emanating from the use of art 13(b), the ICC stated that in making such referrals, 'the Security Council of the United Nations has also accepted that the investigation into the said situation, as well as any prosecution arising therefrom, will take place in accordance with the statutory framework provided for in the Statute, the Elements of Crimes and the Rules as a whole'.[8] This might imply that the SC decided to apply the substantive criminal law of the Statute to the situation referred to the ICC. However, as I will show later, the legal limits of the SC to customary ICL means that the referral must be understood as covering only existing law. The Chambers also assume that

> [i]f it triggers the Court's jurisdiction, the Council must live within the parameters of the Rome Statute with respect to such matters such as jurisdiction. It 'accepts' that investigation and prosecution will be conducted pursuant to the Statute, respecting the division of functions and responsibilities between the Prosecutor and the Chambers.[9]

Here, too does the Chamber not offer any further arguments why that is indeed the case.

The concrete obligations for cooperation are therefore found in part IX of the Statute under the heading 'International Cooperation and Judicial Assistance'. Article 86 lays out the general obligation to cooperate, stating

---

from Diversification and Expansion of International Law' (13 April 2006) UN Doc A/CN.4/L.682, para 39.

6 Ibid. para 37. See also Andreas L. Paulus and Johann Leiß, 'Article 103' in Bruno Simma (ed), *The Charter of the United Nations: A Commentary* (3rd edn, Oxford University Press 2012) 2123; Joost Pauwelyn, *Conflict of Norms in Public International Law: How WTO Law Relates to Other Rules of International Law* (Cambridge studies in international and comparative law, Cambridge University Press 2003) 240–244.

7 See further Chapter 7.

8 *Prosecutor v Omar Hassan Al-Bashir, Situation in Darfur* (Decision on the Prosecution's Application for a Warrant of Arrest against Omar Hassan Ahmad Al-Bashir) ICC-02/05-01/09-3 (4 March 2009) para 45; Situation in Darfur Sudan, ICC, Pre-Trial Chamber I, Decision on Application under Rule 103, ICC-02/05 (4 February 2009) para 31.

9 Situation in Darfur, Sudan (ICC-02/05), Decision on Application under Rule 103 (4 February 2009) para 31.

that 'States Parties shall, in accordance with the provisions of this Statute, cooperate fully with the Court in its investigation and prosecution of crimes within the jurisdiction of the Court'. Even though specifically only addressing state parties, the SC referral must be read as imposing the same obligations to the non-party states addressed, insofar as they are presumed to be within the powers of the SC.[10] This may include art 88, according to which states 'shall ensure that there are procedures available under their national law for all of the forms of cooperation which are specified under this Part', and other far-reaching obligations regarding requests by the court for the taking of evidence, service of documents, etc. (see art 93).

It is of course a well-known feature of the ICC that it lacks any significant enforcement powers and is thus dependent on the cooperation of states to give effect to its decisions and orders.[11] In a recent decision, however, the ICC Appeals Chamber held that it does possess subpoena powers.[12] Without language in the referral that would support another conclusion, it must be assumed that the SC also conferred subpoena powers to the ICC in the referral.

5.1.2 The Preconditions of the Rome Statute

As stated above, art 13(b) of the Statute contains no detailed language of any conditions or any particular mechanism for its operation.[13] It sets out two

---

10 See further on the practice of the SC in that regard in Chapter 6.

11 Leila N. Sadat, *The International Criminal Court and the transformation of international law: Justice for the New Millennium* (International and comparative criminal law series, Transnational Publishers 2002) 120; Akande (n 4) 300. Cf arts 70, 71, 87 (7), 52 (2)(e), 57 (3)(d) Rome Statute.

12 *The Prosecutor v William Samoei Ruto and Joshua Arap Sang*, Judgment on the appeals of William Samoei Ruto and Mr Joshua Arap Sang against the decision of Trial Chamber V (A) of 17 April 2014 entitled 'Decision on Prosecutor's Application for Witness Summonses and resulting Request for State Party Cooperation', ICC-01/09-01/11-1598 (9 October 2014). For commentary see Charles C. Jalloh, 'Prosecutor v Ruto. Case No. ICC-01/09/11. Appeals Judgment on Witness Summonses' (2015) 109 *American Journal of International Law* 610. This is not without controversy; see William Schabas, *The International Criminal Court: A Commentary on the Rome Statute* (Oxford commentaries on international law, Oxford University Press 2010) 768 (arguing that '[t]here can be no real doubt that the *Rome Statute* does not contemplate the compulsory appearance of witnesses, though a mechanism such as a *subpoena'*.) See also Göran Sluiter, '"I Beg You, Please Come Testify" – The Problematic Absence of Subpoena Powers at the ICC' (2009) 12(4) *New Criminal Law Review* 590 (also a proponent of the 'voluntary appearance' principle.).

13 Luigi Condorelli and Santiago Villalpando, 'Referral and Deferral by the Security Council' in Antonio Cassese, Paola Gaeta and John R. Jones (eds), *The Rome Statute of the International Criminal Court* (Oxford University Press 2002) 629; Schabas (n 12) 293.

preconditions that must be satisfied from the perspective of the Rome Statute. First, there must exist a situation in which one or more of such crimes (as referred to in art 5 of the Statute) appear to have been committed. Second, this situation must be referred to the Prosecutor of the ICC by the SC acting under Chapter VII of the UN Charter.

The first precondition refers to '[a] situation in which one or more of such crimes [referred to in art 5] appears to have been committed'. As the preparatory work regarding this provision demonstrates,[14] the wording 'situation' must be distinguished from 'case'. In a late draft at the Rome Conference, the word 'situation' and 'matter' were presented as alternatives.[15] Why the word 'situation' was eventually adopted instead of 'matter' is not answerable based on the official records of the Rome Conference.[16] One participant of the negotiations suggests that 'situation' was considered to be of a more general nature, compared to 'matter' which was 'too specific for the functioning of the Court'.[17] The Pre-Trial Chamber held that

> [s]ituations, which are generally defined in terms of temporal, territorial and in some cases personal parameters, such as the situation in the territory of the Democratic Republic of the Congo since 1 July 2002, entail the proceedings envisaged in the Statute to determine whether a particular situation should give rise to a criminal investigation as well as the investigation as such.[18]

Several arguments are made in this context. For example, one could argue that the limitation grounded in the Chapter VII powers of the SC provides that it should be used to address entire 'situations' and not only certain individuals.[19] However, the recent practice of the SC to adopt targeted sanctions against certain individuals,[20] for example, or the establishment of the STL (set up for prosecuting individuals responsible for the attack of 14 February 2005 resulting in the death of former Lebanese Prime Minister Rafik Hariri and

---

14 See generally in Chapter 2.

15 See Bureau Discussion Paper, UN Doc A/CONF183/C1/L53.

16 Schabas (n 12) 297–98.

17 Lionel Yee, 'The International Criminal Court and the Security Council' in Roy S. Lee (ed), *The International Criminal Court: The Making of the Rome Statute; Issues, Negotiations, Results* (Kluwer Law International 2002) 148.

18 Situation in the Democratic Republic of the Congo (ICC-01/04), Decision on Applications for the Participation in the Proceedings of VPRS-1, VPRS-2, VPRS-3, VPRS-4, VPRS-5, VPRS-6, 17 January 2006, para 65.

19 Condorelli and Villalpando (n 13) 632.

20 See generally Matthew Happold, 'Targeted Sanctions and Human Rights' in Matthew Happold and Paul Eden (eds), *Economic Sanctions and International Law* (Studies in international law, Hart Publishing 2016).

others)[21] appear to contradict this view. In fact, the single case of an individual could sometimes have an impact on an entire situation addressed by the SC.[22] As a result, the vague concept of 'situation' ensures that the SC has sufficient discretionary powers to define and delineate a situation that would be in accordance with the Rome Statute.

Furthermore, from the perspective of the Rome Statute, the SC, when referring a situation to the ICC, must be acting under Chapter VII of the UN Charter. This means that only a binding decision by the SC under Chapter VII shall have any legal consequences for the ICC. Consequently, a President's statement or a resolution containing only a recommendation for the prosecution of crimes are not sufficient from the perspective of the ICC.[23] The same is true for a resolution of the GA, all of which are not legally binding on states and thus cannot produce the necessary legal effects.

5.1.3 Jurisdiction *Ratione Materiae* – Is the ICC Bound to Apply Only Customary Law?

In principle, the jurisdiction *ratione materiae* in case of SC referrals appears to be defined by the general rules on jurisdiction as provided for in the Statute. The heading of art 13 clearly states that the court exercises its jurisdiction 'in accordance with the provisions of this Statute'.[24] Since no specific rules or exceptions are provided for in the Statute regarding its jurisdiction *ratione materiae*, it follows prima facie that the jurisdiction *ratione materiae* extends over the crimes as provided for in art 5.[25] However, as concluded above considering the powers of the SC,[26] legislation of ICL should not be presumed and without explicit language to that effect, the ICC is bound to apply its definitions of crimes only insofar that it is recognized as customary international

---

21 See Bardo Fassbender, 'Reflections on the International Legality of the Special Tribunal for Lebanon' (2007) 5 *Journal of International Criminal Justice* 1091; Frédéric Mégret, 'A Special Tribunal for Lebanon: The UN Security Council and the Emancipation of International Criminal Justice' (2008) 21(02) *Leiden Journal of International Law*; M. Nikolova and M. J. Ventura, 'The Special Tribunal for Lebanon Declines to Review UN Security Council Action: Retreating from Tadic's Legacy in the Ayyash Jurisdiction and Legality Decisions' (2013) 11(3) *Journal of International Criminal Justice* 615.

22 Condorelli and Villalpando (n 13) 632.

23 Ibid. 630–31.

24 Article 13 Rome Statute.

25 Condorelli and Villalpando (n 13) 630.

26 Chapter 4.5.2.

law (or any other international treaty law applicable in the territory of the state concerned).[27]

5.1.3.1 Customary law status of the Rome Statute

Opinions regarding the customary status of the crimes as defined in the Rome Statute are divided. In *Prosecutor v Furundzija*, the ICTY stated '[d]epending on the matter at issue, the Rome Statute may be taken to restate, reflect or clarify customary rules or crystallise them, whereas in some areas it creates new law or modifies existing law'.[28] With the wide ratification of the Rome Statute and its open intent to be universally ratified, it is not implausible that all the Statute's criminal provisions may be reflective of customary international law in the near future.[29] At present, however, several important states from different geographical regions still have yet to ratify the Rome Statute.[30]

---

[27] Critical of such conclusion, Michael P. Scharf, 'Jurisdiction with Respect to Crime: Universal Jurisdiction and the Harvard Research' in John P. Grant and J. C. Barker (eds), *The Harvard Research in International Law: Contemporary Analysis and Appraisal* (Fred B. Rothman & Co 2007) 290 (arguing that '[s]imilarly, whether or not a defendant's state of nationality is a party to the Hostage Taking Convention, the Hijacking Convention, or the Aircraft Sabotage Convention, the perpetrator cannot seriously argue that he did not know that hostage taking or hijacking or blowing up an aircraft was a crime. And he is on notice by the existence of these multilateral conventions (whether or not they are widely ratified) that he can be called to answer for such crimes in the courts of State Parties to these treaties. Thus, the nullem crimen principle is not violated by the exercise of treaty-based jurisdiction over the nationals of non-party states').

[28] *Prosecutor v Anto Furundzija* (Judgment) IT-95-17/1-T (10 December 1998) para 227; *Tadic Case* (Decision on the Defence Motion for Interlocutory Appeal on Jurisdiction) ICTY-IT-94-l-A (2 October 1995) para 223. See also Leila Sadat who states that the 'delegates were not prepared to accept wholesale adopted that each and every definition was perfectly reflective of custom'; Sadat, 'Custom, Codification and Some Thoughts about the Relationship between the Two: Article 10 of the ICC Statute' (2000) 49 *De Paul Law Review* 909, 916. Similarly, William Schabas considers that 'while the correspondence with customary international law is close, it is far from perfect'; Schabas, *Introduction to the International Criminal Court* (3rd edn, Cambridge University Press 2007) 28. See also, Leena Grover, who submits that 'Articles 6, 7, and 8 of the Rome Statute . . .are not completely exhaustive of custom and may depart from custom in places'; Grover, 'A Call to Arms: Fundamental Dilemmas Confronting the Interpretation of Crimes in the Rome Statute of the International Criminal Court' (2010) 21(3) *European Journal of International Law* 543, 568.

[29] See however, Robert Cryer, *Prosecuting International Crimes: Selectivity and the International Criminal Law Regime* (Cambridge University Press 2005) 327–28.

[30] David Bosco, *Rough Justice: The International Criminal Court in a World of Power Politics* (Oxford University Press 2014). See also the statement of the head of the Indian delegation in Rome after the Rome Statute was adopted, remarking that 'the draft adopted a definition of crimes against humanity with which the representatives of

On the other hand, the establishment of the ICC has prompted some scholars to affirm that the definition process at Rome was viewed by some as a 'quasi-legislative event that produced a criminal code for the world'.[31] Indeed, Sadat and Carden argue that the states' delegations at the Rome Conference assumed the role of the international community's legislator.[32] According to this narrative, the Rome Statute asserts prescriptive jurisdiction beyond its state parties. This overreach of the law contained in the Rome Statute is premised on the theory of universal prescriptive jurisdiction.[33] Then if the Rome Statute bound all individuals since its entry into force, it is always applied prospectively.[34] Indeed, this seems to be the view of the ICC. The reasoning of Pre-Trial Chamber I in the Confirmation of Charges against Lubanga is illustrative of how the principle of legality operates before the ICC. The Chamber stated that

> [T]here is no infringement of the principle of legality if the Chamber exercises its power to decide whether Thomas Lubanga ought to be committed for trial on the basis of written (*lex scripta*) pre-existing criminal norms approved by the States Parties to the Rome Statute (*lex praevia*), defining prohibited conduct and setting out the related sentence (*lex certa*), which cannot be interpreted by analogy in *malam parten* (*lex stricta*).[35]

The ICC has never distinguished the applicability of criminal norms contained in the Statute under a retroactive SC referral from situations where the accused, at the time of the conduct, was a national or had committed the alleged crime in the territory of a state party to the Statute. While it was the

---

over half of humanity did not agree'. Dilip Lahiri, 'Explanation of Vote by Mr. Dilip Lahiri, Head of Delegation of India, on the Adoption of the Statute of the International Court' (Rome Conference, 17 July 1998).

31 On this see Sadat (n 28) 923.

32 Leila N. Sadat and S. R. Carden, 'The New International Criminal Court: An Uneasy Revolution' (2000) 88 *Georgetown Law Journal* 381, fn 35.

33 Sadat and Carden (n 32), 406–409; 412–13.

34 Among those who consider the crimes in the ICC Statute to be reflective of customary law is the former chair-man of the Rome Conference and first president of the ICC, Philippe Kirsch: see Philippe Kirsch, 'Customary International Humanitarian Law, its Enforcement, and the Role of the International Criminal Court' in Larry Maybee and Benarji Chakka (eds), *Custom as a Source of International Humanitarian Law: Proceedings of the Conference to Mark the Publication of the ICRC Study 'Customary International Humanitarian Law'* (International Committee of the Red Cross 2006) 79, 80. Others include Gerhard Werle, *Völkerstrafrecht* (2nd edn, Mohr Siebeck 2007); Herman von Hebel and Darryl Robinson, 'Crimes within the Jurisdiction of the Court' in Lee (n 17) 79, 126.

35 *Prosecutor v Lubanga* (Decision on the Confirmation of Charges) ICC-01/04-01/06 (29 January 2007) para 304.

intention of some states during the negotiations in Rome that the Statute would reflect customary international law,[36] most scholarly commentaries consider the definition of crimes in the Rome Statute as not entirely reflective of customary international law.[37] Following a strict interpretation of the principle of legality,[38] the possibility cannot be excluded that certain definitions of international crimes included in the Statute and further elaborated in the Elements of Crimes deviate from customary international law.[39] According to international jurisprudence, the principle of legality 'requires that the offence with which an accused is charged was sufficiently foreseeable and that the law providing for such liability was sufficiently accessible to the accused at the relevant time'.[40]

---

[36] Report of the Preparatory Committee on the Establishment of an International Criminal Court (13 September 1996) UN Doc A/51/22, para 54. Philippe Kirsch, 'Foreword' in Knut Dörmann (ed), *Elements of War Crimes under the Rome Statute of the International Criminal Court: Sources and Commentary* (Cambridge University Press 2003) viii. Most authoritatively see the International Committee of the Red Cross (ICRC)'s study on the Elements of Crimes of the ICC, where it is argued that there was 'general agreement that the definitions of crimes in the ICC Statute were to reflect existing customary international law, and not to create new law'; Kirsch (this note) viii.

[37] See e.g. Mohamed Bennouna, 'The Statute's Rules on Crimes and Existing or Developing International Law' in Cassese (n 13) 1102; Rogier Bartels, 'Dealing with the Principle of Proportionality in Armed Conflict in Retrospect: The Application of the Principle in International Criminal Trials' (2013) 46 *Israel Law Review* 271, 313–14; Robert Cryer, 'Elements of Crimes (in the ICC)' in Antonio Cassese (ed), *The Oxford Companion to International Criminal Justice* (Oxford University Press 2009) 308; Alexandre Galand, 'Security Council Referrals to the International Criminal Court as Quasi-Legislative Acts' (2015) 19 *Max Planck Yearbook of United Nations Law* 142, 143. Leila Sadat writes that "the delegates in Rome were not prepared to accept that each and every definition was perfectly reflective of custom"; Sadat (n 28) 916; William Schabas considers that 'while the correspondence with customary international law is close, it is far from perfect'; Schabas, *An Introduction to the International Criminal Court* (4th edn, Cambridge University Press 2011) 92; José Alvarez, *International Organizations as Law-makers* (Oxford University Press 2005) 300; Robert Cryer and others, *An Introduction to International Criminal Law and Procedure* (3rd edn, Cambridge University Press 2014) 151–152.

[38] The political scientist Judith N. Shklar articulated the centrality of the principle of legality in international criminal justice aptly by writing: 'The principle of legality – that there shall be no crime without law, and no punishment without a crime – *is* criminal justice.' She adds, 'No principle of legality means no justice'. Shklar, *Legalism: Law, Morals, and Political Trials* (Harvard University Press 1986) 152, 160.

[39] Cryer (n 37) 308.

[40] *Prosecutor v Milutinović et al.* (Decision on Dragoljub Ojdanić's Motion Challenging Jurisdiction – Joint Criminal Enterprise) IT-99-37-AR72 (21 May 2003) para 38; see also *S.W. v United Kingdom* (Judgment) ECtHR no. 20166/92 (22 November 1995) paras 35–36 (indicating that the term 'law' in art 7 of the European Convention of Human Rights (ECHR) 'comprises written as well as unwritten law and implies qualitative requirements, notably those of accessibility and foreseeability'). On

This – without doubt – includes customary international law crimes[41] that are applicable at the time of the offence.[42] An example of where the Statute might create new law is, as maintained in Cassese's *International Criminal Law*, art 7(2)(i) Rome Statute. The Statute's provision on enforced disappearance of persons as a crime against humanity 'has not codified customary international law but contributed to the crystallisation of a nascent rule'.[43] It is further argued that art 7(1)(h)(i), art 8(2)(b)(iii), (iv) and (xxvi), (c) and (e) go beyond customary international law.[44]

In addition to the substantive law, the modes of liability that the ICC applies to find an individual criminally responsible is arguably also going beyond customary international law. Particularly, the approach adopted by the ICC regarding indirect perpetration of crimes (art 25(3)(a) Rome Statute) based on the theory of 'control over the crime' is a case in point, as the criticism in separate and dissenting opinions of ICC judges suggest.[45] The ICTY Appeals

---

the question of whether the definition of crimes against humanity satisfies this requirement, see this critical study: Sarah Erne, *Das Bestimmtheitsgebot im nationalen und internationalen Strafrecht am Beispiel des Straftatbestands der Verfolgung* (Nomos 2016).

41 In case of the Extraordinary Criminal Chambers of Cambodia, the Court pointed out that 'the Chamber may rely on both customary and conventional international law, including the general principles of law recognised by the community of nations'. *Duch Case* (Judgment) No. 001/18-07-2007/ECCC/TC (26 July 2010) para 30 (2010) (Extraordinary Criminal Chambers of Cambodia). See further *Aleksovski Appeal Judgement*, para 126 (relying on customary and conventional law sources); *Prosecutor v Kordić et al*, Judgement IT-95-14/2-A (17 December 2004) paras 41–42; *Prosecutor v Milutinović et al*, Decision on Dragoljub Ojdanić's Motion Challenging Jurisdiction – Joint Criminal Enterprise, IT-99-37-AR72 (21 May 2003) paras 38–42.

42 *Kononov v Latvia*, Judgment, ECtHR App No 36376/04 (24 July 2008) para 114(e) 40. See also e.g. *Prosecutor v Milutinović et al*, Decision on Dragoljub Ojdanić's Motion Challenging Jurisdiction – Joint Criminal Enterprise, ICTY Appeals Chamber, IT-99-37-AR72 (21 May 2003) paras 34–44 (as applied to joint criminal enterprise); *Prosecutor v Aleksovski*, Judgement, ICTY Appeals Chamber, IT-95-14/1-A (24 March 2000) para 126 (as applied to grave breaches of the Geneva Conventions of 1949). As regards the integral requirements of the principle of legality, i.e. foreseeability and accessibility: 'An assessment of the foreseeability and accessibility requirements integral to the principle of legality should take into account the particular nature of international law, including its reliance on unwritten custom.' *Duch Case* (Judgment) No. 001/18-07-2007/ECCC/TC (26 July 2010) para 31.

43 Cassese et al, *Cassese's International Criminal Law* (Oxford University Press 2013) 98; See also Bartels (n 37) 313. Also the sexual crimes included in the definition of crimes in the Statute might not reflect customary law; see Caelo Focarelli, 'International Criminal Justice (2009)' in Conforti (n 3) 325.

44 Bartels (n 37) 313.

45 See also the criticism in *Prosecutor v Lubanga* (Judgment pursuant to Article 74 of the Statute, Separate Opinion of Judge Adrian Fulford) ICC-01/04-01/06-2842 (14

Chamber also noted that '[t]his mode of liability . . . does not have support in customary international law or in the settled jurisprudence of this Tribunal, which is binding on the Trial Chambers'.[46] Furthermore, the Appeals Chamber of the STL held, confirming the ICTY Appeals Chamber's reasoning, that '[t]he problem with the doctrine of perpetration by means [i.e., control over the crime theory] is that it is not recognized in customary international law'.[47] In response to the challenge that the 'control over the crime' theory was not part of customary international law, the ICC Pre-Trial Chamber I noted that 'since the Rome Statute expressly provides for this specific mode of liability, the question as to whether customary law admits or discards the "joint commission through another person" [i.e. control over the crime theory] is not relevant for this Court'.[48] Taken together it is questionable whether these modes of liability reflect customary international law.

5.1.3.2 Emerging customary status of the Elements of Crimes

The fact that the Elements of Crimes of the ICC Statute were adopted by the ASP of the ICC by consensus, including non-party states, may change this assessment.[49] Indeed, it was the aim of the drafters to codify existing customary law. This consensus could be taken as evidence for *opinio juris* of the international community and thus possibly developing into customary international law.[50] If the adoption of the Elements of Crimes by consensus are being

---

March 2012); *Prosecutor v Katanga and Ngudjolo Chui* (Decision on the Confirmation of Charges) ICC-01/04-01/07 (30 September 2008); *Prosecutor v Ngudjolo Chui* (Concurring Opinion of Judge Christine Van den Wyngaert to the Judgment pursuant to Article 74 of the Statute) ICC-01/04-02/12 (18 December 2012).

[46] *Prosecutor v Stakic* (Appeals Chamber Judgment) IT-97-24-A (22 March 2006) para 62.

[47] Special Tribunal for Lebanon (Interlocutory Decision on the Applicable Law: Terrorism, Conspiracy, Homicide, Perpetration, Cumulative Charging) STL-11-01/1/I/AC/R176bis, F00010 (16 February 2011) para 256.

[48] Prosecutor v Katanga and Ngudjjolo Chui (Decision on the Confirmation of Charges) ICC-01/04-01/07 (30 September 2008) para 508. See also Galand (n 37) 152–53.

[49] See Official Records of the Assembly of States Parties to the Rome Statute of the International Criminal Court (3–10 September 2002) part II.B. For the recent amendment of the Elements of Crimes during the 2010 Review Conference see Resolution RC/Res.5 (Adopted at the 12th plenary meeting, 10 June 2010), 2010 Review Conference are replicated from the Official Records of the Review Conference of the Rome Statute of the International Criminal Court, Kampala, 31 May–11 June 2010 (International Criminal Court publication, RC/11). See the Official Records, ICC Doc RC/9/11, available at https://asp.icc-cpi.int/iccdocs/asp_docs/ASP9/OR/RC-11-ENG.pdf (accessed 22 June 2016).

[50] Larissa Van den Herik, 'The Decline of Customary International Law as a Source of International Criminal Law' (Grotius Centre Working Paper 2014/038-ICL) 10,

viewed as an expression of *opinio juris* as regards the customary international law nature of the definition of these crimes, it is a different question whether actual practice exists in that regard. Identifying the status of customary international law would additionally require a comprehensive analysis of the practice of states and the organs of the ICC, which would go beyond the scope of this study.[51] It would also require an analysis of the *opinio juris* and state practice of states not parties to the ICC. Those states outside the court include the world's superpowers, the United States and China. Similarly, Russia, India and regional powers including Turkey, Egypt, Israel, Saudi Arabia, Pakistan and Indonesia are outside the court.[52] Suffice it to note that the ICTY Trial Chamber addressed the status of the ICC Statute by stating that

> In many areas the Statute may be regarded as indicative of the legal views, i.e. opinio juris of a great number of States . . . Depending on the matter at issue, the Rome Statute may be taken to restate, reflect or clarify customary rules or crystallise them, whereas in some areas it creates new law or modifies existing law. At any event, the Rome Statute by and large may be taken as constituting an authoritative expression of the legal views of a great number of States.[53]

Thus, it is an open question whether all of the crimes defined in the Elements of Crimes reflect customary international law. Still, it is important to explain why the adoption of the Elements of Crimes, by itself, cannot create customary international law. This is for the following reasons. First, pursuant to art 9 of the Rome Statute, the Elements of Crimes shall assist the Court in the interpretation and application of arts 6, 7 and 8, consistent with the Statute. The Elements of Crimes are mere interpretive aides and cannot be invoked to inappropriately broaden, modify or override the plain meaning of the definition of crimes as included in the Articles of the Rome Statute.[54] Furthermore, as noted above, art 10 of the Statute expressly provides that '[n]othing in this Part shall be interpreted as limiting or prejudicing in any way existing or developing rules of international law for purposes other than this Statute'. In

---

available at http://ssrn.com/abstract=2587622 (accessed 29 June 2016). In this sense arguably also, Bruno Simma and Stephan Wittich, 'Das Völkergewohnheitsrecht' in August Reinisch (ed), *Österreichisches Handbuch des Völkerrechts* (5th edn, MANZ 2013) 34.

[51] It is not the purpose of this study to survey the relevant state practice. Suffice it to note here that consensus at a diplomatic conference does not by itself constitute state practice; see also Simma and Wittich (n 50) 34.

[52] Bosco (n 30).

[53] *Prosecutor v Anto Furundzija* (Judgment) IT-95-17/1-T (10 December 1998) para 227.

[54] Grover (n 28) 557.

other words, art 10 confirms the view that the Rome Statute itself does not claim to codify customary international law.[55] This is further supported by the fact that art 21 of the Rome Statute deals with the applicable law of the ICC. Here, the Statute itself makes a clear distinction between the Statute and the Elements of Crimes and 'the principles and rules of international law, including the established principles of the international law of armed conflict', i.e. customary international law, establishes a hierarchy of law that judges are to apply if interpretation of the Rome Statute and Elements of Crimes fails to resolve an issue.[56]

5.1.3.3 Interpretation of the referral as covering only customary international law

The SC referral must be interpreted as only referring jurisdiction *ratione materiae* of customary international law crimes to the ICC. Such narrow interpretation is supported by the fact that generally, the conferral of powers from one entity to another is to be construed narrowly,[57] and the presumption that the SC does not intend to impose obligations that force member states to breach fundamental principles of human rights,[58] to which the principle of legality belongs.[59] This interpretation is also reinforced by the ILC, which found in the context of its study on the fragmentation of international law that SC resolutions must be construed as 'producing and intending to produce effects in accordance with existing law and not in violation of it'.[60] This rule of interpretation warrants a strong presumption against a conflict with the principle of legality and calls for techniques of harmonious interpretation to be used so that the conflict does not materialize into a genuine one.[61]

---

55 Similarly, Sadat (n 11) 262.

56 Grover (n 28) 553.

57 See *mutatis mutandis* Dan Sarooshi, *The United Nations and the Development of Collective Security: The Delegation by the UN Security Council of its Chapter VII Powers* (Clarendon Press; Oxford University Press 1999) 46.

58 Rosalyn Higgins and others, *Oppenheim's International Law: United Nations* (vol 1, Oxford University Press 2017) 422.

59 The principle of legality is enshrined in several international instruments, including art 11(2) of the Universal Declaration of Human Rights and Art 15 of the ICCPR, as well as several regional human rights conventions, such as the American Convention on Human Rights (art 9), African Charter on Human and Peoples' Rights, art 7(2), and the ECHR art 7(1).

60 ILC, 'Report of the Study Group of the ILC on Fragmentation of International Law: Difficulties Arising from Diversification and Expansion of International Law' (13 April 2006) UN Doc A/CN.4/L.682, para 39.

61 Paulus and Leiß (n 6) 2123. See also ILC, 'Report of the Study Group of the ILC on Fragmentation of International Law: Difficulties Arising from Diversification

As a result, a presumption exists that unless the SC explicitly and clearly states the contrary,[62] it intended that rights to non-retroactivity of the accused be respected. An implicit intent to the contrary is not sufficient. This reasoning has been adopted by the European Court of Human Rights (ECtHR), for instance. In *Al-Jedda v United Kingdom*, the court found that in the absence of clear and explicit language to the contrary, 'there must be a presumption that the Security Council does not intend to impose any obligation on Member States to breach fundamental principles of human rights'.[63] This principle of interpretation was reiterated in *Nada v Switzerland*,[64] and again in *Al-Dulimi v Switzerland*[65] even despite clear and explicit language that was used in the SC resolution. This also means that the wording 'acting under Chapter VII' in art 13(b) of the Rome Statute must be interpreted as meaning those SC referrals that are in accordance with its Chapter VII powers, hence as only referring jurisdiction over crimes as recognized under customary international law.

As a result, the ICC is directed to only apply the definitions of crimes in its Statute insofar as they reflect customary international law or those international crimes under a treaty to which the state concerned is a party.[66]

5.1.3.4 Consequences for the applicable law under the Rome Statute

This conclusion raises the question of whether the ICC, under its constituent treaty, is authorized to apply customary international law definitions of crimes that deviate from the definition as included in its Statute. This does not appear to be problematic. It is clear from the provisions of the Statute that it disclaims an intent to define substantive ICL, for purposes other than the operation of the ICC.[67] Article 10 Rome Statute clearly states that '[n]othing in this Part

---

and Expansion of International Law' (13 April 2006) UN Doc A/CN.4/L.682, para 37; Pauwelyn (n 6) 204–44.

62 See the reasoning of the ECtHR to this effect; see e.g. *Al-Jedda v United Kingdom*, ECtHR, Grand Chamber, Judgment, APP No 27021/08 (7 July 2011) para 102; *Nada v Switzerland, ECtHR*, Grand Chamber, Judgment, APP No 10593/08 (12 September 2012) para 172; *Al-Dulimi and Montana Management Inc v Switzerland*, ECtHR, Grand Chamber, Judgment, APP No 5809/08 (21 June 2016) paras 138–40.

63 *Al-Jedda v United Kingdom* (n 62) para 102. This also follows from the rule of interpretation to presume that the SC is not deviating from general international law unless the contrary intent is clear; see Alexander Orakhelashvili, *Peremptory Norms in International Law* (Oxford University Press 2008) 80.

64 *Nada v Switzerland* (n 62) para 172.

65 Al-Dulimi and Montana Management Inc v Switzerland, Judgment, Application No 5809/08 (21 June 2016) paras 145–49.

66 But see Alexandre Galand, who considers the SC referral a 'quasi-legislative' act; Galand (n 37).

67 Kenneth S. Gallant, 'The International Criminal Court in the System of States and International Organizations' (2003) 16(3) *Leiden Journal of International Law*

[Jurisdiction, Admissibility and Applicable Law] shall be interpreted as limiting or prejudicing in any way existing or developing rules of international law for purposes other than this Statute'.[68] Furthermore, a reference to the rules of customary international law is found in art 21(b) of the Statute (although the Rome Statute does not explicitly mention 'customary international law').[69]

Also, art 21(3) states that the application and interpretation of the law pursuant to this article must be consistent with internationally recognized human rights.[70] Without doubt the major universal human rights instruments fall in this category,[71] which include the principle of legality, including the prohibition of retroactive application of criminal law.[72] Even without such explicit reference to internationally recognized human rights, several authors suggest that customary human rights law is binding upon international organizations (such as the ICC) by virtue of the rules of general international law.[73] And art 22 of the Statute itself provides for the principle of non-retroactivity (also known as *nullum crimen sine lege*). As a result, the ICC must apply customary international law rules and might be called to deviate from the definitions included in arts 6–8 Rome Statute insofar as those definitions are not reflective of customary law or otherwise applicable treaty law in the case of a SC referral involving a non-states party.

In practice, I propose[74] that the ICC Chambers should apply the so-called '*Tadic* principles' in its exercise of jurisdiction over situations in non-party

553, 577. For a comprehensive account see M. Milanovic, 'Is the Rome Statute Binding on Individuals? (And Why We Should Care)' (2011) 9(1) *Journal of International Criminal Justice* 25.

[68] See also art 22(3) stipulating that '[t]his article shall not affect the characterization of any conduct as criminal under international law independently of this Statute'.

[69] Van den Herik (n 50) 8.

[70] For a comprehensive analysis of this provision see Gerhard Hafner and Christina Binder, 'The Interpretation of Article 21 (3) ICC Statute Opinion Reviewed' (2004) 9 *Austrian Review of International and European Law* 163.

[71] Hafner and Binder (n 70) 190.

[72] Cherif M. Bassiouni, 'The Need for an International Criminal Court in the New International World Order' (1992) 25(2) *Vanderbilt Journal of Transnational Law* 151, 176. It is important to stress that the principle of legality is also politically of infinite value, as pointed out by political scientist Judith Shklar (n 38) 152l. 'No principle of legality means no justice', ibid. 160.

[73] Cedric Ryngaert and others (eds), *Judicial Decisions on the Law of International Organizations* (Oxford University Press 2016) 233; Henry G. Schermers, 'The Legal Bases of International Organization Action' in René-Jean Dupuy (ed), *A Handbook on International Organizations* (2nd edn, Nijhoff 1998) 402.

[74] See, in support, Bartels (n 37) 313–14. Similarly, Antonio Cassese, 'The Statute of the International Criminal Court: Some Preliminary Reflections' (1999) 10 *European Journal of International Law* 144, 151. Cassese appears to be of a similar view when he notes that the ICC for certain crimes 'would first have to establish (i)

states.[75] These principles are the four conditions that, according to the Appeals Chamber of the ICTY, must be met in order for criminal conduct to fall within the jurisdiction of the ICTY Statute.[76] These conditions are as follows:

> (i) the violation must constitute an infringement of a rule of international humanitarian law; (ii) the rule must be customary in nature or, if it belongs to treaty law, the required conditions must be met . . . (iii) the violation must be 'serious', that is to say, it must constitute a breach of a rule protecting important values, and the breach must involve grave consequences for the victim . . . (iv) the violation must entail, under customary or conventional law, the individual criminal responsibility of the person breaching the rule.

With regard to (ii), the appeals chamber considered that

> the International Tribunal is authorised to apply, in addition to customary international law, any treaty which: (i) was unquestionably binding on the parties at the time of the alleged offence; and (ii) was not in conflict with or derogating from peremptory norms of international law, as are most customary rules of international humanitarian law.[77]

It is submitted that the ICC should apply these principles even in those cases where this issue is not raised by the defence. This should already be done in the confirmation decision by a Pre-Trial Chamber on the prosecution's document containing the charges against one or more individuals. Unfortunately, the ICC's practice to date, however, shows that this is not being done at that stage of the proceedings.[78]

---

whether under general international law such [conduct] . . . is considered a breach of international humanitarian law of armed conflict, and in addition (ii) whether under customary international law such a breach would amount to a war crime'; ibid.

[75] In his report on the proposed ICTY Statute, the UN Secretary-General had already stated that 'the application of the principle nullem crimen sine lege requires that the international tribunal should apply rules of international humanitarian law which are beyond any doubt part of customary law so that the problem of adherence of some but not all states to specific conventions does not arise'; Report of the Secretary-General Pursuant to Paragraph 2 of Security Council Resolution 808 (1993) (3 May 1993) UN Doc S/25704, 34.

[76] *Tadic Case* (Decision on the Defence Motion for Interlocutory Appeal on Jurisdiction) ICTY-IT-94-l-A (2 October 1995) paras 94 and 143; Bartels (n 37) 312.

[77] *Tadic Case* (Decision on the Defence Motion for Interlocutory Appeal on Jurisdiction) ICTY-IT-94-l-A (2 October 1995) paras 94 and 143.

[78] In the Decisions on the Confirmation of Charges in the cases related to an alleged attack on AU peacekeepers in Darfur, the Pre-Trial Chambers did not pronounce on this issue. It must be said that the defence in these cases did not raise the issue: see *Prosecutor v Bahar Idriss Abu Garda*, Decision on the Confirmation of Charges, ICC-02/05-02/09, Pre-Trial Chamber, 8 December 2010 (ICC-02/05-02/09-243-Red); and

In any case, the ICC has avoided addressing these issues directly by assuming that

> the Security Council of the United Nations has also accepted that the investigation into the said situation, as well as any prosecution arising therefrom, will take place in accordance with the statutory framework provided for in the Statute, the Elements of Crimes and the Rules as a whole.[79]

The ICC does not provide, however, any reasons for this assumption and, as shown, this view appears to be rather questionable. Practically speaking, the ICC might of course simply overlook this issue.[80] As one commentator put it, 'the Court will normally determine simply that the crime is one contained in the Statute and that it was within the temporal, geographical and personal jurisdiction of the Court at the time that the relevant alleged acts took place'.[81]

5.1.4 *Ratione Temporis*

The jurisdiction *ratione temporis* of the ICC Statute similarly faces challenges stemming from the principle of legality. The Statute itself provides for an absolute limit in art 24, stating that 'no person shall be criminally responsible under this Statute for conduct prior to the entry into force of the Statute'. The Rome Statute entered into force on 1 July 2002 in accordance with art 123.[82] No situation prior to that may be referred to the ICC by the SC under the Statute.

Prosecutor v Abdallah Banda Abakaer Nourain and Saleh Mohammed Jerbo Jamus, Corrigendum of the 'Decision on the Confirmation of Charges', ICC-02/05-03/09, Pre-Trial Chamber, 8 March 2011 (ICC-02/05-03/09-121-CORR-RED). However, compare *Prosecutor v Thomas Lubanga Dyilo*, Decision on the Confirmation of Charges, ICC-01/04-01/06, Pre-Trial Chamber, 29 January 2007 (ICC-01/04-01/06-803), paras 294–316 in which Pre-Trial Chamber I did go into the issue of jurisdiction over the alleged conduct – even though here it involved a situation on the territory of a state party that had ratified Additional Protocol I.

79 *Prosecutor v Al-Bashir* (Decision on the Prosecution's Application for a Warrant of Arrest against Omar Al-Bashir) ICC-02/05-01/09 (4 March 2009) para 45; Situation in Darfur, Sudan (Decision on Application under Rule 103) ICC-02/05 (4 February 2009) para 31.

80 In the same vein see Bartels (n 37), 313–14.

81 Bruce Broomhall, 'Article 22' in Otto Triffterer and Kai Ambos (eds), *Commentary on the Rome Statute of the International Criminal Court: Observers' Notes, Article by article* (2nd edn, C.H. Beck; Hart; Nomos 2008) 33.

82 See United Nations Treaty Series (vol 2187, 3), available at https://treaties.un.org/doc/Publication/MTDSG/Volume%20II/Chapter%20XVIII/XVIII-10.en.pdf (accessed 3 July 2016).

However, the Statute does not provide any guidance as to whether a 'situation' may be prospective as well as retrospective. For example, could a SC referral adopted on 31 March 2005, as was the case of the first referral of the SC to the ICC,[83] refer to 'the situation in Darfur since 1 July 2002'? From the perspective of the Rome Statute, this does not cause a problem since it is not referring to a date prior to the entry into force of the Rome Statute. The jurisdiction *ratione temporis* of the ICC is generally based on the entry into force of the Statute and its ratification by the state concerned, but the SC referral specifically does not depend on the acceptance of the state concerned.[84]

However, this would be in conflict with the principle of legality if the crimes went beyond those that were crimes under customary international law (or otherwise applicable treaties or domestic law) at the time of their commission. Again, a presumption exists that the SC did not legislate new ICL that goes beyond recognized customary rules.[85] To avoid the retroactive application of criminal law, the ICC should apply only customary international law or otherwise applicable treaty law or domestic law that was in force at the time of the commission of the crime.[86]

It is interesting to note that this issue had already been raised during the work of the ILC. As James Crawford writes about the work of the ILC,

> The other challenge [for the work of the ILC on a draft statute] was juridical and involved an issue of principle: that is to say respect for the fundamental principle of legality as embodied in Article 15(1) of the International Covenant on Civil and Political Rights of 1966 . . . If the jurisdiction of the Court, or at least its operation, was to depend on the consent of States concerned, or on a 'triggering' mechanism under Chapter VII of the Charter, then it was probable that the jurisdiction would only be brought into play after the alleged crime(s) had been committed (or at least had started to be committed). As a practical matter, it was thought that States were

---

83 SC Res 1593 (2005).

84 See also Stephané Bourgon, 'Jurisdiction Ratione Temporis' in Cassese (n 13) 552–53.

85 See Chapter 5.1.3. Similarly, Robert Frau, 'Das Völkerstrafrecht in der jüngsten Praxis des VN-Sicherheitsrates' (2011) 10 *Zeitschrift für Internationale Strafrechtsdogmatik* 784, 789.

86 In this sense also Condorelli and Villalpando, who even argue that that 'the terms of Article 11, read as a whole and in the logic of the overall system of the ICC, would not preclude the Security Council from referring a situation to the Court in which crimes appear to have been committed before the entry into force of the Statute, provided that, in strict accordance with the general principle of non-retroactivity, such conduct was held to be criminal under valid rules of international law at the time of its commission'; see Condorelli and Villalpando (n 13) 637. In contrast, Stephané Bourgon argues that while such a situation would appear contrary to the *ratione temporis* jurisdiction of the ICC, this is justified by keeping with the powers of the Security Council under Chapter VII, without giving further reasons for this conclusion; see Bourgon (n 84) 552–53.

> unlikely to agree in advance to the international prosecution of unspecified international crimes in unspecified circumstances, and the Security Council would refer situations only after an initial breach of the peace or act of aggression had occurred. But if that were so, then the principle of legality dictated that the applicable law should be the international law in force at the time the acts were committed, i.e. existing international criminal law, and not any new lex specialis associated with a Statute of the ICC.[87]

Another issue relates to the question of prospective jurisdiction. May the SC refer a situation which prospectively means covering not just crimes committed until the date of the SC referral but also all crimes committed after that date? If so, can a referral that is silent on this issue (and in practice all referrals have been silent on this point) be construed as having this effect? William Schabas suggests an interpretation in light of the objective of ending impunity that arrives at the permissibility of a prospective definition of a 'situation'.[88] However, as noted above, a SC referral of a situation that implies it continues without temporal limitation is not without its problems.[89] If the SC referral does not specify an end date (and in practice it did not), then the only way to rectify the situation would be another resolution. However, in most cases it will be clear from the fact that the SC refers a specific situation that it can be delimited (by way of looking at the preamble and other mentions of the situation). In practice, the Pre-Trial Chamber assumed that the SC referral provided for prospective jurisdiction in SC Res 1593 (2005), without directly addressing this issue.[90]

In conclusion, the SC referral must be interpreted as providing the ICC with prospective jurisdiction unless expressly decided otherwise in the SC resolution referring the situation, extending to what can be reasonably inferred from the description of the situation addressed (but construed narrowly).[91] It follows from the legal nature of the SC referral that the ICC can only exercise

---

87 James Crawford, 'The Work of the International Law Commission' in Cassese (n 13) 27.

88 Schabas (n 12) 298–99.

89 Similarly, ibid.

90 *Bashir* (ICC-02/05-01/09), Decision on the Prosecution's Application for a Warrant of Arrest against Omar Hassan Ahmad Al-Bashir (4 March 2009) para 37. Also: *Abu Garda* (ICC-02/05-02/09), Decision on the Prosecutor's Application under Article 58 (7 May 2009) para 2.

91 See, however, William Schabas who suggests that '[i]n the absence of an acceptable manner by which the Court can address the end date of a Security Council referral that is silent on the matter, it might be preferable to deny such resolutions any prospective effect'. Schabas (n 12) 298–99.

its jurisdiction to that extent, provided the SC has not terminated the referral expressly.[92]

5.1.5 Jurisdiction *Ratione Personae* and the Question of Personal Immunities

According to arts 1 and 25 Rome Statute, the ICC only has jurisdiction over natural persons. This personal jurisdiction is generally limited to instances where the accused possesses the nationality of a state party to the ICC or where the alleged crime has been committed in the territory of a state party.[93] However, these limitations based on the nationality of the accused or the territory where the alleged crime had been committed do not apply in case of a SC referral. The Rome Statute allows the court to proceed even if none of the states concerned have ratified the Statute or accepted its jurisdiction. Difficult legal issues arise from immunity *ratione personae* (also called personal immunity). The effect of the SC referral in accordance with the Statute in this respect is disputed.

5.1.5.1 Clarifying the basic concept

Immunity *ratione personae* is a procedural bar to the exercise of jurisdiction based on the notion that any activity of an incumbent head of state, head of government, foreign minister and diplomatic agent must be immune from any interference from a foreign state.[94] It covers official and private acts committed prior to and during office.[95] It grants only *procedural* immunity.[96] However, it can only be enjoyed by incumbent heads of state and other high-ranking state

---

[92] Contra this view but without explaining why the ICC would still be authorized to exercise jurisdiction once the SC has terminated the referral, see Condorelli and Villalpando (n 13) 642–44.

[93] Micaela Frulli, 'Jurisdiction Ratione Personae' in Cassese (n 13) 535.

[94] Cryer and others (n 37) 542; Dapo Akande, 'International Law Immunities and the International Criminal Court' (2004) 98(3) *American Journal of International Law* 407, 409; Manisuli Ssenyonjo, 'The International Criminal Court and the Warrant of Arrest for Sudan's President Al-Bashir: A Crucial Step Towards Challenging Impunity or a Political Decision?' (2009) 78 *Nordic Journal of International Law* 397, 405.

[95] See Salvatore Zappala, 'Do Heads of State in Office Enjoy Immunity from Jurisdiction for International Crimes? The Ghaddafi Case Before the French Cour de Cassation' (2001) 12(3) *European Journal of International Law* 595.

[96] ILC, 'Preliminary report on the immunity of State officials from foreign criminal jurisdiction' (31 May 2012) UN Doc A/CN.4/654, para 11. See also the explanation in the commentary to *The Princeton Principles on Universal Jurisdiction* (Program in Law and Public Affairs, Princeton University 2001) 48–52.

representatives;[97] when they cease to hold office the immunity also ceases, and only immunity *ratione materiae*, i.e. immunity for official state acts, remains.[98]

For the ICC, art 27(2) of the Rome Statute provides for jurisdiction over any state official, irrespective of their immunity. Therefore, art 27(2) explicitly removes immunity *ratione personae*. In this respect the Rome Statute departs from other ICL instruments.[99] The provisions of the ad hoc tribunals, for example, removed immunity *ratione materiae* but arguably not immunity *ratione personae*.[100]

The existence of personal immunity before international courts is not uncontested. Issues are further complicated by the fact that immunity vis-à-vis the ICC has to be separated from the question of personal immunities of state officials in national jurisdictions, i.e. those immunities applicable with respect to national authorities. This is important because the ICC does not have independent powers of arrest and must therefore rely on states to arrest and surrender wanted persons.[101]

---

[97] See Draft Article 4, ILC Text of draft articles 1, 3 and 4 provisionally adopted by the Drafting Committee at the sixty-fifth session of the International Law Commission (6 May–7 June and 8 July–9 August 2013) UN Doc A/CN.4/L.814 (4 June 2013); Second Report of the Special Rapporteur, Ms. Concepcion Escobar Hernandez, (4 April 2013) UN Doc A/CN4/661, provisionally adopted at the 65th session of the International Law Commission.

[98] Antonio Cassese, 'When May Senior State Officials be Tried for International Crimes? Some Comments on the Congo v. Belgium Case' (2002) 13 *European Journal of International Law* 853, 864–65. See also ILC, 'Preliminary report on immunity of State officials from foreign criminal jurisdiction' (Roman Anatolevich Kolodkin, Special Rapporteur) UN Doc A/CN.4/601 (29 May 2008) paras 78–83.

[99] Schabas (n 12) 446.

[100] The respective provisions of the ICTY and ICTR read '[t]he official position of any accused person, whether as Head of State or Government or as a responsible Government official, shall not relieve such person of criminal responsibility nor mitigate punishment'; see Schabas (n 12) 450–52; William Schabas, 'The Special Tribunal for Lebanon: Is a "Tribunal of an International Character" Equivalent to an "International Criminal Court"?' (2008) 21(02) *Leiden Journal of International Law*, 526–27.

[101] Akande (n 94) 420. See the proposed language to clarify this during the preparatory work by the delegation of Austria that '[i]n the course of investigations or procedures performed by, or at the request of the court, no person may make a plea of immunity from jurisdiction irrespective of whether on the basis of international or national law'. Summary of the Proceedings of the Preparatory Committee during the Period 25 March–12 April 1996, UN Doc A/AC.249/1 (7 May 1996) 77.

5.1.5.2 International practice

International practice is not conclusive in regard to personal immunity before international courts.[102] To date, no international criminal court has exercised jurisdiction over officials entitled to immunity *ratione personae* at the time of the trials.[103] The first serving head of state to appear before an international criminal court was Uhuru Kenyatta in 2014.[104] All trials involving high-ranking state officials before this case occurred when the official ceased to hold office or personal immunities were arguably implicitly waived by that official's state. For example, the conclusion of the Treaty of Versailles (arts 227–28) and Treaty of Sèvres (arts 226–27) must be seen as implicit waivers of the personal immunities. The Nuremberg Tribunal did not prosecute any serving high-ranking officials. Joachim Von Ribbentrop, Reich Minister for Foreign Affairs (1938–45) and Karl Doenitz, Reich Head of State (2–23 May 1945) were tried and sentenced by the Nuremberg Tribunal but the proceedings took place after they ceased to be in office; thus they only enjoyed immunity *ratione materiae*. The same applies to Mamoru Shigemitsu, Japanese Minster of Foreign Affairs (1943–45) and Hiroshi Oshima, Japanese Ambassador to Berlin (1938–45), who were tried and sentenced by the International Military Tribunal for the Far East. Note that Emperor Hirohito was not tried, adding to the uncertainty relating to personal immunities. The ICTY indicted Slobodan Milosevic in May 1999 while he was the Head of State of the Federal Republic of Yugoslavia from July 1997 to October 2000. No state objected to that based on an alleged violation of his immunity *ratione personae*. The arrest warrant was enforced and Milosevic was transferred into the custody of the ICTY only in June 2001, i.e. when he enjoyed immunity *ratione materiae* but not personal immunity. In the Decision on Preliminary Motions, the Trial Chamber referred to Milosevic's criminal responsibility and not to questions relating to the jurisdiction of the Tribunal when the indictment was first issued. The ICTY did not review whether the indictment of June 1999 was in accordance with international law, but whether it lacked jurisdiction due to Milosevic's status as *former* Head of State. Accordingly, it is debatable whether there are any

---

[102] The ILC has not dealt with this question in 'Preliminary report on the immunity of State officials from foreign criminal jurisdiction' (31 May 2012) UN Doc A/CN.4/654, para 12.

[103] The only instance was the indictment against sitting President Slobodan Milosevic; see Princeton University (n 96) 48–52. Since Milosevic died before the closing of the trial, this precedent is arguably inconclusive. For discussion of this precedent see (n 105) below. For the proceedings against Charles Taylor see below with the discussion of the international courts theory.

[104] BBC News, 'Kenyatta Appears at ICC in Hague for Landmark Hearing' (8 October 2014), available at http://www.bbc.com/news/world-africa-29530638 (accessed 12 May 2016).

precedents of an international criminal court explicitly overruling the immunity *ratione personae* of an incumbent high-ranking State official.[105]

The provisions as well as the precedents of the international criminal courts were essentially focused on establishing that officials bore criminal responsibility for crimes that were within these tribunals' jurisdiction, but not necessarily on securing the criminal jurisdiction of the tribunals over officials enjoying immunity *ratione personae*.[106]

To reiterate, the principle that an official position cannot relieve the accused of their criminal responsibility for international crimes is contained in art 27(1), not in art 27(2) of the Rome Statute. Article 27(1) ensures that criminal responsibility can be found without any distinction based on official capacity, and art 27(2) ensures that the ICC has jurisdiction over officials normally entitled to procedural immunity from criminal jurisdiction.[107] Indeed, the ICJ noted 'immunity from criminal jurisdiction and individual responsibility are quite separate concepts'.[108] Indeed, the difference between these two separate concepts is encapsulated in art 27 of the Rome Statute.[109]

---

[105] Similarly, the ICTR did not address the immunity of Jean Kambanda, former Prime Minister of Rwanda from April 1994 to July 1994, sentenced to life imprisonment for crimes against humanity and genocide, as when indicted in 1997 he had not been Prime Minister for three years; *Prosecutor v Kambanda* (Judgment and Sentence) ICTR-97-23-S (4 September 1998); *Prosecutor v Kambanda* (Judgment) ICTR-97-23-I (19 October 2000). Regarding the ICTY and President Milosevic, see Gaeta (n 1) 315–22; see also Ssenyonjo (n 94) 407–408; *Prosecutor v Milosevic* (Decision on Preliminary Motions) IT-02-52 (8 November 2001) paras 26–34. See also Claus Kress, 'The International Criminal Court and Immunities under International Law for States not Party to the Court's Statute' in Morten Bergsmo and Yan Ling (eds), *State Sovereignty and International Criminal Law* (FICHL publication series no. 15 (2012). Torkel Opsahl Academic EPublisher 2012) 253; S. Williams and L. Sherif, 'The Arrest Warrant for President al-Bashir: Immunities of Incumbent Heads of State and the International Criminal Court' (2009) 14(1) *Journal of Conflict and Security Law* 71, 73. Also sharing this view with an extensive discussion of these issues, see e.g. Alexandre Galand, 'Conflicts of Norms in Situations Referred to the International Criminal Court by the United Nations Security Council' (PhD Thesis, European University Institute 2015) 149–55. For the historical precedents see Geoffrey Robertson, 'Ending Impunity: How International Criminal Law Can Put Tyrants on Trial' (2005) 38(3) *Cornell International Law Journal* 649, 655.

[106] Kress (n 105) 252.

[107] Bruce Broomhall, *International Justice and the International Criminal Court: Between Sovereignty and the Rule of Law* (Oxford University Press 2004) 138.

[108] *Arrest Warrant Case* (Judgment) [2002] ICJ Rep 3, para 60.

[109] The Statutes of the ICTY, ICTR and SCSL contain no similar provision on the issue of head of state immunity; see William Schabas, *The UN International Criminal Tribunals: The Former Yugoslavia, Rwanda, and Sierra Leone* (Cambridge University Press 2006) 328.

5.1.5.3 International courts theory

The so-called 'international courts theory' posits that immunities generally, including personal immunities, are simply not available in international courts.[110] In *Taylor*, the Special Court for Sierra Leone (SCSL) held in 2004 that the SCSL was an 'international court' and as such not barred from prosecuting serving heads of state because, according to the SCSL, personal immunities only apply in the relations between states.[111] On this point, the SCSL relied primarily on a passage in the ICJ's *Arrest Warrant Case* in which the court noted that 'an incumbent or former Minister for Foreign Affairs may be subject to criminal proceedings before *certain international criminal courts*, where they have jurisdiction'.[112] From it, the SCSL deduced that personal immunities are generally inapplicable before any 'international' tribunal.[113]

This conclusion was rightly questioned by many on several grounds.[114] First, it is rather unconvincing to sidestep immunity by simply asserting that a tribunal is not a state. Domestic courts have consistently upheld personal immunities, regardless of the nature of the charges, and it is generally uncontested that personal immunities exist before foreign states.[115] In light of the maxim *nemo dat quod non habet* it appears implausible that

---

[110] Paola Gaeta, 'Official Capacities and Immunities' in Cassese (n 13) 991. Contra, Cryer and others (n 37) 561.

[111] *Prosecutor v Charles Taylor* (Decision on Immunity from Jurisdiction) No SCSL-03-01-I (31 May 2004) paras 51–53.

[112] Cited in *Prosecutor v Charles Taylor* (Decision on Immunity from Jurisdiction) No SCSL-03-01-I (31 May 2004) para 50. Emphasis in original.

[113] Paola Gaeta and Patryk Labuda argue that the customary international rules on personal immunities do not apply before international criminal tribunals, but that art 98(1) of the Rome Statute restricts the authority of the ICC in this respect; see Paola Gaeta and Patryk I. Labuda, 'Trying Sitting Heads of State: The African Union versus the ICC in the Al-Bashir and Kenyatta Cases' in Charles Jalloh and Ilias Bantekas (eds), *The International Criminal Court and Africa* (Oxford University Press 2017) 149.

[114] See e.g. Cryer and others (n 37) 562–63; Zsuzsanna Deen-Racsmany, 'Prosecutor v. Taylor: The Status of the Special Court for Sierra Leone and its Implications for Immunity' (2005) 18 *Leiden Journal of International Law* 299; Micaela Frulli, 'The Question of Charles Taylor's Immunity' (2004) 2 *Journal of International Criminal Justice* 1118; David S. Koller, 'Immunities of Foreign Ministers: Paragraph 61 of the Yerodia Judgment as it Pertains to the Security Council and the International Criminal Court' (2004) 20 *American University International Law Review* 7; Hugh King, 'Immunities and Bilateral Immunity Agreements: Issues Arising from Articles 27 and 98 of the Rome Statute' (2006) 4 *New Zealand Journal of Public International Law* 269.

[115] See e.g. *The Minister of Justice and Constitutional Development v The Southern African Litigation Centre* (Judgment of the South African Supreme Court) [2016] (867/15) ZASCA 17 (15 March 2016) paras 84–85; *Gaddafi*, Court of Cassation, Criminal Chamber (13 March 2001) ILR 125, 508, 509; Castro (1999) 32 ILM 596; see

> [i]f neither the United Kingdom nor Canada has the power to ignore the personal immunity of a third State without consent, then the two together cannot create an international court and bestow upon it a power that they do not possess. The problem remains whether it is two States, or twenty, or sixty: they cannot bestow a power that they do not possess.[116]

Indeed, since the ICC as an international organization operates based on the conferral of powers from its states parties, the personal immunities of non-party states apply also in relation to the ICC itself, as art 98 of the Rome Statute makes clear.[117] In light of the above, the better reading of the passage in the ICJ *Arrest Warrant Case* that referred to the lack of personal immunities before 'certain international courts'[118] points to the fact that the ICJ merely observed *obiter dicta* that international courts exist with the power to supersede personal immunities.[119] Also, the *jus cogens* nature of the crimes allegedly committed

---

also the UK decision regarding President Mugabe in January 2004; see Colin Warbrick, 'Immunity and International Crimes in English Law' (2004) 53 *International and Comparative Law Quarterly* 769; see also ILC, 'Preliminary Report on Immunity of State Officials from Foreign Criminal Jurisdiction' (5 May–6 June 2008 and 7 July–8 August 2008) UN Doc A/CN.4/601, para 34. See also Dapo Akande and Sangeeta Shah, 'Immunities of State Officials, International Crimes, and Foreign Domestic Courts' (2010) 21(4) *European Journal of International Law* 815, 819–820. The ILC reports in this regard: 'With respect to the absolute or restricted nature of immunity *ratione personae*, two opposing positions have been expressed to date. For some, there are no exceptions to this type of immunity, which is therefore opposable to any act carried out by the persons enjoying immunity. For others, on the contrary, certain acts performed by a Head of State, Head of Government, Minister for Foreign Affairs or, where appropriate, any other person who might potentially enjoy immunity would not be covered if the act was contrary to *jus cogens* norms or could be characterized as an international crime.' ILC, 'Preliminary report on the immunity of State officials from foreign criminal jurisdiction' (31 May 2012) UN Doc A/CN.4/654, para 64. See also Zappala (n 95).

116 Cryer and others (n 37) 563. Similarly, Akande (n 94) 417–18. See also the dissenting opinion of Judge Shahabuddeen in Krstic stating '[i]n my view . . . there is no substance in the suggested automaticity of disappearance of the immunity just because of the establishment of international criminal courts . . . International criminal courts are established by States acting together, whether directly or indirectly as in the case of the Tribunal [ICTY], which was established by the Security Council on behalf of States members of the United Nations. There is no basis for suggesting that by merely acting together to establish such a court States signify an intention to waive their individual functional immunities. A presumption of continuance of their immunities as these exist under international law is only offset where some element in the decision to establish such a court shows that they agreed otherwise.' *Prosecutor v Krstic* (Decision on Application for Subpoenas) IT-98-33-A (1 July 2003) paras 11–12.

117 Akande (n 94), 421.

118 *Arrest Warrant Case* (Judgment) [2002] ICJ Rep 3, para 61.

119 Cryer and others (n 37) 563.

does not remove personal immunities.[120] The ICJ seems to have held exactly that in the *Arrest Warrant Case*.[121]

Indeed, the preparatory work of art 27(2) suggests that states generally thought it necessary to include such a provision.[122] This is further supported by the fact that during the negotiations of the RA between the ICC and the UN, Belgium sought to insert a provision regarding the immunity of United Nations officials, stating '[p]aragraph 1 of this article [on immunity] shall be without prejudice to the relevant norms of international law, particularly . . . article 27 of the Statute, in respect of crimes that come under the jurisdiction of the Court'.[123] This proposal was rejected and in art 19 of the RA the UN agrees to waive its immunities to which UN officials are entitled. William Schabas rightly pointed out that 'if article 27(2) removed such immunity, there would be no need for any such provision, and this was precisely the point that Belgium unsuccessfully tried to confirm'.[124]

---

[120] Akande (n 94) 414. See for this conclusion *Minister of Justice and Constitutional Development and Others v Southern African Litigation Centre and Others* (867/15) [2016] ZASCA 17 (15 March 2016) para 84. See also Akande and Shah (n 115). See also Article 2 of the Resolution of the Institute de droit international, 'Immunities from Jurisdiction and Execution of Heads of State and of Government in International Law' (Vancouver, 24 August 2001).

[121] *Arrest Warrant Case* (Judgment) [2002] ICJ Rep 3, para 58 ('[The Court] has been unable to deduce from . . . practice that there exists under customary international law any form of exception to the rule according immunity from criminal jurisdiction and inviolability to incumbent Ministers for Foreign Affairs, where they are suspected of having committed war crimes or crimes against humanity.'). This has been subsequently confirmed by the ICJ in *Djibouti v France* (Judgment) [2008] ICJ Rep 177, para 170. See also Erika de Wet, 'The Implications of President Al-Bashir's Visit to South Africa for International and Domestic Law' (2015) 13(5) *Journal of International Criminal Justice* 1049, 1052. For domestic courts adopting the same view, see the case law cited in *Prosecutor v Omar Hassan Ahmad Al-Bashir* (Minority Opinion of Judge Marc Perrin de Brichambaut) No ICC-02/05-01/09 (6 July 2017) para 86 fn 119. But see for an international crimes exception, OLG (Köln) (Beschluss) 2 Zs 1330/99, *German citizen of Iranian origin v Department of Public Prosecution Bonn and Chief Public Prosecutor of Cologne (joining)*, Proceeding to force criminal prosecution, 2 Zs 1330/99, (16 May 2000) Germany; North Rhine-Westphalia; Cologne; Higher Regional Court [OLG].

[122] While some states thought it initially unnecessary to include art 27(2), this provision was adopted without debate at the Rome Conference; see UN Doc A/CONF.183/C.1/SR.2, paras 75–83; UN Doc A/CONF.183/C.1/SR.8, para 75; Report of the Working Group on General Principles of Criminal Law, UN Doc A/CONF.183/C.1/WGGP/L.4.

[123] See Proposal submitted by Belgium concerning document PCNICC/2000/WGICC-UN/L.1, PCNICC/2000/WGICC-UN/DP.18.

[124] Schabas (n 12) 451.

5.1.5.4 Personal immunities and non-party states

Immunity *ratione personae* becomes irrelevant if the state of the official is deemed to have waived it.[125] In *Prosecutor v Uhuru Muigai Kenyatta*, the first case where an incumbent head of state appeared before an international criminal court, the ICC never addressed the immunity of the defendant[126] because Kenya is a state party; by ratifying the Rome Statute, including art 27(2), Kenya, of which Kenyatta is the head of state, has waived the right it was entitled to under international law.[127]

Personal immunities of heads of state and other high-ranking officials are rights belonging to the state of the official.[128] Accordingly, the legal basis for the court to exercise jurisdiction over a situation would provide an answer as to whether a particular state has waived the immunity of its officials in respect of the proceedings in question.

This has important consequences for the application of immunities in case of SC referrals involving non-party states. The legal basis for the jurisdiction of the ICC over these state officials[129] is the SC resolution referring the situation to the ICC. It follows that as a treaty norm, the removal of personal immunity included in the Rome Statute is not as such applicable to the state that is not party to that treaty. Nothing in the Rome Statute can remove the immunity belonging to non-party states since that treaty cannot create obligations or

---

[125] *Arrest Warrant Case* (Judgment) [2002] ICJ Rep 3, para 61.

[126] *Prosecutor v Francis Kirimi Muthaura and Uhuru Muigai Kenyatta* (Decision on the Confirmation of Charges Pursuant to Article 61(7(a) and (b) of the Rome Statute) ICC-01/09-02/11-382-Red ICC (23 January 2012); *Prosecutor v Uhuru Muigai Kenyatta* (Decision on Defence request for excusal from attendance at, or for adjournment of, the status conference scheduled for 8 October 2014) ICC-01/09-02/11 (30 September 2014).

[127] See also Article 7(1) of the Resolution of the Institute de droit international, 'Immunities from Jurisdiction and Execution of Heads of State and of Government in International Law' (Vancouver, 24 August 2001) which states: 'The Head of State may no longer benefit from the inviolability, immunity from jurisdiction or immunity from measures of execution conferred by international law, where the benefit thereof is waived by his or her State. Such waiver may be explicit or implied, provided it is certain'.

[128] Dapo Akande, 'The Legal Nature of Security Council Referrals to the ICC and its Impact on Al-Bashir's Immunities' (2009) 7(2) *Journal of International Criminal Justice* 333, 339.

[129] According to the work of the ILC, personal immunity is restricted to heads of state, heads of government and foreign ministers. See art 3 of the text of draft articles 1, 3 and 4 provisionally adopted by the Drafting Committee at the sixty-fifth session of the International Law Commission, Immunity of State officials from foreign criminal jurisdiction (4 June 2013) UN Doc A/CN.4/L.814; Second report on the immunity of State officials from foreign criminal jurisdiction (Special Rapporteur Concepción Escobar Hernández) (4 April 2013) UN Doc A/CN.4/611, paras 56–68.

modify rights for third states.[130] For example, in the case of the SC referral concerning Darfur, Sudan has not become a party to the Rome Statute. As a result, as pointed out by Paola Gaeta, 'one fails to see how the fact that the jurisdiction of the ICC over the crimes in Darfur was triggered by the SC can make a treaty provision, namely art 27, applicable to Sudan, if this state has not accepted the regulation contained therein'.[131]

However, the SC referral itself could provide for the removal of personal immunities under its Chapter VII powers. The question then arises of whether the SC referral in accordance with the Statute must be interpreted as removing the immunity *ratione personae* implicitly, when the referral is silent on the issue. This is now the opinion of the ICC.[132]

One could raise several objections against this view. Without an explicit removal of personal immunity for state officials, the SC referral should be interpreted as not deviating from the customary international law rules on personal immunities.[133] As a conferral of powers from the SC to the ICC, a referral should be interpreted narrowly.[134] Therefore, the obligation expressly provided in the SC referrals of Darfur and Libya to 'cooperate fully' with the ICC might not be enough to imply a removal of personal immunities of the states concerned.[135]

---

[130] Akande (n 128), 339; Ssenyonjo (n 94) 405; de Wet (n 121) 1056. See also *Prosecutor v Omar Hassan Ahmad Al-Bashir* (Decision on the Cooperation of the Democratic Republic of the Congo regarding Omar Al-Bashir's Arrest and Surrender to the Court) ICC-02/05-01/09-195 (9 April 2014) para 26.

[131] Gaeta (n 1) 324. In a similar vein also William Schabas, 'The International Criminal Court and Non-Party States' (2010) 28 *Windsor Yearbook of Access to Justice* 1, 6–7.

[132] See for a very convincing argument to this effect Akande (n 128) Similarly de Wet (n 121).

[133] See however Erika de Wet arguing that 'the submission that the Security Council must stipulate all deviations from international law explicitly in the text of the resolution is not in accordance with the established and accepted practice of the Security Council, which supports the opposite conclusion. Instead of explaining the extent to which states must deviate from international law under a Security Council resolution, resolutions under Chapter VII indicate what states may not do when deviating from international law in accordance with the resolution'; de Wet (n 121) 1061.

[134] Similar to the principle in agency law that the scope of the agency should be interpreted conservatively in the absence of a clear mandate (*potestas stricte interpretatur*), see Aaron X. Fellmeth and Maurice Horwitz (eds) *Guide to Latin in International Law* (Oxford University Press 2009).

[135] Cryer and others (n 37) 560; Göran Sluiter, 'Obtaining Cooperation from Sudan – Where is the Law?' (2008) 6 *Journal of International Criminal Justice* 871, 877–78; Gaeta (n 1) 330. But see the opinion of the South African Supreme Court rejecting immunity *ratione personae* of Sudanese President Al-Bashir: The Supreme Court of Appeal of South Africa (Judgment of 15 March 2016) Case No 867/15. For a brief

Another argument could be raised in this respect. The SC obliged Sudan to 'cooperate fully with and provide any necessary assistance to the Court and the Prosecutor pursuant to this resolution'. The question is whether this includes the application of art 27(2) but not art 98(1) of the Statute. As Roger O'Keefe points out, art 98(1) remains applicable in this situation, and it would

> doubtless be open to the Security Council, acting under chapter VII of the UN Charter, to decide that the state party in question must surrender the person to the Court notwithstanding article 98(1) and the immunity and inviolability owed by the state party to the third state in respect of the person. But the Security Council has not done this in this case.[136]

In fact, a presumption exists that the SC does not intend to deviate from international law and equally does not intend to force members to violate international law when carrying out SC resolutions.[137] Furthermore, the interpretation that the SC does not intend to remove personal immunities is also warranted by the fact that the issue of immunity of state officials from criminal jurisdiction concerns not only state officials' smooth functioning but also the very core function of the SC, namely the peaceful relations between states and stable international relations (see art 1 UN Charter).[138] In fact, the ICJ described the inviolability of diplomatic envoys, which is to be seen as analogous to the present issue, as the most fundamental prerequisite for the conduct of relations between states in the *Case concerning United States Diplomatic*

---

discussion see http://www.ejiltalk.org/the-bashir-case-has-the-south-african-supreme-court-abolished-immunity-for-all-heads-of-states/ and http://jurist.org/hotline/2015/07/netsanet-sacco-immunity-ICC.php (accessed 1 June 2018). It must be noted however that this judgement is primarily based on the domestic law in force in South Africa that sought to implement its obligations under the Rome Statute, and while the Court also discusses its legal obligations under international law, the conclusion that the Court reached must be rejected for the reasons provided in this chapter. For a discussion of the South African North Gauteng High Court decision that was upheld by the South African Supreme Court, see de Wet (n 121); Manuel J. Ventura, 'Escape from Johannesburg?' (2016) 13(5) *Journal of International Criminal Justice* 995.

[136] Roger O'Keefe, *International Criminal Law* (Oxford University Press 2015) 573.

[137] Anne Peters, 'Article 25' in Simma (n 6) para 28.

[138] Huikang Huang, 'On Immunity of State Officials from Foreign Criminal Jurisdiction' (2014) 13 *Chinese Journal of International Law* 1, 1; Akande (n 94) 410; de Wet (n 121) 1052. See however for the argument that the special nature of international criminal tribunals provides an explanation why the traditional rules of immunities in inter-state relations should not apply: Rémy Prouvèze, 'Immunities' in William Schabas and Nadia Bernaz (eds), *Routledge Handbook of International Criminal Law* (Routledge handbooks, Routledge 2011) 361.

and Consular Staff in Tehran.[139] Personal immunities do not shield individuals from criminal responsibility but merely provide for a procedural bar that is removed once the official leaves office, thus not frustrating the objective of the ICC to end impunity.

Furthermore, such interpretation is also supported by the presumption provided in art 8(2) of the 2001 Resolution of the Institute de droit international : '[s]i la dérogation n'est pas explicite, il convient de présumer qu'il n'est pas dérogé à l'inviolabilité et aux immunités visées au paragraphe précédent; l'existence et l'étendue de cette dérogation doivent être établies sans ambiguïté par toutes voies de droit.'[140] The requirement to expressly remove personal immunities is also confirmed *mutatis mutandis* by the ILC, which stated that 'when applied to a serving Head of State . . . a waiver of immunity should be explicitly stated'.[141] In light of these reasons, it is questionable whether personal immunities can be deemed to be removed through the SC referral without an express provision to that effect.[142]

Nevertheless, the obligation for the situation state (Sudan, for example) to 'cooperate fully with and provide any necessary assistance to the Court and the Prosecutor' may include the obligation to surrender individuals, regardless of their status, if so requested by the ICC, or 'to do anything that enables the surrender by another State if the latter is requested by the Court'.[143] That obli-

---

139 *Case Concerning United States Diplomatic and Consular Staff in Tehran (US v Iran)* [1980] ICJ Rep 3, para 91.

140 'In the absence of an express derogation, there is a presumption that no derogation has been made to the inviolability and immunities referred to in the preceding paragraph; the existence and extent of such a derogation shall be unambiguously established by any legal means' (the French text is authoritative, the English text is a translation by the Institute), Institute de droit international, 'Les immunités de juridiction et d'exécution du chef d'État et de gouvernement en droit international' (Vancouver, 26 August 2001).

141 See ILC, 'Third Report on immunity of State Officials from Foreign Criminal Jurisdiction', by Roman Anatolevich Kolodkin, Special Rapporteur, A/CN.4/646, para 55, to which also Judge Brichambaut refers in his minority opinion.

142 Sharing this view, Gaeta (n 1) 323. Contra this view see *Prosecutor v Omar Hassan Ahmad Al-Bashir* (Decision on the Cooperation of the Democratic Republic of the Congo regarding Omar Al-Bashir's Arrest and Surrender to the Court) ICC-02/05-01/09-195 (9 April 2014) para 29; Robert Uerpmann-Wittzack, 'Immunität vor internationalen Strafgerichten' (2006) 44 *Archiv des Völkerrechts* 33, 42; Akande (n 128) 342; Nerina Boschiero, 'The ICC Judicial Finding on Non-cooperation Against the DRC and No Immunity for Al-Bashir Based on UNSC Resolution 1593' (2015) 13(3) *Journal of International Criminal Justice* 625.

143 *Prosecutor v Omar Al-Bashir*, Request by Max du Plessis, Sarah Nouwen and Elizabeth Wilmshurst for leave to submit observations on the legal questions presented in 'The Hashemite Kingdom of Jordan's appeal against the 'Decision under article 87(7) of the Rome Statute on the non-compliance by Jordan with the request by the

gation may require the state to surrender the individual or to waive immunities to give effect to such request. However, the failure of the state to do so is a violation of an obligation imposed by the SC and does not mean that personal immunities have been removed.[144]

5.1.5.5 Personal immunities and national authorities

It is a separate issue whether personal immunities are applicable on the national level to national authorities acting to support the ICC (the ICC has not made such a distinction).[145] Even if one is following the international court theory (i.e. adopting the view that personal immunities are simply not available before the ICC) the problem of personal immunities before national authorities remains. This is because the ICC does not possess independent powers of arrest and therefore relies on states to arrest and surrender persons wanted by the ICC.[146] As Dapo Akande notes with respect to the SC referral in Sudan:

> In order for the ICC to exercise jurisdiction in practice, it will need to obtain custody of [Sudanese President] Al-Bashir. Unless Al-Bashir chooses to surrender himself voluntarily (which is most unlikely), the Court needs a state to arrest him and turn him over to the Court. At that stage, the question will arise whether Al-Bashir is immune from arrest by national authorities acting to support the Court. Where the request is to arrest a person who is, as is the case here, ordinarily entitled to immunity from the exercise of foreign criminal jurisdiction (including immunity from arrest), the question is how to reconcile the tension between the obligation of states to accord immunity and the statement that immunity shall not bar the Court from exercising jurisdiction.[147]

This tension is resolved by art 98 of the Rome Statute.[148] Article 98(1) provides:

> The Court may not proceed with a request for surrender or assistance which would require the requested State to act inconsistently with its obligations under international law with respect to the State or diplomatic immunity of a person or property of a third State, unless the Court can first obtain the cooperation of that third State for the waiver of the immunity.

Court for the arrest and surrender o[f] Omar Al-Bashir' of 12 March 2018 (ICC-02/05-01/09-326) in accordance with the Order of the Appeals Chamber dated 29 March 2018 (ICC-02/05-01/09 OA2) (27 April 2018) para 7.

[144] Similarly ibid.

[145] Akande (n 128) 336.

[146] Akande (n 94) 420.

[147] Akande (n 128) 336.

[148] See also *Prosecutor v Omar Hassan Ahmad Al-Bashir* (Decision on the Cooperation of the Democratic Republic of the Congo regarding Omar Al-Bashir's Arrest and Surrender to the Court) ICC-02/05-01/09-195 (9 April 2014) para 27.

This provision and its relationship with art 27 of the Statute is important for several reasons. First, art 27 removes immunities for actions taken by national authorities when acting in response to a request by the ICC.[149] This is because reading art 27 as applying only to actions by the ICC would render parts of that provision practically meaningless.[150] As noted above, the ICC has no independent powers of arrest and therefore relies on national authorities. An interpretation that leaves immunities intact with respect to actions by national authorities is difficult to reconcile with the proclamation that immunities shall not bar the exercise of jurisdiction by the ICC. The ICC would only be in a position to apply art 27 in cases where a person entitled to immunity surrendered voluntarily, in which case the person is unlikely to claim immunity. In other situations, for example where such persons are surrendered by their state or (in case of heads of states) through voluntarily surrendering their immunity, art 27 would be irrelevant. As Dapo Akande notes, '[t]his would confine Article 27 to the rare case. The effect of the argument would be to make an important provision directed at combating impunity inoperable for most practical purposes'.[151]

Therefore, such an interpretation cannot be accepted in light of the principle of effectiveness in treaty interpretation that requires all applicable provisions of a treaty to be read in a way which gives meaning to all of them harmoniously and the interpreter is thus 'not free to adopt a reading that would result in reducing whole clauses or paragraphs of a treaty to redundancy or inutility'.[152] Furthermore, the text of art 27(2) refers not only to international law immunities but also national law immunities that shall not bar the exercise of the ICC's jurisdiction. Only national authorities apply national law and not the ICC. Therefore, to give effect to this part of the provision it must be read as being directed at national authorities who would otherwise be bound by national law rules on immunities. Lastly, the reading that art 27 applies also to immunities with respect to national authorities is further evidenced by the implementation legislation of states parties to the ICC removing immunities also at the national

---

149 Akande (n 94) 419–26; Akande (n 128) 338.

150 Akande (n 128) 338.

151 Ibid.

152 *United States v Standards for Reformulated and Conventional Gasoline* (Appellate Body Report, 29 April 1996) WTO Doc.WT/DS2/AB/R, 23. See also *Corfu Channel Case* [1949] ICJ Rep 4, 24; *Territorial Dispute Case (Libyan Arab Jamahiriya v Chad)* [1994] ICJ Rep 6, 23; UNAT Judgment No 4 [1951] Judgments of the United Nations Administrative Tribunal Nos 1.70, 8. Michael Wood, 'The Interpretation of Security Council Resolutions' (1998) 2 *Max Planck Yearbook of United Nations Law* 73, 86; sharing this view, Akande (n 128), 338; Akande (n 94) 419–26.

level.[153] As a result, art 27 of the Rome Statute also applies to immunities with respect to national authorities.

This means that with respect to actions to support the ICC, art 27 constitutes also a waiver of national law immunities by states parties to the ICC. For states parties, this means that they are obliged to arrest and surrender their officials in relation to each other regardless of whether they would otherwise be entitled to national law immunities.[154]

However, as noted above, art 27 cannot remove immunities owed to non-party states. With respect to non-party states, art 98 expressly allows state parties to the ICC to give effect to the immunity obligations they owe to those non-party states.[155] Indeed, as Dapo Akande notes, 'Article 98 directs the Court not to take action that would result in the violation by states of their international obligations to accord immunity to foreign officials'.[156]

This clearly establishes that with respect to officials from non-party states, personal immunities remain untouched.[157] That is the clear function of art 98,[158] as this has also been recognized by the Pre-Trial Chamber II.[159] As a result, the

---

[153] See particularly the reasoning of the South African Supreme Court to this effect regarding the immunity of Sudanese President Al-Bashir: *The Minister of Justice and Constitutional Development v The Southern African Litigation Centre* (Judgment of the South African Supreme Court) [2016] (867/15) ZASCA 17 (15 March 2016) paras 96–102; For the implementation legislation see e.g. Canada: s 6.1 Extradition Act (1999, as amended by Crimes Against Humanity and War Crimes Act 2000); New Zealand: ss 31(1), 66 and 120 International Crimes and International Criminal Court Act (2000); United Kingdom: s 23, International Criminal Court Act (2001); Switzerland: art 6, Federal Law on Cooperation with the International Criminal Court (2001); Malta: art 26s Extradition Act (amended by c 453 International Criminal Court Act 2002); South Africa: s 10(9) Implementation of the Rome Statute of the International Criminal Court Act (2002); Croatia: art 6(3) Law on the Application of the Statute of the International Criminal Court (2003); Ireland: s 61 International Criminal Court Act (2006); Estonia: art 489 Code of Criminal Procedure (2003). See also s 25 of the Commonwealth's Model Law to Implement the Rome Statute of the International Criminal Court. See also Akande (n 128) 338.

[154] Akande (n 94) 420.

[155] Akande (n 128) 339.

[156] Akande (n 94) 420.

[157] See however the Appeals Chamber of the Special Court for Sierra Leone holding in regard to the prosecution of sitting Head of State Charles Taylor that 'the principle seems now established that the sovereign equality of states does not prevent a Head of State from being prosecuted before an international criminal tribunal or court'. *Prosecutor v Charles Taylor* (Decision on Immunity from Jurisdiction) No SCSL-03-01-I (31 May 2004) para 52. This seems to oversimplify the matter since stated in general terms this is not correct; see also Akande (n 94) 416–17.

[158] de Wet (n 121) 1056.

[159] *Prosecutor v Omar Hassan Ahmad Al-Bashir* (Decision on the Cooperation of the Democratic Republic of the Congo regarding Omar Al-Bashir's Arrest and

removal of immunity *ratione personae* cannot be presumed, for the reasons given above, unless the SC explicitly waives the immunity.[160]

5.1.5.6 The ICC's approach towards personal immunities

The practice of the ICC rejects any claim to personal immunities,[161] but has offered very different arguments for the very same conclusion that have changed over time. For example, in its decision on the arrest warrant against President of Sudan, Omar Al-Bashir, the Chamber put forward the following arguments for this conclusion. First, it referred to the goal of the Statute to put an end to impunity for the perpetrators of the most serious crimes of concern to the international community as a whole;[162] second, it referred to art 27;[163] third, it referred to consistent case law of the Chamber that according to art 21 of the Statute, the other sources of law

> provided for in paragraphs (l)(b) and (l)(c) of article 21 of the Statute, can only be resorted to when the following two conditions are met: (i) there is a lacuna in the written law contained in the Statute, the Elements of Crimes and the Rules; and (ii) such lacuna cannot be filled by the application of the criteria of interpretation provided in articles 31 and 32 of the Vienna Convention on the Law of the Treaties and article 21(3) of the Statute.[164]

And finally, that by virtue of art 13(b) the SC has accepted that the investigation takes place in accordance with the statutory framework provided for in the

---

Surrender to the Court) ICC-02/05-01/09-195 (9 April 2014) para 26. With this decision, the Pre-Trial Chamber distanced itself (implicitly) from previous decisions of Pre-Trial Chamber I, in which the Chamber argued that a special customary international law exception exists for personal immunities without acknowledging art 98 of the Statute; see *Prosecutor v Omar Hassan Ahmad Al-Bashir* (Decision Pursuant to Art. 87(7) of the Rome Statute on the Failure by the Republic of Malawi to Comply with the Cooperation Requests Issued by the Court with Respect to the Arrest and Surrender of Omar Hassan Ahmad Al-Bashir) ICC-02/05-01/09-139 (12 December 2011). See on this further de Wet (n 121), 1056.

[160] Contra *Prosecutor v Omar Hassan Ahmad Al-Bashir* (Decision on the Cooperation of the Democratic Republic of the Congo regarding Omar Al-Bashir's Arrest and Surrender to the Court) ICC-02/05-01/09-195 (9 April 2014) para 29; see also Akande (n 128), who similarly argues that the SC referral must be interpreted as implicitly removing the personal immunity; Cryer and others (n 37) 559.

[161] *Prosecutor v Omar Hassan Ahmad Al-Bashir* (Decision on the Prosecution's Application for a Warrant of Arrest against Omar Hassan Ahmad Al-Bashir) ICC-02/05-01/09-3 (4 March 2009) paras 40–45.

[162] Ibid. para 42.

[163] Ibid. para 43.

[164] Ibid. para 44.

Statute, the Elements of Crimes and the Rules as a whole.[165] Then, it argued in its *Malawi*[166] and *Chad*[167] decisions, dealing with the failure of these states to enforce an ICC arrest warrant against the President of Sudan, Al-Bashir, a non-party state to the ICC, that

> customary international law creates an exception to Head of State immunity when international courts seek a Head of State's arrest for the commission of international crimes. There is no conflict between Malawi's obligations towards the Court and its obligations under customary international law; therefore, article 98(1) of the Statute does not apply.

Evidence for this conclusion was found in the fact that 120 states ratifying the Statute have thereby renounced their immunities. However, this is certainly no proof that all other states, in this case Sudan, have also lost their immunities.[168] Therefore, the better explanation is that under existing international law, 'it is not the international nature of the court as such but the waiver by the parties . . . that accounts for the irrelevance of immunities before it'.[169] Any other conclusion would render art 98 of the Statute meaningless.

The ICC Decision on the Failure by Malawi to Arrest and Surrender Al-Bashir[170] was directly criticized by Paola Gaeta, who raised several problems with the arguments presented by the ICC. First, the reference to the purpose of the ICC to put an end to impunity cannot be construed as the legal basis for the non-application of the immunity of a Head of State.[171] As to the second and third argument, it must be noted that art 27(2) (removing personal immunities) only applies with respect to persons who are nationals of states parties to the Statute. This is also the reasoning adopted by the states that failed

---

165 Ibid. para 45.

166 *Prosecutor v Omar Hassan Ahmad Al-Bashir* (Decision Pursuant to Article 87(7) of the Rome Statute on the Failure by the Republic of Malawi to Comply with the Cooperation Requests Issued by the Court with Respect to the Arrest and Surrender of Omar Hassan Ahmad Al-Bashir) ICC-02/05-01/09-139 (12 December 2011).

167 *Prosecutor v Omar Hassan Ahmad Al-Bashir* (Decision on the Non-compliance of the Republic of Chad with the Cooperation Requests Issued by the Court Regarding the Arrest and Surrender of Omar Hassan Ahmad Al-Bashir) ICC-02/05-01/09-151 (26 March 2013).

168 Cryer and others (n 37) 564; Dire Tladi, 'The ICC Decisions on Chad and Malawi: On Cooperation, Immunities, and Article 98' (2013) 11(1) *Journal of International Criminal Justice* 199. See also Akande (n 94) 417.

169 Deen-Racsmany (n 114) 318; sharing this view see also Akande (n 94) 417; Cryer and others (n 37) 564; King (n 114); Schabas (n 12) 450.

170 *Prosecutor v Omar Hassan Ahmad Al-Bashir* (Decision on the Failure by Malawi to Arrest and Surrender Al-Bashir) ICC-02/05-01/09 (12 December 2011) paras 13–43.

171 Gaeta (n 1) 323.

to arrest and surrender Al-Bashir and the African Union (AU) in its decisions not to cooperate with the ICC despite the ICC's decisions.[172] Personal immunities are inapplicable only if one demonstrates that the content of art 27(2) Rome Statute corresponds to a rule of customary international law, which the Chamber did not establish.[173] In fact, the ICJ and other courts have consistently held that the personal immunity of heads of state is absolute in nature.[174] The fourth argument (i.e. the implicit removal of immunities by the SC referral) pertains to the discussion above and has to be similarly rejected, because the SC referral cannot be interpreted in this way.[175]

In an apparent reaction to the criticism of the reasons given by the Pre-Trial Chamber, the Pre-Trial Chamber II issued its decision regarding the Democratic Republic of Congo's failure to arrest President Al-Bashir of Sudan based on different grounds. The Chamber correctly noted that

---

[172] See e.g. *Prosecutor v Omar Hassan Ahmad Al-Bashir* (Decision Pursuant to Article 87(7) of the Rome Statute on the Failure by the Republic of Malawi to Comply with the Cooperation Requests Issued by the Court with Respect to the Arrest and Surrender of Omar Hassan Ahmad Al-Bashir) ICC-02/05-01/09-139 (12 December 2011) para 8; *Prosecutor v Omar Hassan Ahmad Al-Bashir* (Decision on the Cooperation of the Democratic Republic of the Congo regarding Omar Al-Bashir's Arrest and Surrender to the Court) ICC-02/05-01/09-195 (9 April 2014) paras 12–14. See also the various resolutions of the AU not to cooperate with the ICC in arresting Al-Bashir, which also relies on this argument, e.g. AU, Assembly, 'Decision on the Meeting of African States Parties to the Rome Statute of the International Criminal Tribunal (ICC) Doc.Assembly/AU/13(XIII)', 3 July 2009, Assembly/AU/Dec.245(XIII) Rev.1, para 10; AU, Assembly, 'Decision on the Progress Report of the Commission on the Implementation of Decision Assembly/AU/Dec.270(XIV) on the Second Ministerial Meeting on the Rome Statute of the International Criminal Court (ICC) Doc. Assembly/AU/10(XV)', 27 July 2010, Assembly/AU/Dec.296(XV), paras 5–6; AU, Assembly, 'Decision on the Implementation of the Decisions on the International Criminal Court (ICC) Doc. EX.CL/639(XVIII)', 30–31 January 2011, Assembly/AU/Dec.334(XVI), para 5; AU, Assembly, 'Decision on the Implementation of the Assembly Decisions on the International Criminal Court Doc.EX.CL/670(XIX)', 30 June–1 July 2011, Assembly/AU/Dec.366(XVII), para 5.

[173] Gaeta (n 1) 323. Similarly Schabas (n 131) 6–7. See also the ICJ which held that '[the Court] has been unable to deduce . . . that there exists under customary international law any form of exception to the rule according immunity from criminal jurisdiction and inviolability to incumbent Ministers for Foreign Affairs, where they are suspected of having committed war crimes or crimes against humanity'. *Arrest Warrant Case* (Judgment) [2002] ICJ Rep 3, para 58.

[174] See *Arrest Warrant Case* (Judgment) [2002] ICJ Rep 3, para 58. Confirming this view see *Djibouti v France* (Judgment) [2008] ICJ Rep 177, para 170. See also the ECtHR in *Al-Adsani v United Kingdom* (Judgment) [2001] Application No 35763/97, para 61.

[175] Sharing this view see Gaeta (n 1) 323. Contra Boschiero (n 142) 640–51.

> Given that the Statute is a multilateral treaty governed by the rules set out in the Vienna Convention on the Law of Treaties, the Statute cannot impose obligations on third States without their consent. Thus, the exception to the exercise of the Court's jurisdiction provided in article 27(2) of the Statute should, in principle, be confined to those States Parties who have accepted it.[176]

The Court then noted the function of Article 98(1) in this respect:

> This provision directs the Court to secure the cooperation of the third State for the waiver or lifting the immunity of its Head of State. This course of action envisaged by article 98(1) of the Statute aims at preventing the requested State from acting inconsistently with its international obligations towards the non-State Party with respect to the immunities attached to the latter's Head of State.[177]

However, the Chamber arrived at the conclusion that the immunities attached to Sudan's President were removed by virtue of the SC referral, arguing that

> by issuing Resolution 1593 (2005) the SC decided that the 'Government of Sudan . . . shall cooperate fully with and provide any necessary assistance to the Court and the Prosecutor pursuant to this resolution'. Since immunities attached to Omar Al-Bashir are a procedural bar from prosecution before the Court, the cooperation envisaged in said resolution was meant to eliminate any impediment to the proceedings before the Court, including the lifting of immunities. Any other interpretation would render the SC decision requiring that Sudan 'cooperate fully' and 'provide any necessary assistance to the Court' senseless. Accordingly, the 'cooperation of that third State [Sudan] for the waiver of the immunity', as required under the last sentence of article 98(1) of the Statute, was already ensured by the language used in paragraph 2 of SC Resolution 1593(2005). By virtue of said paragraph, the SC implicitly waived the immunities granted to Omar Al-Bashir under international law and attached to his position as a Head of State. Consequently, there also exists no impediment at the horizontal level between the DRC and Sudan as regards the execution of the 2009 and 2010 Requests.[178]

As noted above, this argument is not entirely convincing since the implicit removal of personal immunities is not without problems.[179]

---

[176] *Prosecutor v Omar Hassan Ahmad Al-Bashir* (Decision on the Cooperation of the Democratic Republic of the Congo regarding Omar Al-Bashir's Arrest and Surrender to the Court) ICC-02/05-01/09-195 (9 April 2014) para 26 (footnotes omitted).

[177] Ibid. para 27.

[178] Ibid. para 29 (footnotes omitted).

[179] See *Prosecutor v Omar Hassan Ahmad Al-Bashir* (Minority Opinion of Judge Marc Perrin de Brichambaut) No ICC-02/05-01/09 (6 July 2017) paras 64–83 (raising concerns regarding this conclusion), para 83. For the view that the SC referral implicitly removes immunities and the resulting questions regarding potential obligations or rights of non-party states to disregard immunities generally accorded by international

In another recent decision, the ICC reconsidered the reasons given in previous decisions and put forward another argument in support of the same conclusion. The Pre-Trial Chamber II held, by majority, that

> because the rights and obligations as provided for in the Statute, including article 27(2), are applicable to Sudan (by imposition of the Security Council acting under Chapter VII of the UN Charter), the immunities of Omar Al-Bashir as Head of State do not bar States Parties to the Rome Statute from executing the Court's request of his arrest and surrender.[180]

Judge Brichambaut disagreed and wrote a detailed minority opinion, in which he found that 'the current state of the law does not allow a definite answer to be reached in relation to the question of whether this resolution removes the immunities of Omar Al-Bashir'.[181] He did consider the Genocide Convention as resolving the issue, stating that

> [t]he combined effect of a literal and contextual interpretation of article IV of the Genocide Convention, in conjunction with an assessment of the object and purpose of this treaty, lead to the conclusion that Omar Al-Bashir does not enjoy personal immunity, having been 'charged' with genocide within the meaning of article VI of the Genocide Convention.[182]

---

law, see Akande (n 128) 342–48. See however O'Keefe (n 136) 572–73: 'It is not apparent why a decision by the Security Council that Sudan must co-operate fully with and provide any necessary assistance to the Court should be taken to mean that such co-operation and assistance has ipso facto been obtained, as article 98(1) requires in relation to a third state's waiver of immunity before the Court may proceed with a request to a state party for the surrender of a serving or former official of the third state. It would doubtless be open to the Security Council, acting under chapter VII of the UN Charter, to decide that the state party in question must surrender the person to the Court notwithstanding article 98(1) and the immunity and inviolability owed by the state party to the third state in respect of the person. But the Security Council has not done this in this case. As the Pre-Trial Chamber implicitly acknowledges, article 98(1) remains applicable'.

180 *Prosecutor v Omar Hassan Ahmad Al-Bashir* (Decision under article 87(7) of the Rome Statute on the non-compliance by South Africa with the request by the Court for the arrest and surrender of Omar Al-Bashir) ICC-02/05-01/09 (6 July 2017) para 107.

181 *Prosecutor v Omar Hassan Ahmad Al-Bashir* (Minority Opinion of Judge Marc Perrin de Brichambaut) ICC-02/05-01/09 (6 July 2017) para 83.

182 Ibid. para 100. For a further discussion see Gabriel M. Lentner, 'Why the ICC won't get it right – The Legal Nature of UN Security Council Referrals and Al-Bashir's Immunities' (2017), available at https://www.ejiltalk.org/why-the-icc-wont-get-it-right-the-legal-nature-of-un-security-council-referrals-and-al-bashir-immunities/ (accessed 1 June 2018).

5.1.5.7 Subsequent practice of affected states and UN organs

In 2009 the AU adopted a resolution calling for AU member states not to cooperate with the ICC in relation to the arrest of Omar Al-Bashir.[183] Later, in 2017, the AU passed another resolution adopting an 'ICC Withdrawal Strategy' partly based on the conviction that personal immunities are applicable in cases of heads of state or government under customary international law, even when referred to by the SC.[184]

As regards the reaction from other countries, several indicated that states are under an obligation to arrest and surrender Omar Al-Bashir on the basis of the Statute and/or SC Resolution 1593, having adopted provisions in their national law implementing the obligations arising out of the Rome Statute to that effect.[185] Furthermore, in SC meetings, certain states have emphasized the need to execute warrants of arrest issued by the Court, which could indicate that these states do not consider that the existing rule of customary international law relating to heads of state immunity constitutes an obstacle vis-à-vis the ICC.[186] Others, especially states represented in the AU and the Arab League, have taken the opposite view.[187]

The SC itself did not adopt any measures against Sudan that could be taken as expecting Sudan to lift the immunities against President Omar Al-Bashir.[188] The SC has not dealt with the requests by the AU to defer the situation in Darfur in accordance with art 16 of the Statute.[189] The AU requested the deferral due to its view that sitting heads of state enjoy immunities under

---

[183] African Union Assembly Decision, Thirteenth Session (3 July 2009) Doc Assembly/AU-/245(XIII) Rev 1, para 10. See further Ottilia A. Maunganidze and Anton Du Plessis, 'The ICC and the AU' in Carsten Stahn (ed), *The Law and Practice of the International Criminal Court* (Oxford University Press 2015); Dapo Akande, Max Du Plessis and Charles C. Jalloh, 'Assessing the African Union Concerns about Article 16 of the Rome Statute of the International Criminal Court' (2011) 4(1) *African Journal of Legal Studies* 5.

[184] African Union, Draft 2 Withdrawal Strategy Document (12 January 2017), available at https://www.hrw.org/sites/default/files/supporting_resources/icc_withdrawal_strategy_jan._2017.pdf (accessed 3 March 2018).

[185] *Prosecutor v Omar Hassan Ahmad Al-Bashir* (Minority Opinion of Judge Marc Perrin de Brichambaut) ICC-02/05-01/09 (6 July 2017) para 87 fn 121.

[186] E.g. Australia, Columbia, France, Germany, Guatemala, Ukraine; see *Prosecutor v Omar Hassan Ahmad Al-Bashir* (Minority Opinion of Judge Marc Perrin de Brichambaut) ICC-02/05-01/09 (6 July 2017) para 87 fn 122.

[187] E.g. Egypt, Morocco, Russia, Rwanda, Venezuela see *Prosecutor v Omar Hassan Ahmad Al-Bashir* (Minority Opinion of Judge Marc Perrin de Brichambaut) ICC-02/05-01/09 (6 July 2017) para 89 fn 124.

[188] *Prosecutor v Omar Hassan Ahmad Al-Bashir* (Minority Opinion of Judge Marc Perrin de Brichambaut) ICC-02/05-01/09 (6 July 2017) para 81.

[189] Ibid. para 82.

international law.[190] The fact that the SC did not adopt such a resolution could be evidence for the position that the immunities did *not* form an obstacle for the exercise of the jurisdiction of the ICC, based on the argument that the SC referral has removed such immunities.[191]

Summing up, the practice and *opinio juris* of affected states and UN organs appear to be rather inconclusive.

5.1.5.8 Conclusion

In conclusion, strong arguments exist for the view that states parties as well as non-party states must respect the personal immunity afforded to nationals of non-party states, when the SC referral is silent on the matter. These personal immunities are applicable to the ICC as well as national authorities acting in support of the ICC, unless the SC referral expressly removes them. In any case, it should be always borne in mind that immunity from jurisdiction does not mean impunity. Immunity *ratione personae* ends when the high-ranking state official ceases to hold office.

5.1.6 Jurisdiction *Ratione Loci* – Territorial Jurisdiction

With regards to the jurisdiction *ratione loci*, art 13(b) of the Rome Statute is a clear exception to the territorial jurisdiction of art 12(2) and is therefore not limited to the territories of state parties to the ICC.[192] Hence, on the basis of a SC referral, the ICC enjoys jurisdiction over crimes even if they are committed on the territory of non-party states by the nationals of non-party states and in the absence of consent by the territorial state or the state of nationality of the accused.[193] Accordingly, the SC referral allows the Court to exercise its jurisdiction in spite of the principle of the sovereignty of states.[194]

The SC will need to define in the referral the territorial scope of the jurisdiction *ratione loci*. In the Darfur referral, the SC referral merely mentioned 'the situation in Darfur' as the territorial scope of jurisdiction. Similarly, the referral adopted in 2011 regarding Libya mentioned 'the situation in the Libyan

---

[190] Taken together, the practice and *opinio juris* of states represented in the AU could therefore be considered as emerging (perhaps even constituting) regional customary international law.

[191] Brichambaut (n 188) para 82.

[192] Stephané Bourgon, 'Jurisdiction ratione loci' in Cassese (n 13) 565.

[193] Mahnoush H. Arsanjani, 'Reflections on the Jurisdiction and Trigger Mechanism of the International Criminal Court' in Herman von Hebel, J. G. Lammers and Jolien Schukking (eds), *Reflections on the International Criminal Court: Essays in Honour of Adriaan Bos* (T.M.C. Asser Press; Kluwer Law International 1999).

[194] Bourgon (n 192) 566.

Arab Jamahiriya'. The jurisdiction of the ICC will be limited to the prosecution of crimes committed on the territory mentioned in the resolution.

5.1.7 Legal Consequences for the Prosecution

Once the preconditions of art 13(b) are met, the normal requirements of the Rome Statute will apply, including the independent prosecution.[195] Article 42 of the Statute requires that the

> Office of the Prosecutor shall act independently as a separate organ of the Court. It shall be responsible for receiving referrals and any substantiated information on crimes within the jurisdiction of the Court, for examining them and for conducting investigations and prosecutions before the Court. A member of the Office shall not seek or act on instructions from any external source.

The SC referral obliges the Prosecutor to initiate investigations as provided for in the referral, but it does not oblige her to prosecute.[196] By virtue of Article 53, the Prosecutor decides independently whether there is sufficient basis for prosecution, taking particular account of the 'interests of justice'. Whenever she decides not to proceed, following a referral under art 13(b), the SC shall be informed pursuant to art 53(2), but it can only request a review of that decision by a Pre-Trial Chamber according to art 53(3)(a) Rome Statute.[197]

The state concerned is obliged under art 93 of the Statute under the heading 'other forms of cooperation' to

> comply with requests by the Court to provide the following assistance in relation to investigations or prosecutions including the taking of evidence (b); the service of documents, including judicial documents (d); the execution of searches and seizures (h); the identification, tracing and freezing or seizure of proceeds, property and assets (k).

---

[195] James Crawford, 'The ILC's Draft Statute for an International Criminal Tribunal' (1994) 88(1) *American Journal of International Law* 140, 147. See further Dan Sarooshi, 'The Peace and Justice Paradox: The International Criminal Court and the UN Security Council' in Dominic McGoldrick, Peter Rowe and Eric Donnelly (eds), *The Permanent International Criminal Court: Legal And Policy Issues* (Hart Publishing 2004) 98.

[196] Condorelli and Villalpando (n 13) 642–44. For a more reluctant voice, see Cherif M. Bassiouni, *The Legislative History of the International Criminal Court* (International and comparative criminal law series, Transnational Publishers 2005) 140.

[197] Condorelli and Villalpando (n 13) 642–44; Luca Schicho, 'The Security Council and the International Criminal Court: An Awkward Partnership?' (2008) 13 *Austrian Review of International and European Law* 115, 125.

5.2 ADMISSIBILITY

Admissibility of a case is subject to the principle of complementarity. According to this principle, included in art 17 of the Rome Statute, a case is inadmissible where:

> (a) The case is being investigated or prosecuted by a State which has jurisdiction over it, unless the State is unwilling or unable genuinely to carry out the investigation or prosecution;
> (b) The case has been investigated by a State which has jurisdiction over it and the State has decided not to prosecute the person concerned, unless the decision resulted from the unwillingness or inability of the State genuinely to prosecute;
> (c) The person concerned has already been tried for conduct which is the subject of the complaint, and a trial by the Court is not permitted under article 20, paragraph 3;
> (d) The case is not of sufficient gravity to justify further action by the Court.

While certain ambiguities in the text of the Rome Statute exist,[198] a SC referral in accordance with the Statute must be interpreted as being subject to the principle of complementarity as provided in art 17.[199] Article 17 does not distinguish between different 'trigger' mechanisms, and furthermore pursuant to art 19 of the Statute, '[t]he Court shall satisfy itself that it has jurisdiction in any case brought before it. The Court may, on its own motion, determine the admissibility of a case in accordance with article 17'.[200] Additionally, under art 53, the Prosecutor, in deciding whether to initiate an investigation, has to also

---

[198] It appears that this was intentionally left unresolved at the Rome Conference; see Schabas (n 12) 275. Schabas (n 28) 169–70.

[199] *Prosecutor v Saif Al-Islam Gaddafi and Abdullah Al-Senussi* (Decision Requesting Further Submissions on Issues Related to the Admissibility of the Case against Saif Al-Islam Gaddafi) ICC-01/11-01/11 (7 December 2012) para 6. In this sense also Nouwen, who points out that 'Complementarity must be assessed irrespective of whether the situation was referred to the Court by the Security Council or by a state party to the Rome Statute or whether the Prosecutor opened an investigation *proprio motu* with PTC permission'; Sarah M. H. Nouwen, *Complementarity in the Line of Fire: The Catalysing Effect of the International Criminal Court in Uganda and Sudan* (Cambridge University Press 2013) 75.

[200] Sharing this view, see Condorelli and Villalpando (n 13) 630; Marta Bo, 'The Situation in Libya and the ICC's Understanding of Complementarity in the Context of UNSC-Referred Cases' (2014) 25(3–4) *Criminal Law Forum* 505, 509.

consider the issue of admissibility in the case of referral under art 13(b).[201] This is also the position of the Office of the Prosecutor.[202]

In practice, the ICC has not drawn a distinction between admissibility in cases involving states parties to the ICC and those situations referred to it by the SC.[203]

5.3 THE SC REFERRAL NOT IN ACCORDANCE WITH THE STATUTE

A SC referral that is not in accordance with the Statute raises several legal issues. Such a SC referral can take two forms in practice. First, the SC referral could limit the jurisdiction of the Court in a way not foreseen in the Rome Statute with respect to, for example, providing jurisdiction only over certain crimes or limiting personal jurisdiction to those of a certain nationality. Second, the SC referral could extend the ICC's jurisdiction not in accordance with the Statute by e.g. extending temporal jurisdiction before the entry into force of the Rome Statute, or extending the crimes under the jurisdiction of the Court.

As concluded above, the legal nature of the SC referral as a conferral of powers from the SC to the ICC does not establish that the ICC can lawfully exercise such powers. In order to take up these conferred powers, the constituent treaty, i.e. the Rome Statute, must provide such a right.[204] As an international court endowed with limited jurisdiction, the ICC cannot 'depart from the terms of the Statute', as the Permanent Court of Justice noted in the

---

[201] The omission of a reference to art 13(b) in art 18 regarding the procedure to be followed by the Court does not change this. This interpretation is supported by the fact that neither the Draft Statute proposed by the ILC in 1994 nor the first works by the Preparatory Committee envisaged any exception to the principle of complementarity in the case of referral by the Security Council; see Condorelli and Villalpando (n 13) 630.

[202] See UN Docs S/PV.5216, 2; S/PV.5321, 3; S/PV.5459, 4; S/PV.5589, 2.

[203] See *Prosecutor v Saif Al-Islam Gaddafi and Abdullah Al-Senussi* (Judgment on the appeal of Libya against the decision of Pre-Trial Chamber I of 31 May 2013 entitled 'Decision on the admissibility of the case against Saif Al-Islam Gaddafi') ICC-01/11-01/11-547-Red (21 May 2014); *Prosecutor v Saif Al-Islam Gaddafi and Abdullah Al-Senussi* (Decision Requesting Further Submissions on Issues Related to the Admissibility of the Case against Saif Al-Islam Gaddafi) ICC-01/11-01/11 (7 December 2012) para 6 referring to *Prosecutor v Germain Katanga and Mathieu Ngudjolo Chui* (Judgment on the Appeal of Mr. Germain Katanga against the Oral Decision of Trial Chamber II of 12 June 2009 on the Admissibility of the Case) ICC-01/04-01/07-1497 (25 September 2009) paras 75–79.

[204] In this sense also Rod Rastan, 'Jurisdiction' in Stahn (n 181) 157. Similarly, see Sarooshi (n 57) 252–53 regarding the delegation of Chapter VII powers to regional arrangements.

Free Zones of Upper Savay case.[205] It can only act within its framework, which both confers and limits the Court's jurisdiction.[206] In other words, the conferral of powers through the SC referral cannot provide the ICC with the right to exercise these conferred powers beyond its constituent treaty.[207] Hence, the ICC can arguably only exercise jurisdiction in accordance with its Statute.[208]

From the perspective of the ICC, this resulting superiority of the Statute compared with all other sources of applicable law (art 21) is, prima facie, justifiable.[209] This is because of the nature of the constituent instrument of the ICC: the Rome Statute is a multilateral treaty 'having certain special characteristics'[210] including that of being the 'supreme norm' of a subject of international law endowed with its own legal personality.[211]

Nevertheless, as the ICJ stated, '[i]nternational organizations are subjects of international law and, as such, are bound by any obligations incumbent upon them under general rules of international law, under their constitutions or under international agreements to which they are parties'.[212] This means that general rules of international law must be considered as well. The question arises whether the obligations stemming from the SC resolution referring a situation to the ICC, even if not in accordance with the Statute, are still obligations under international law. This is relevant because nothing in the Rome Statute can be read as subordinating the ICC to the SC.[213] The ICC, as a separate international organization, cannot directly be bound by obligations stemming from a SC resolution, since only the member states of the UN are bound by it (art 25 UN Charter).[214]

---

[205] *Free Zones of Upper Savay and the District of Gex* (PCIJ, Judgment) PCIJ Rep A/N22, 12 (19 August 1929) 12.

[206] Alain Pellet, 'Applicable Law' in Cassese (n 13) 1079.

[207] Cf Sarooshi (n 57) 252–53.

[208] Sharing this conclusion. e.g. Gaeta (n 1) 324. This conclusion does not affect the lawfulness of the delegation or the exercise of delegated powers from the perspective of the United Nations Charter.

[209] Pellet (n 206) 1078–79.

[210] *Certain Expenses Case* (Judgment) [1962] ICJ Rep 1962, 151, 157.

[211] Pellet (n 206) 1078–79. See on this Chapter 1.5.

[212] ICJ, *Interpretation of the Agreement*, Advisory Opinion, 21 May 1980, Reports 1980, § 37.

[213] Luigi Condorelli and Santiago Villalpando, 'Can the Security Council Extend the ICC's Jurisdiction?' in Cassese (n 13) 574. Similarly, Akande (n 128) 341. Arguably sharing this view see Bourgon (n 84) 552–553 regarding the extension of the temporal scope of jurisdiction beyond the provisions of the Rome Statute.

[214] Nico Krisch, 'Introduction to Chapter VII: The General Framework' in Simma (n 6 para 67. See with respect of SC sanctions and the legal order of the European Union, Case T-85/09 *Kadi v Commission* [2010] ECR II-5177; Joined Cases C-584/10 P, C-593/10 P and C-595/10 P *European Commission and Others v Yassin Abdullah*

Still, any exercise of jurisdiction of the ICC involving non-states parties to the ICC must be based on the SC referral, even if not in accordance with the Statute. The legal nature of the SC referral prevents the ICC from taking action beyond the scope of jurisdiction as defined in the SC resolution referring a situation to the Court. In other words, since the legality of the exercise of jurisdiction by the ICC depends (in case of non-party states) on the powers conferred to it by the SC, the ICC cannot exercise more than is given to it.

This has important legal consequences. If the SC limits the jurisdiction in a way that is clearly not in accordance with the Statute (e.g. by only referring a single case to the jurisdiction of the court), the ICC cannot 'carve out' this limitation from the referral and act on the basis of its Statute as if the SC referral did not include special limitations to its jurisdiction.[215] This means that the ICC is obliged to recognize that it *only* enjoys jurisdiction as conferred to it by the SC referral.

5.3.1 Limiting the ICC's Jurisdiction

The SC referral could try to limit the jurisdiction of the ICC by providing jurisdiction only over certain and not all the crimes which are included in the Statute, or limiting personal jurisdiction to those of a certain nationality.

Kadi (CJEU, 18 July 2013). On this point, see Lentner (n 2). The literature on this is extensive; see e.g. Eric Stein, 'The United Nations, the European Union, and the King of Sweden: Economic Sanctions and Individual Rights in a Plural World Order' (2009) 46 *Common Market Law Review* 13; A. Gattini, 'Joined Cases C-402/05 P & 415/05 P, Yassin Abdullah Kadi, Al Barakaat International Foundation v Council and Commission, judgment of the Grand Chamber of 3 September 2008' (2009) 46 *Common Market Law Review* 213; P. De Sena and M. Vitucci 'The European Courts and the Security Council: Between Dédoublement Fonctionnel and Balancing of Values' (2009) 1 *European Journal of International Law* 194; G. De Burca 'The ECJ and the International Legal Order: A Re-evaluation' in G. De Burca and J. H. H. Weiler (eds), The Worlds of European Constitutionalism (Cambridge University Press 2012), 105; M. Bothe, 'Security Council's Targeted Sanctions against Presumed Terrorists: The Need to Comply with Human Rights Standards' (2008) 6 *Journal of International Criminal Justice* 541; Jean d'Aspremont and Frédéric Dopagne, 'Kadi: The ECJ's Reminder of the Elementary Divide between Legal Orders' (2008) 5 *International Organizations Law Review* 371; J. M. Farrall, *United Nations Sanctions and the Rule of Law* (Cambridge University Press 2009); P. Hilpold, 'UN Sanctions Before the ECJ: the Kadi Case' in August Reinisch (ed), *Challenging Acts of International Organizations before National Courts* (Oxford University Press 2010); Luis Hinojosa Martínez, 'Bad Law for Good Reasons: The Contradictions of the Kadi Judgment' (2008) 5 *International Organizations Law Review* 339.

[215] This will be discussed in detail with respect to the practical question arising out of the jurisdictional exemption included in the first two ever SC referrals to the ICC.

The question arises whether such limitation is operational for the Court. In light of the principle of systemic integration[216] and the presumption of compatibility[217] to avoid a conflict of norms and application of art 103 of the Charter,[218] a presumption against conflict exists in international law. Defining a conflict of norms, Hans Kelsen wrote that '[a] conflict between two norms occurs if in obeying or applying one norm, the other one is necessarily or possibly violated'.[219] In other words, a conflict of norms does not exist if the applicable norms leave room for interpretation that allows both norms to apply without the other being necessarily or possibly violated.

This points to the fact that compatibility with the Rome Statute of limitations to the jurisdiction of the ICC in cases of SC referrals should be interpreted in light of the existing principles and presumptions (against conflict). As established above, the legal nature of the SC referral is a conferral of powers from the SC to the ICC. The SC referral confers the power to the ICC to act within the confines of the jurisdiction as referred to the ICC. This means that unless clear wording of the Statute renders an interpretation to give effect to the SC referral impossible, the ICC must be understood as competent under its constituent treaty to act upon the SC referral.[220] With regards to the limitations stemming from the UN Charter with respect to the principle of legality, compatibility with the Rome Statute is ensured by art 21 dealing with the applicable law.[221]

As a result, the inclusion of art 13(b) providing for the SC referral must be read as making the SC referrals operational for the ICC, and that insofar as the SC remains within the constitutional confines of the UN Charter generally and the conditions of Chapter VII action specifically, broad discretion as to

216 Codified in art 31(3) (c) VCLT; see further Paulus and Leiß (n 6) 17–18 with further references, concluding 'contradiction should only be assumed when norms stand in clear conflict with each other or in the case that the contradictory intent is clearly expressed'.

217 *Case Concerning the Right of Passage (Portugal v India)* (Merits) [1960] ICJ Rep 6.

218 Paulus and Leiß (n 6) 17–18. See also ILC, 'Report of the Study Group of the ILC on Fragmentation of International Law: Difficulties Arising from Diversification and Expansion of International Law' (13 April 2006) UN Doc A/CN.4/L.682.

219 Hans Kelsen, 'Derogation' in H. Klecatsky, R. Marcic and H. Schambeck (eds) *Die Wiener Rechtstheoretische Schule* (Europa Verlag 1968) 1438; Similarly Pauwelyn (n 6) 199.

220 In this sense arguably Andreas Zimmermann, '"Acting under Chapter VII (…)" – Resolution 1422 and Possible Limits of the Powers of the Security Council' in Jochen A. Frowein (ed), *Verhandeln für den Frieden: Negotiating for Peace: Liber Amicorum Tono Eitel* (Beiträge zum ausländischen öffentlichen Recht und Völkerrecht vol 162, Springer 2003) 275–76.

221 See on this above Chapter 5.1.3.

the concrete parameters of the jurisdiction to be exercised by the ICC must be assumed. This interpretation is supported by the doctrine of implied powers. Making use of the referral by the SC allows the ICC to perform its functions in situations where it otherwise would not have jurisdiction.[222]

In case of clear incompatibility of the SC referral resolution and the Rome Statute, the conclusions from the following section must apply *mutatis mutandis*.

5.3.2 Extending or Otherwise Modifying ICC Jurisdiction

The extension of the ICC's jurisdiction (*ratione materiae*, *ratione personae*, *ratione loci* and *ratione temporis*) beyond the provisions of the Rome Statute or otherwise modifying its jurisdiction is the clear case of incompatibility of the SC referral and the Rome Statute. A situation might arise in which the SC views it as being in the interest of the maintenance of international peace and security to adopt a SC referral that extends the jurisdiction of the ICC beyond its Statute. The question arises of whether the ICC is legally authorized to exercise the extended jurisdiction based on the binding nature of Chapter VII resolutions in accordance with art 25 in combination with arts 48(2) and 103 of the UN Charter, even if it is in conflict with its obligations under its constituent treaties.[223] However, art 48(2) solely presupposes that the only requirement is

---

[222] According to the ICJ, it is presumed that an act appropriate for the fulfilment of an attributed function of the organization is not ultra vires; see *Certain Expenses Case* (Advisory Opinion) [1962] ICJ Rep 151, 168. As a result, few judgments determine the ultra vires quality of an act of an international organization (see *Constitution of the Maritime Safety Committee of the Inter-Governmental Maritime Consultative Organization* (Advisory Opinion) [1960] ICJ Rep 150, 171; with regard to the WHO see *Nuclear Weapons in Armed Conflict* (Advisory Opinion) [1996] ICJ Rep 226, para 22.

[223] Rejecting this argument, see Danesh Sarooshi, 'Aspects of the Relationship between the International Criminal Court and the United Nations' (2001) 32 *Netherlands Yearbook of International Law* 27, 40. This question was at issue during the drafting of the 1986 VCLT between states and international organizations or between international organizations (not yet entered into force). One view proposed that art 103 of the Charter should equally apply to international organizations in order not to be used as a vehicle to circumvent collective action of states through the escape into the international organization. On the other hand it was opined that art 103 does not mention international organizations, which cannot be parties to the UN and are thus under no obligation under the UN Charter. See UN Conference on the law of treaties between states and international organizations or between international organizations (Vienna 18 February–21 March 1986) Official Records, vol II, Documents of the Conference (New York 1986) UN Doc A/CONF.129/4, 5, 25–26 and Official Records, vol I, Summary Records of the plenary meetings and of the meetings of the Committee of the Whole (1986) 119–22. As regards the analogous situation of obligations stemming from SC sanctions and

that member states of the UN take appropriate action in those organizations in which they are members.[224] Thus, the only requirement arising from art 48 of the Charter is that the contracting parties of the ICC should, as UN members, take in the ASP appropriate action to the extent possible to comply with the obligations arising out of the SC's decisions.[225]

However, art 103 can only address UN member states, and the UN Charter cannot impose obligations on another international organization that go beyond its constitutional treaty.[226] The resulting legal situation is unsatisfactory but clear: the member states are bound by the SC resolution to accept the exercise of jurisdiction by the ICC in the way it is included in the referral (and the ICC receives the conferred powers from the SC to that extent). But, the ICC is prevented from acting upon this conferred authority, i.e. the referral of jurisdiction, by its constituent treaty (the Rome Statute). Article 103 just makes clear that, from the perspective of the UN Charter, its provisions will prevail over any other conflicting obligations of member states.[227] But in case of SC referrals involving a non-states party, no such conflicting obligations exist, since the state concerned over which the SC provides jurisdiction to the ICC is not bound by the provisions of the Rome Statute, because it is not a state party.[228] As a result, art 103 is not applicable to this situation. To construct

---

the EU legal order see Gabriel M. Lentner, 'Kadi II before the ECJ – UN Targeted Sanctions and the European Legal Order' (2013) 6 *European Law Reporter* 202. See further, Alexander Orakhelashvili, 'Article 30 (1986)' in Olivier Corten and Pierre Klein (eds), *The Vienna Conventions on the Law of Treaties: A Commentary* (Oxford commentaries on international law, Oxford University Press 2011) 801–803.

[224] Brun-Otto Bryde and August Reinisch, 'Article 48' in Bruno Simma and others (eds), *The Charter of the United Nations, A Commentary* (2nd edn, C.H. Beck 2002) para 10.

[225] For a different view see Zimmermann who argues that this would hardly be compatible with the object and purpose of the Charter as member states of the UN could circumvent their obligations by entering into a multilateral treaty; Zimmermann (n 220) 275–76. However, such interpretation goes against the clear wording of art 48.

[226] Sarooshi (n 223) 40; Paulus and Leiß (n 6) 2130; Michael E. Kurth, *Das Verhältnis des Internationalen Strafgerichtshofes zum UN-Sicherheitsrat: Unter besonderer Berücksichtigung von Sicherheitsratsresolution 1422 (2002)* (Nomos 2006) 117.

[227] See d'Aspremont who correctly points out that art 103 simply addresses a conflict of norms 'from the vantage point of the UN Charter. This mechanism does not resolve conflicts of norms that may arise within the legal order of member states or within the legal order of international organizations'; Jean d'Aspremont, 'The Multifaceted Concept of Autonomy of International Organizations and International Legal Discourse' in Richard Collins and Nigel D. White (eds), *International Organizations and the Idea of Autonomy: Institutional Independence in the International Legal Order* (Routledge research in international law, Routledge 2011) 75.

[228] Sharing this view see Akande (n 4) 308.

art 103 in a way that would make the ICC bound by SC resolutions imposing obligations on the ICC to act beyond its constituent treaty has no basis in law, as art 48(2) of the Charter appears to confirm. Addressees of the obligations stemming from the UN Charter are the member states, and they have the obligation to carry out the decisions of the SC directly and through their action in the appropriate international organizations of which they are members.[229]

Therefore, the conferred powers to the ICC as prescribed in the SC resolution are the only source for the ICC to exercise jurisdiction over situations in non-party states. Whether the authority provided to the ICC is in conflict with the provisions of the Rome Statute is a question of the internal law of the ICC. This internal law should be interpreted, if possible, to provide the legal basis to give effect to the SC resolutions. But if the interpretation of the SC referral leads to an extension of the ICC's jurisdiction beyond the provisions of the Rome Statute, the ICC cannot act upon such referral in that it would constitute ultra vires acts. The Rome Statute is clear in this respect: it can only be amended by states parties and adopted by the ASP or a Review Conference (art 121).[230]

One way to arrive at an acceptable interpretation could be to view the extension of the ICC's jurisdiction, like the SC referral in general, as an authorization to use the conferred powers within the parameters as provided for in the SC referral.[231] Taking art 2 of the RA together with the prosecutorial discretion inherent in such a conferral (the Prosecutor is not obliged to prosecute a case pursuant to arts 42 and 53 Rome Statute), the conferral of powers to the ICC should not be read as requiring the ICC to go beyond its constituent treaty. As a result, the ICC may exercise such conferred authority, but only insofar as it is not going beyond the Statute.[232]

---

229 Sarooshi (n 223) 40–43; Condorelli and Villalpando (n 213) 578.

230 Condorelli and Villalpando (n 213) 574.

231 On the question of whether art 103 also applies to authorizations adopted by the SC, see e.g. R. Kolb, 'Does Article 103 of the Charter of the United Nations Apply only to Decisions or also to Authorizations Adopted by the Security Council' (2004) 64 *ZaöRV* 21.

232 Also arriving at this conclusion, but on the basis of the RA binding the UN to the Statute, see Condorelli and Villalpando (n 213) 575–80. However, the RA nowhere imposes such an obligation on the UN or the SC. Even if it would, the authors do not consider the discussion of art 103 UN Charter under which UN obligations prevail over any other international agreement.

In any case, the SC is of course entitled to provide for specific coercive measures[233] in the SC referral in order to ensure effective state cooperation by the states concerned.[234]

5.3.3 Admissibility not in Accordance with the Rome Statute

As pointed out, issues of admissibility will be considered in a subsequent phase of the prosecution of crimes by the organs of the ICC (notably the Prosecutor and the competent Pre-Trial or Trial Chamber). However, it is possible that the SC considers that a particular national judicial authority – though available and willing to prosecute and thus in a position to successfully challenge admissibility before the ICC – is unable to deal with the crimes committed in their entirety. In situations where crimes cannot be geographically located in one single state or where there is a controversy between states on the *forum conveniens*, the SC may consider the ICC as being the most appropriate jurisdiction to investigate and judge certain crimes. In these situations, the SC decisions to refer the situation to the Court could be justified by the determination that the inherent characteristics of the crimes concerned are the cause of the inability of single states to obtain the necessary evidence or otherwise carry out the proceedings impartially and appropriately.[235]

It is clear from the legal relationship between the SC and the ICC established here[236] that the SC is not bound by the principle of complementarity.[237] But the ICC is bound by the provision of its constituent treaty, including the rules on complementarity. Therefore, a SC resolution imposing an obligation

---

[233] In regard to the obligations of cooperation of states not party to the ICC, an expert paper of the Office of the Prosecutor of the ICC contemplated that the SC referral could impose obligations that are greater than those provided for in the Rome Statute. In this respect, the report stated: 'A Security Council referral under Article 13(b) can greatly enhance the Prosecutor's authority to compel co-operation from States, including those not party to the Statute. As Article 13(b) entails Security Council action under the extensive powers conferred upon it by Chapter VII of the UN Charter, the Security Council could also use its Article13(b) referral power to specify particular measures to enable the Prosecutor to avoid strict requirements for state co-operation and to act with more authority to investigate a situation.' Office of the Prosecutor, 'Informal Expert Paper: Fact-finding and investigative functions of the office of the Prosecutor, including international co-operation' (2003) paras 92–93, available at https://www.icc-cpi.int/NR/rdonlyres/20BB4494-70F9-4698-8E30-907F631453ED/281983/state_cooperation.pdf (accessed 12 March 2018).

[234] Akande (n 4) 308–309.

[235] Condorelli and Villalpando (n 13) 630.

[236] See above Chapter 3.

[237] For the view that the SC is bound by the principle of complementarity, see Condorelli and Villalpando (n 213) 581.

on national authorities to refrain from the prosecution of crimes and instead cooperate with the ICC could be rendering the national judicial systems 'unavailable' in legal terms, with the result that the state is effectively (due to its obligations under the resolution) 'unable to carry out' the proceedings accordingly. The ICC could then, on the basis of the Rome Statute, determine the admissibility of the relevant cases by virtue of art 17.[238]

5.4 SC ACTING ULTRA VIRES

In line with a significant part of scholarship, this study proceeds on the premise that acts of the SC are ultra vires are devoid of any binding force.[239] While the legal consequences of ultra vires acts are highly complex,[240] the wording of art

---

[238] Condorelli and Villalpando (n 13) 630.

[239] See Karl Doehring, 'Unlawful Resolutions of the Security Council and their Legal Consequences' (1997) 1 *Max Planck Yearbook of United Nations Law* 91; Bernd Martenczuk, 'The Security Council, the International Court and Judicial Review: What Lessons from Lockerbie?' (1999) 10(3) *European Journal of International Law* 517, 534; Jochen A. Frowein and Nico Krisch, 'Chapter VII. Action with Respect to Threats to the Peace, Breaches of the Peace, and Acts of Aggression' in Simma (n 224) para 29; Salvatore Zappala, 'Are Some Peacekeepers Better Than Others? UN Security Council Resolution 1497 (2003) and the ICC' (2003) 1 *Journal of International Criminal Justice* 671, 675; Jochen A. Frowein, 'The UN Anti-Terrorism Administration and the Rule of Law', in Pierre-Marie Dupuy and others (eds) *Common Values in International Law: Essays in Honour of Christian Tomuschat* (NP Engel Verlag 2006) 785–95; contra Peters (n 137) paras 175ff.

[240] Excess of powers are generally considered a ground for nullity; see W. M. Reisman and Dirk Pulkowski, 'Nullity in International Law' in Rüdiger Wolfrum (ed), *Max Planck Encyclopedia of Public International Law* (Oxford University Press Online) para 21. However, the legal consequences of ultra vires acts of international organizations are highly disputed; see Chittharanjan F. Amerasinghe, *Principles of the Institutional Law of International Organizations* (2nd edn, Cambridge University Press 2005) 194–98; Kirsten Schmalenbach, 'International Organizations or Institutions, General Aspects' in Wolfrum (this note, above) para 50. However, scholarship has suggested that SC resolutions that are manifestly ultra vires or in open violation of *jus cogens* norms are void or not legally binding; see Jan Klabbers, *An Introduction to International Organizations Law* (3rd edn, Cambridge University Press 2015) 185; Doehring (n 239) 91–109; Frowein and Krisch (n 239) para 29; Ebere Osieke, 'The Legal Validity of Ultra Vires Decisions of International Organizations' (1983) 77(2) *American Journal of International Law* 239, 244–45. See also the opinion of ad hoc Judge Lauterpacht in the Genocide case (*Application of the Convention on the Prevention and Punishment of the Crime of Genocide* (Judgment) [2007] ICJ Rep 43 (separate opinion of ad hoc Judge Lauterpacht) paras 98–104, particularly at para 103). See however for the view that the SC itself determines the legality of its acts, e.g. Anthony Aust, 'The Role of Human Rights in Limiting the Enforcement Powers of the Security Council: A Practitioners View', in Erika de Wet and André Nollkaemper

25 of the UN Charter clearly establishes that only such decisions of the SC are binding that are adopted 'in accordance with the present Charter'.[241] It follows preliminarily that SC referrals not in accordance with the Charter (and hence ultra vires) are not legally binding. Resulting from the legal nature of the SC referral, the ICC is then not authorized to exercise jurisdiction over situations in non-party states in such cases. A SC referral that is ultra vires has therefore no legal effects.[242]

In practice, it is important to recognize the tendency of the ICJ to minimize claims of acts being ultra vires through a twofold presumption.[243] First, there is a presumption of acts not being ultra vires in case they may be considered 'appropriate for the fulfilment' of the stated purposes of the organization.[244] Second, acts based on one of its assigned functions are presumed to be within the constitutional powers of the organization.[245] It must also be noted that each organ must determine its own powers.[246] It follows that an act must arguably be presumed not to be ultra vires.[247]

The SC cannot easily be considered to be acting ultra vires, as Sir Michael Wood correctly points out:

> Much of the writing about the Security Council by international lawyers has an air of unreality. It is based neither on the practice of states nor on the practice of the organs of the United Nations, nor yet on decisions of courts and tribunals. It reflects the authors' dogmatic reading of the text of the United Nations Charter, and often

---

(eds), *Review of the Security Council by Member States* (Intersentia/Metro 2003) 34. See also critically Karl Zemanek, 'Is the Security Council the Sole Judge of its Own Legality?' in A. Reinisch and U. Kriebaum (eds), *The Law of International Relations – Liber Amicorum Hanspeter Neuhold* (Eleven International Publishing 2007) 483–505; August Reinisch, 'Should Judges Second-Guess the UN Security Council?' (2009) 6(1) *International Organizations Law Review* 257, 259–60.

241 Contra Jean-Pierre Cot, *La Charte des Nations Unies: Commentaire article par article* (3rd edn, Economica 2005) 916–17. On the various interpretations of this wording see Peters (n 137) 807.

242 See further Higgins (n 58) 351–54.

243 Reisman and Pulkowski (n 240) para 22.

244 *Certain Expenses Case* (Advisory Opinion) [1962] ICJ Rep 151, 168. See also Schmalenbach (n 240) para 51.

245 *Certain Expenses Case* (n 244) 168; Reisman and Pulkowski (n 240) para 22.

246 *Certain Expenses Case* (n 244) 168; see also the *Namibia Case*, 1971 ICJ Rep 22, where this position was affirmed. See however for doubt cast on this point by the opinions of Judge Morelli, 1962 ICJ Reports at 222 (separate opinion) and Judge Winiarski, ibid. at 232 (dissenting). Niels Blokker, 'Constituent Instruments: Creating a Genie that May Escape from the Bottle?' in Katz J. Cogan, Ian Hurd and Ian Johnstone (eds), *The Oxford Handbook of International Organizations* (Oxford University Press 2016) 13; Schmalenbach (n 240) para 54.

247 See also Peters (n 137) paras 177–82.

> attempts, unrealistically, to apply domestic or 'European' constitutional principles to the field of international relations. It seems to be asserted that much that the Council has done since the end of the Cold War is ultra vires, beyond its powers under the Charter, or otherwise unlawful. This is not, of course, the case.[248]

Eventually, the crucial issue is, then, who has the power to determine whether or not the SC acted ultra vires? The presumption established above points to the burden of proof on the party challenging the validity of the SC action.[249] However, no procedure exists in order to establish the ultra vires nature of an act of the SC. With respect to the SC referral, the ICC might have the capacity to determine that the SC acted ultra vires. This follows from the ICC's constituent instrument. The ICC would be barred from exercising jurisdiction in such a case since art 13(b) expressly provides for the referral to stem from SC action acting under Chapter VII of the Charter of the UN. It is not permissible to construe this express wording to include actions of the SC which would be ultra vires.

5.5 JUDICIAL REVIEW OF SC REFERRALS BY THE ICC

The ICC is empowered to determine its own jurisdiction pursuant to art 19(1) of the Statute.[250] This is an inherent power of the *competence de la competence* of an international court such as the ICC and is further reflected in art 119(1) of the Rome Statute. This provision states that '[a]ny dispute concerning the judicial functions of the Court shall be settled by the decision of the Court'. In fact, as the ICTY Appeals Chamber clearly established, this power 'is a major part of the incidental or inherent jurisdiction of every judicial or arbitral tribunal'[251] and allows the Court to examine the legality of the decisions of other organs as a matter of incidental jurisdiction over the matter before it.[252] On this

---

[248] Michael Wood, 'The Law of Treaties and the UN Security Council: Some Reflections' in Enzo Cannizzaro (ed), *The Law of Treaties Beyond the Vienna Convention* (Oxford University Press 2011) 247. See also Georg Ress, 'The Interpretation of the Charter' in Simma (n 222) para 5.

[249] Schmalenbach (n 240) para 54.

[250] Condorelli and Villalpando (n 13) 640–42.

[251] *Tadic Case* (Decision on the Defence Motion for Interlocutory Appeal on Jurisdiction) ICTY-IT-94-l-A (2 October 1995) para 18.

[252] See *Tadic Case* (Decision on the Defence Motion for Interlocutory Appeal on Jurisdiction) ICTY-IT-94-l-A (2 October 1995) paras 14–22. See however the Appeals Chamber of the STL declining to review its own legality: *Prosecutor v Ayyash* et al (Decision on the Defence Appeals against the Trial Chamber's 'Decision on the Defence Challenges to the Jurisdiction and Legality of the Tribunal') STL-II-OIIPT/

basis, it has been argued that the ICC is thus entitled to establish whether or not the exercise of its jurisdiction under art 13(b) respected the conditions laid down by the Statute (supporting the possibility of judicial review of SC referrals for the purpose of the Rome Statute see, inter alia, Stahn[253] and Trahan[254]). However, two consequences must be distinguished, first considering the basis of the internal law of the ICC, and second its status under general international law.

The first legal consequence is the incidental judicial review of the SC referral by the ICC. The ICC must determine its own jurisdiction. This means that, as a practical matter, the ICC is competent under its constituent treaty, the Rome Statute, to review a SC referral insofar as it has to satisfy itself that the requirements of art 13(b), which is the constitutional basis for its exercise of jurisdiction, are met.[255] As a result, the ICC, 'acting by virtue of Article 19, shall have jurisdiction to verify the legality of the SC action under Chapter VII of the Charter'.[256] It is doing so on the basis of its internal law, since art 13(b) of the Statute refers to the SC acting under Chapter VII of the Charter.

The second legal consequence is sometimes overlooked. Such incidental judicial review cannot determine the legality of the SC referral under UN law.[257] It must be noted that judicial review by the ICC has effects only for the internal law of the ICC. The ICC cannot, therefore, perform a substantive review of whether the bases for the SC to act under Chapter VII are indeed fulfilled.[258] This does carry significant practical implications since the ICC will, depending on its determination, either exercise jurisdiction pursuant to

---

AC/AR90.1 (24 October 2012) paras 11–23. See on this Nikolova and Ventura (n 21); Mégret (n 21).

[253] Carsten Stahn, 'The Ambiguities of Security Council Resolution 1422 (2002)' (2003) 14 *European Journal of International Law* 85, 102.

[254] Jennifer Trahan, 'The Relationship Between the International Criminal Court and the U.N. Security Council: Parameters and Best Practices' (2013) 24(4) *Criminal Law Forum* 417, 472.

[255] Gabriël H. Oosthuizen, 'Some Preliminary Remarks on the Relationship Between the Envisaged International Criminal Court and the UN Security Council' (1999) 46(3) *Netherlands International Law Review* 313–42, 318ff.

[256] Condorelli and Villalpando (n 13) 630. See also on the indirect review by the ICTY, Susan Lamb, 'Legal Limits to United Nations Security Council Powers' in Guy S. Goodwin-Gill (ed), *The Reality of International Law: Essays in Honour of Ian Brownlie* (repr. Clarendon 2003) 364.

[257] Contra, Condorelli and Villalpando, who argue on the basis of the acceptance of the judicial review of SC measures through the ICTY. As has been pointed out above (Chapter 4.1.2.2) this argument is not convincing because the ICC is not a subsidiary organ of the UN; Condorelli and Villalpando (n 13) 640–42.

[258] Franklin Berman, 'The Relationship between the International Criminal Court and the Security Council' in von Hebel (n 193) 321.

the SC referral or refuse to exercise such jurisdiction based on its determination that the SC referral is ultra vires and therefore void. Still, the ICC lacks the competence to exercise direct control over SC measures with a view to annulling them.[259]

This means that from the perspective of international law[260] the ICC cannot determine that a conferral of powers from the SC to the ICC has taken place in a legally effective way. And since the source of the jurisdiction exercised by the ICC over non-party states in case of referrals is the binding nature of SC measures under Chapter VII, the finding of the ICC cannot establish whether the SC measure actually is binding on the UN members that are, in case of a situation involving the territory of the state subject to the referral, addressed and obliged to accept the exercise of the ICC's jurisdiction. This is further supported by the fact that the entity endowed with conferred powers is subject to their limits and, unless otherwise stated, not entitled to give an authoritative interpretation of their scope.[261] This means that, in practice, the ICC is not competent to determine a SC referral to be void on the basis that it did not make an express determination under art 39 before adopting Chapter VII measures, for example. In practice, given that no compulsory judicial review exists in the UN system[262] (the ICJ may deliver an authoritative, even though not legally binding, advisory opinion),[263] the dispute will require a political

---

[259] See for the analogous situation of authoritative interpretations of the UN Charter by organs of the UN, Antonios Tzanakopoulos, *Disobeying the Security Council: Countermeasures against Wrongful Sanctions* (Oxford University Press 2011) 112.

[260] For a similar, arguably analogical situation, see Antonios Tzanakopoulos, 'Collective Security and Human Rights' in Erika de Wet and Jure Vidmar (eds), *Hierarchy in International Law: The Place of Human Rights* (Oxford University Press 2012) 67.

[261] Jochen A. Frowein and Nico Krisch, 'Article 39' in Simma (n 222) 33.

[262] See José Alvarez, 'Judging the Security Council' (1996) 90 *American Journal of International Law* 1; Dapo Akande, 'The International Court of Justice and the Security Council: Is There Room for Judicial Control of Decisions of the Political Organs of the United Nations?' (1997) 46(2) *International and Comparative Law Quarterly* 309; Thomas M. Franck, 'The "Powers of Appreciation": Who is the Ultimate Guardian of UN Legality' (1992) 86(3) *American Journal of International Law* 519, 520. See however Reinisch, who argues that the ICJ has in fact reviewed SC measures: Reinisch (n 240) (with further references). But see the ICJ in its advisory opinion in the *Namibia* case, stating 'Undoubtedly, the Court does not possess powers of judicial review or appeal in respect of the decisions taken by the United Nations organs concerned'. *Legal Consequences for States of the Continued Presence of South Africa in Namibia (South West Africa) Notwithstanding Security Council Resolution 276 (1970)* (Advisory Opinion) ICJ Rep 1971, 16, para 89.

[263] See however Peters, who argues that a 'successful rebuttal of the presumption of legality and validity of a Council decision *in a proceeding before the ICJ* is that the

solution. The lack of effective law enforcement will leave the last resort to UN member states.[264]

In conclusion, the ICC may only incidentally review the SC referral to establish whether the conditions set out in art 13(b) of the Statute have been met on the basis of its power to determine its own jurisdiction pursuant to art 19(1) of the Statute.

5.6 THE REFERRAL AND THE CRIME OF AGGRESSION

The crime of aggression was included in the amendments adopted at the first review conference of the ICC in Kampala, Uganda.[265] In accordance with art 121(5) in conjunction with art 15 *bis* and *ter* paras (2) and (3) respectively, the ICC will not be able to exercise jurisdiction over the crime of aggression until at least 30 states parties have ratified or accepted the amendments, and a decision is taken by two-thirds of states parties to activate the jurisdiction at any time after 1 January 2017.[266] On 14 December 2017, the ASP decided by consensus to 'activate the Court's jurisdiction over the crime of aggression as of 17 July 2018'.[267]

---

members are entitled to ignore such a decision and may refuse to carry it out'; Peters (n 137) para 188 (emphasis in the original).

[264] Schmalenbach (n 240) para 53.

[265] The amendments are contained in Resolution RC/Res.6 as adopted at the 13th plenary meeting of the Review Conference, on 11 June 2010, available at http://www.icc-cpi.int/iccdocs/asp_docs/Resolutions/RC-Res.6-ENG.pdf (accessed 3 January 2012) and related Annexes I (Amendments to the Rome Statute of the International Criminal Court on the Crime of Aggression), II (Amendments to the Elements of Crime) and III (Understandings regarding the amendments to the Rome Statute of the International Criminal Court on the Crime of Aggression). The process of implementing art 5 of the Rome Statute (which includes aggression among the crimes made subject to the Court's jurisdiction) started in 2002 within the Working Group on Aggression created by the Preparatory Commission for the ICC (see the Discussion Paper prepared by the Coordinator in July 2002, in UN Doc. PCNICC/2002/WGCA/RT.1/Rev.2., 11 July 2002). Following the establishment by the Assembly of States Parties, in September 2002, of the Special Working Group on the Crime of Aggression, the Group met from 2003 to 2009, and elaborated the 2009 Proposals that formed the basis for the discussions, and for the compromise reached, in Kampala (see Report of the Special Working Group on the Crime of Aggression, ICC-ASP/7/20/Add.1). For a comprehensive account of the Crime of Aggression and the ICC, see Mauro Politi, 'The ICC and the Crime of Aggression: A Dream that Came Through and the Reality Ahead' (2012) 10(1) *Journal of International Criminal Justice* 267.

[266] Article 15 *bis* (3).

[267] ASP, ICC-ASP/16/L.10 (14 December 2017).

Article 15 *ter* provides for the SC referral regarding the crime of aggression that the 'Court may exercise jurisdiction over the crime of aggression in accordance with article 13, paragraph (b), subject to the provisions of this article'.[268] Moreover, paragraph 2 of the Understandings[269] explicitly states that 'it is understood that the Court shall exercise jurisdiction over the crime . . . irrespective of whether the State concerned has accepted the Court's jurisdiction in this regard'.[270] It must be noted that this clarification is merely a restatement of the legal nature of such SC referral.[271]

Pursuant to art 25(4) Rome Statute, the responsibility of states under international law is not affected by the criminal responsibility of individuals. Furthermore, under art 15 *ter* (4), the amendment establishes that a determination of an act of aggression by an organ outside the Court shall be without prejudice to the Court's own findings under this Statute.[272] It therefore provides for 'fair and effective investigations and prosecution'[273] and this is further strengthened by the fact that there is no external filter envisaged, i.e.

---

[268] For a discussion of the definition of aggression adopted and its tension with the principle of legality, see M. Milanovic, 'Aggression and Legality: Custom in Kampala' (2012) 10(1) *Journal of International Criminal Justice* 165.

[269] Understandings regarding the amendments to the Rome Statute of the International Criminal Court on the Crime of Aggression, Annex III, RC/10/Add.1.

[270] Ibid. para 3.

[271] This applies also with regard to the crime of aggression. Concerning general international law, the *monetary gold* consent principle is considered not applicable in the case of an authoritative decision taken by the Security Council: see Dapo Akande, 'Prosecuting Aggression: The Consent Problem and the role of the Security Council' (Working Paper May 2010, Oxford Institute for Ethics, Law, and Armed Conflict), available at http://www.elac.ox.ac.uk/downloads/dapo%20akande%20working%20paper%20may%202010.pdf (accessed 12 May 2016); Carsten Stahn, 'The "End", the "Beginning of the End" or the "End of the Beginning"? Introducing Debates and Voices on the Definition of "Aggression"' (2010) 23(4) *Leiden Journal of International Law* 875, 878. The theoretical question of whether the SC could do so without such a provision in the Statute, must be answered in the negative: as an international court set up by a treaty outside the UN system, the SC has no such power; see further e.g. Corinna Contag, *Der Internationale Strafgerichtshof im System Kollektiver Sicherheit* (Saarbrücker Studien zum Internationalen Recht vol 41, Nomos 2009) 110.

[272] David Scheffer, 'The Complex Crime of Aggression under the Rome Statute' (2010) 23(4) *Leiden Journal of International Law* 897, 899. On the different interpretations of the legal consequences of a SC determination of aggression pursuant to art 39 in light of the supremacy provision of art 103 of the Charter, see Michael J. Glennon, 'The Blank-Prose Crime of Aggression' (2010) 35 *Yale Journal of International Law* 71, 104–105.

[273] Para 4 of the preamble and art 54(1)(b) of the Rome Statute.

no need for a prior determination by the GA of the UN (as a political filter) or the ICJ.[274]

Still, without the ability to politically influence the investigation, the SC will be rather reluctant to make use of the possibility to refer a situation involving the crime of aggression to the ICC.

5.7 CONCLUSION

The legal relationship between the SC and the ICC is complex. I have analyzed the most important legal scenarios that could arise in practice, ranging from the SC acting within its competences and in accordance with the Rome Statute; not in accordance with the Statute; and the SC acting ultra vires.

When acting intra vires and referring a situation in accordance with the Rome Statute, it is important to stress that this does not mean per se that the situation state is put in exactly the same legal position as a state party to the ICC. In this regard, two key legal issues are highly relevant for practice. First, as I have argued, the SC referral should not be presumed to be seeking to retroactively apply ICL that goes beyond customary (or for the situation state otherwise existing) law in force at the time of the commission of the alleged crime. Furthermore, without clear wording to the opposite effect, the SC referral should not be presumed as attempting to legislate prospectively ICL as included in the Rome Statute (and the Elements of Crimes) that goes beyond customary ICL at the time of the referral. The ICC in these situations must ensure only to apply existing ICL in the situation referred to it by the SC.

Second, I concluded that personal immunities of heads of state and other high-ranking government officials under international law are still applicable for the ICC and states in cases of SC referrals, where the referral has not removed such immunities under customary international law. While the ICC Chambers take the opposite view, the inconsistencies in the arguments provided for their conclusion that personal immunities do not apply in such cases seriously undermine the authority of their decisions. It will be interesting to see how this issue will play out in the future, as most states affected refuse to give effect to the decisions of the ICC.

As regards SC referrals that clearly deviate from the provisions of the Statute (i.e. an interpretation of the SC referral leads to an extension of the ICC's jurisdiction beyond the provisions of the Rome Statute), the ICC cannot act upon such referral. However, as a matter of principle, art 13(b) of the Rome Statute must be read as giving broad discretion as to the concrete parameters of the jurisdiction to be exercised by the ICC, and limitations to the ICC's

---

[274] Stahn (n 271) 877.

jurisdiction imposed by the referral should not be automatically considered incompatible with the Statute.

Next, the SC acting ultra vires has two important legal consequences for the ICC. First, considering such acts legally void, the ICC would have no legal basis to proceed with any exercise of jurisdiction. And second, the same follows from the perspective of the ICC, since its constituent instrument, art 13(b) of the Statute, expressly conditions the exercise of jurisdiction on action of the SC within the confines of Chapter VII powers imposed by the Charter.

On the question of judicial review of the SC referral, I concluded that the ICC may only conduct incidental review of the SC referral with a view to ascertaining whether the conditions set out in art 13(b) of the Statute have been met.

With respect to the now activated jurisdiction of the ICC over the crime of aggression, the prospect of the SC referring a situation involving the crime of aggression to the ICC seems to be rather slim, and it is likely that in any future referral, the SC will carve out the prosecution of such crimes from the referral.

6. The Security Council referrals in practice

This chapter analyzes the practice of SC referrals to the ICC. It will build on the theoretical outline established in the previous chapters to address the legal issues arising from the SC's practice in relation to referrals. It is not a comprehensive record of the practice of the SC and the ICC. Instead it seeks to address the legal questions that have arisen from such practice insofar as they relate to the particularities of SC referrals and its legal nature. This chapter is consequently confined to the legal issues arising directly out of the SC referrals and will therefore not address more general questions relating to ICL or the internal law of the ICC.[1]

[1] The existing literature on these questions is extensive: Robert Frau, 'Das Völkerstrafrecht in der jüngsten Praxis des VN-Sicherheitsrates' (2011) 10 *Zeitschrift für Internationale Strafrechtsdogmatik* 784; Robert Frau, 'Die Überweisung der Lage in Libyen an den Internationalen Strafgerichtshof durch den Sicherheitsrat der Vereinten Nationen – zugleich ein Beitrag zur Völkerstrafrechtspraxis des Sicherheitsrates' (2011) 49(3) *Archiv des Völkerrechts* 276; Priscilla Hayner, 'Libya: The ICC Enters During War' [2013] ECFR background paper 1; Konstantinos D. Magliveras and Gino J. Naldi, 'The International Criminal Court's Involvement with Africa: Evaluation of a Fractious Relationship' (2013) 82 *Nordic Journal of International Law* 417; Hovhannes Nikoghosyan, 'Government Failure, Atrocity Crimes and the Role of the International Criminal Court: Why not Syria, but Libya' (2015) 19(8) *The International Journal of Human Rights* 1240; Kerstin Odendahl, 'Regimewechsel und Interventionsverbot: die Elfenbeinküste und Libyen als Fallstudien' (2012) 50 *Archiv des Völkerrechts* 318; Carsten Stahn, 'Libya, the International Criminal Court and Complementarity: A Test for "Shared Responsibility"' (2012) 10(2) *Journal of International Criminal Justice* 325; Leslie Vinjamuri, 'The ICC and the Politics of Peace and Justice' in Carsten Stahn (ed), *The Law and Practice of the International Criminal Court* (Oxford University Press 2015); Dapo Akande, Max Du Plessis and Charles C. Jalloh, 'Assessing the African Union Concerns about Article 16 of the Rome Statute of the International Criminal Court' (2011) 4(1) *African Journal of Legal Studies* 5; L. R. Atkinson, 'Knights of the Court: The State Coalition Behind the International Criminal Court' (2011) 7 *Journal of International Law & International Relations* 66; Nerina Boschiero, 'The ICC Judicial Finding on Non-cooperation Against the DRC and No Immunity for Al-Bashir Based on UNSC Resolution 1593' (2015) 13(3) *Journal of International Criminal Justice* 625; Luigi Condorelli and Annalisa Ciampi, 'Comments on the Security Council Referral of the Situation in Darfur to the ICC' (2005) 3(3) *Journal of International Criminal Justice* 590; John R. Crook, 'United States Abstains on Security

To date, there have been only two SC referrals involving non-party states – the SC referral of the situation in Darfur, Sudan in 2005 and that of Libya in 2011.[2] Neither referral is entirely in accordance with the Rome Statute. Both referrals raised legal issues that can be traced back to the so-called 'peacekeeping exemptions', in which the SC sought to limit the ICC's jurisdiction regarding non-party states. Furthermore, both referrals take the view that the ICC and not the UN must bear the costs of these referrals. And as mentioned above, legal issues surround the applicability of heads of state immunity regarding the incumbent President of Sudan, Omar Al-Bashir, against whom two arrest warrants were issued.

Addressing the legal issues arising out of this practice, this study proceeds as follows. First, the so-called 'peacekeeping exemptions' included in SC Res 1422, 1487 and 1497 will be analyzed. It will be demonstrated that the wording of the exemption inspired the language adopted in the SC referrals for both Darfur and Libya. Second and third, the necessary historical background is provided regarding the situation concerning Darfur and Libya, before looking at the proposed draft resolution as regards the situation in Syria. Then, Chapter

---

Council Resolution Authorizing Referral of Darfur Atrocities to International Criminal Court' (2005) 99(3) *American Journal of International Law* 691; Robert Cryer, 'Sudan, Resolution 1593, and International Criminal Justice' (2006) 19(01) *Leiden Journal of International Law* 195; Max Du Plessis and Christopher Gevers, 'Darfur goes to the International Criminal Court (perhaps)' (2005) 14(2) *African Security Review* 23; Fred Grünfeld and Wessel N. Vermeulen, *Failure to Prevent Gross Human Rights Violations in Darfur: Warnings to and Responses by International Decision Makers (2003–2005)* (International Criminal Law Series, BRILL 2014); Matthew Happold, 'II. Darfur, the Security Council, and the International Criminal Court' (2006) 55(1) *International & Comparative Law Quarterly* 226; Corrina Heyder, 'The U.N. Security Council's Referral of the Crimes in Darfur to the International Criminal Court in Light of U.S. Opposition to the Court: Implications for the International Criminal Court's Functions and Status' (2006) 24 *Berkeley Journal of International Law* 650; Matthias Neuner, 'The Darfur Referral of the Security Council and the Scope of the Jurisdiction of the International Criminal Court' (2005) 8 *Yearbook of International Humanitarian Law* 320; Lutz Oette, 'Peace and Justice, or Neither?: The Repercussions of the Al-Bashir Case for International Criminal Justice in Africa and Beyond' (2010) 8(2) *Journal of International Criminal Justice* 345; Göran Sluiter, 'Obtaining Cooperation from Sudan – Where is the Law?' (2008) 6 *Journal of International Criminal Justice* 871; Manisuli Ssenyonjo, 'The International Criminal Court and the Warrant of Arrest for Sudan's President Al-Bashir: A Crucial Step Towards Challenging Impunity or a Political Decision?' (2009) 78 *Nordic Journal of International Law* 397; Nigel White and Robert Cryer, 'The ICC and the Security Council: An Uncomfortable Relationship' in Jose Doria, Hans-Peter Gasser and Cherif M. Bassiouni (eds), *The Legal Regime of the International Criminal Court: Essays in Honour of Professor Igor Blishchenko* (Martinus Nijhoff Publishers 2009).

[2] S/RES/1593 (2005) and S/RES/1970 (2011).

7 will analyze the key legal issues common to both referrals relating to the jurisdictional exemption, the financing of the referral and the obligations of non-party states.

6.1 THE PEACEKEEPING EXEMPTIONS: UN SC RES 1422, 1487 AND 1497

With the entry into force of the Rome Statute of the ICC on 1 July 2002, the US was concerned that its personnel could be subject to 'unwarranted, politically motivated prosecutions' by the ICC.[3] As a result, the US vetoed a SC resolution that would have extended a UN peacekeeping mission in Bosnia-Herzegovina (UNMIBH) on 30 June 2002, due to a lack of SC agreement to include in it the exemption from ICC jurisdiction.[4] The US threatened to veto further peacekeeping missions, should the sought-for exemption not be included in their mandates.[5]

Many states opposed the US effort as an attempt to amend the ICC Statute in excess of the SC's authority. Then Secretary-General Kofi Annan himself expressed concern, sending a letter to US Secretary of State Colin Powell. In this letter, the Secretary-General stated that the US proposal was a dangerous and irresponsible threat to peacekeeping, and would violate the Charter and international treaty law.[6] In an open meeting convened by the SC, nearly all states representatives opposed the US position, but many recognized that compromise could preserve essential peacekeeping operations.[7] The compromise proposed by the US was to defer proceedings against peacekeepers for one year. At the end of that period, if the resolution were not renewed, the Prosecutor could proceed. A variation of this draft was approved by the

---

[3] Bryan MacPherson, 'Authority of the Security Council to Exempt Peacekeepers from international Criminal Court Proceedings', *ASIL Insights* (11 July 2002), available at https://www.asil.org/insights/volume/7/issue/9/authority-security-council-exempt-peacekeepers-international-criminal (accessed 19 June 2018).

[4] Claudia Fritsche, 'Security Council Resolution 1422: Peacekeeping and the International Criminal Court' in Jochen A. Frowein (ed), *Verhandeln für den Frieden: Negotiating for Peace: Liber Amicorum Tono Eitel* (Beiträge zum ausländischen öffentlichen Recht und Völkerrecht vol 162, Springer 2003) 107.

[5] Ibid.

[6] UN Secretary-General Kofi Annan, Letter to Secretary of State Colin Powell (3 July 2002), available at http://www.amicc.org/docs/SG_to_SS.pdf (accessed 11 July 2016).

[7] U.N. SCOR, 4568 mtg., UN Doc S/PV.4568 (2002), available at http://www.un.org/Docs/pv4568e.pdf and http://www.un.org/Docs/pv4568e1.pdf (accessed 11 July 2016). The number of states represented was greater than the number of speakers as the ambassador from Denmark spoke on behalf of the European Union and Costa Rica on behalf of the Rio Group.

SC unanimously,[8] acting under Chapter VII of the UN Charter, in Res 1422 (2002).[9] Right after the passage of Res 1422, the US voted for the renewal of the peacekeeping mission in Bosnia and Herzegovina, and indicated its willingness to continue further peacekeeping missions.[10]

In the operative part of Res 1422, the SC:

> 1. *Requests*, consistent with the provisions of Article 16 of the Rome Statute, that the ICC, if a case arises involving current or former officials or personnel from a contributing State not a Party to the Rome Statute over acts or omissions relating to a United Nations established or authorized operation, shall for a twelve-month period starting 1 July 2002 not commence or proceed with investigation or prosecution of any such case, unless the Security Council decides otherwise;
> 2. *Expresses* the intention to renew the request in paragraph 1 under the same conditions each 1 July for further 12-month periods for as long as may be necessary;
> 3. *Decides* that Member States shall take no action inconsistent with paragraph 1 and with their international obligations.

This wording was controversial, raising serious questions concerning the scope of the SC's powers and whether it would bind the ICC in its exercise of jurisdiction, similar to those addressed in this study.[11] It sought to bar the ICC from exercising jurisdiction in the prescribed situation. Such a 'deferral' by the SC is in theory governed by Article 16 of the Rome Statute, which states:

> No investigation or prosecution may be commenced or proceeded with under this Statute for a period of 12 months after the Security Council, in a resolution adopted

---

[8] UNSC Verbatim Record (12 July 2002) UN Doc S/PV.4572.

[9] S/RES/1422 (2002).

[10] Fritsche (n 4) 107–108.

[11] For a comprehensive analysis see ibid.; Mohamed El Zeidy, 'The United States Dropped the Atomic Bomb of Article 16 of the ICC Statute: Security Council Power of Deferrals and Resolution 1422' (2002) 35 *Vanderbilt Journal of Transnational Law* 1503; Sebastian Heselhaus, 'Resolution 1422 (2002) des Sicherheitsrates zur Begrenzung der Tätigkeit des Internationalen Strafgerichtshof' (2002) 62 *Zeitschrift für ausländisches öffentliches Recht und Völkerrecht*; Carsten Stahn, 'The Ambiguities of Security Council Resolution 1422 (2002)' (2003) 14 *European Journal of International Law* 85; Andreas Zimmermann, '"Acting under Chapter VII (…)" – Resolution 1422 and Possible Limits of the Powers of the Security Council' in Frowein (n 4); Michael E. Kurth, *Das Verhältnis des Internationalen Strafgerichtshofes zum UN-Sicherheitsrat: Unter besonderer Berücksichtigung von Sicherheitsratsresolution 1422 (2002)* (Nomos 2006); William Schabas, 'United States Hostility to the International Criminal Court: It's All About the Security Council' (2004) 15 *European Journal of International Law* 701.

> under Chapter VII of the Charter of the United Nations, has requested the Court to that effect; that request may be renewed by the Council under the same conditions.

A year later, this 'deferral' was renewed with a vote in the SC of 12 in favour, none against and 3 abstentions in SC Res 1487 (2003).[12] During the meeting of the SC, the Secretary-General of the UN again voiced his concern for such request,[13] along with most representatives of states.[14] US concerns about the difficulty of renewing this resolution in 2003 led it to conclude bilateral immunity agreements pursuant to art 98 of the Rome Statute to prevent the extradition of US nationals to the Court. In 2004, the US announced its decision not to renew Res 1487. Among the reasons for doing so was the increasing hostility towards the text that year in light of the revelations of prisoner abuse in Iraq, with numerous countries,[15] including China, saying that they would abstain.[16] As a result, the resolution was not renewed.

In SC Res 1497 (2003),[17] establishing a Multinational Force in Liberia to support the implementation of the 17 June 2003 ceasefire agreement, the predecessor of the jurisdictional exemption included in SC referrals concerning Darfur and Libya years later is found. In August 2003, the US threatened to veto this SC resolution unless it secured an exemption from the ICC for personnel from non-party states,[18] which was granted. In the relevant parts, the SC resolution provides:

> *Determining* that the situation in Liberia constitutes a threat to international peace and security, to stability in the West Africa subregion, and to the peace process for Liberia,
> Acting under Chapter VII of the Charter of the United Nations
> 1. *Authorizes* Member States to establish a Multinational Force in Liberia to support the implementation of the 17 June 2003 ceasefire agreement . . .

---

12 UNSC Verbatim Record (12 June 2003) UN Doc S/PV.4772, 22.

13 Ibid. 2–3.

14 Ibid.

15 Also Secretary-General Kofi Annan stated that 'For the past two years, I have spoken quite strongly against the exemption, and I think it would be unfortunate for one to press for such an exemption, given the prisoner abuse in Iraq', available at http://www.un.org/apps/news/story.asp?NewsID=11081&Cr=ICC&Cr1= (accessed 11 March 2018).

16 US Deputy Ambassador to the UN James B. Cunningham, 'Remarks on the ICC at the Security Council Stakeout' (22 June 2004), available at http://www.amicc.org/docs/CunninghamJune22_04.pdf (accessed 11 May 2016).

17 UNSC Res 1497 (1 August 2003) UN Doc S/RES/1497.

18 Department of State Spokesman Richard Boucher, 'Daily Press Briefing' (31 July 2003), available at http://www.amicc.org/docs/Boucher7_31_03.pdf (accessed 11 May 2016).

5. *Authorizes* the Member States participating in the Multinational Force in Liberia to take all necessary measures to fulfil its mandate . . .
7. *Decides* that current or former officials or personnel from a contributing State, which is not a party to the Rome Statute of the International Criminal Court, shall be subject to the exclusive jurisdiction of that contributing State for all alleged acts or omissions arising out of or related to the Multinational Force or United Nations stabilization force in Liberia, unless such exclusive jurisdiction has been expressly waived by that contributing State.

This resolution was similarly approved by 12 affirmative votes and 3 abstentions (Mexico, Germany, France). In his statement, the Mexican representative sought 'to make it clear that the one and only reason for our abstention is our disagreement with the content of paragraph 7 of the draft resolution'.[19]

Indeed, paragraph 7 goes beyond the previous 'peacekeeping exemptions' by not merely limiting the ICC's jurisdiction but also, as pointed out by the German representative in the SC, by limiting 'the national jurisdiction of third countries with respect to crimes committed by members of the multinational force or a United Nations stabilization force if that member is the national of a State not party to the Rome Statute of the ICC'.[20] With similar concerns, France stated that 'the scope of the jurisdictional immunity thus created is incompatible with the provisions of the Rome Statute of the International Criminal Court, the norms of French law or the principles of international law'.[21] This new resolution conferred on states that are not parties to the Rome Statute the exclusive jurisdiction over crimes committed by their troops serving under a multinational force or UN stabilization force in Liberia, except where such jurisdiction has been explicitly waived.[22] As a result, operative paragraph 7 would prohibit the use of jurisdiction based on the passive personality principle or universal jurisdiction.[23] This exclusive jurisdiction is

---

19 UNSC Verbatim Record (1 August 2003) UN Doc S/PV.4803, 2.

20 Ibid. 4.

21 Ibid. 7.

22 Ademola Abass, 'The Competence of the Security Council to Terminate the Jurisdiction of the International Criminal Court' (2005) 40 *Texas International Law Journal* 263, 263–64. Edith M. Lederer, 'U.S. Drops U.N. Bid for War Crime Shield' (Press Release, 23 June 2004), available at http://freerepublic.com/focus/f-news/1159509/posts (accessed 12 May 2016); Amnesty International, 'U.S. Threats to the International Criminal Court', available at http://web.amnesty.org/pages/icc-US_threats-eng (accessed 22 April 2014). UNSC Res 1487 (2003) UN Doc S/RES/1487 requesting that the ICC not commence or proceed with the investigation or prosecution of any case arising from UN operations against a citizen of a non-ICC state.

23 Cryer (n 1) 209.

> quite plainly contrary to treaty provisions binding upon virtually all UN Member States, including the US. It is well known that the four Geneva Conventions oblige a state party 'to search for persons alleged to have committed, or to have ordered to be committed, such grave breaches, and [to] bring such persons, regardless of their nationality, before its own courts'.[24]

Similar provisions are contained in the Convention Against Torture.[25]

On the basis of these facts it has been suggested that this resolution was arguably ultra vires.[26] For instance, Salvatore Zappala argues that

> the threat to peace which constitutes the underpinning of Chapter VII powers and of resolution 1497 (2003) does not cover or extend to operative paragraph 7. Absent such a link, the serious limitation imposed on the sovereignty of all member States (that which asserts the exclusive jurisdiction of the sending state) might be held to lack any basis under Chapter VII.[27]

Given that the SC enjoys broad discretionary powers under Chapter VII, as established above, this argument is not very strong.[28] The legal consequences of such limited jurisdiction will be discussed below in the context of the SC referrals concerning Darfur and Libya.

---

[24] Sharon A. Williams and William Schabas, 'Article 13' in Otto Triffterer and Kai Ambos (eds), *Commentary on the Rome Statute of the International Criminal Court: Observers' Notes, Article by Article* (2nd edn C.H. Beck; Hart; Nomos 2008) 571. Convention for the Amelioration of the Condition of the Wounded and Sick in Armed Forces in the Field, 75 UNTS 31 (1949), art 49; Convention for the Amelioration of the Condition of Wounded, Sick and Shipwrecked Members of Armed Forces at Sea, 75 UNTS 85 (1950), art 50; Convention Relative to the Treatment of Prisoners of War, 75 UNTS 135 (1950), art 129; Convention Relative to the Protection of Civilian Persons in Time of War, 75 UNTS 287 (1950), art 146.

[25] It is another question, however, whether the SC acting under Chapter VII is bound by these treaty norms. For an overview of the scholarly discussion in this regard see Gordon Joy, 'The Sword of Damocles: Revisiting the Question of Whether the United Nations Security Council is Bound by International Law' (2012) 12(9) *Chicago Journal of International Law* 605, 626–33.

[26] Salvatore Zappala, 'Are Some Peacekeepers Better Than Others? UN Security Council Resolution 1497 (2003) and the ICC' (2003) 1 *Journal of International Criminal Justice* 671. A majority of the experts of the 'Committee on the International Criminal Court' of the International Law Associate agrees with this assessment, for an overview of the discussion see Winfried Bausback and Tobias H. Irmseher, 'Bericht von der 71. Konferenz der International Law Association in Berlin' (2004) 42 *Archiv des Völkerrechts* 467, 471–73.

[27] Zappala (n 26) 675.

[28] See above Chapter VII powers of the SC. Sharing this view, Stahn (n 11) 98.

While there have been only two referrals (Darfur and Libya) so far, it is important for the present analysis to review and revisit the general practice of the SC vis-à-vis the ICC.

6.2 UN SC RES 1593

6.2.1 Factual Background

At least 300,000 people[29] were killed in a civil war in Sudan that experts believe led to one of the greatest humanitarian disasters in the world.[30] Specifically, a massive campaign of ethnic violence in Sudan's western region, Darfur, has claimed more than 70,000 civilian victims and uprooted an additional estimated 1.8 million. The roots of the violence are complex and remain partly unclear. The primary perpetrators of the killings and expulsions are government-backed 'Arab' militias, while the victims are mainly members of black 'African' tribes.[31]

In early September 2004, after reviewing the results of a government-sponsored investigation of the crimes committed in Darfur, US Secretary of State Colin Powell described the crimes as genocide, and President George W. Bush used this term in a speech to the UN several weeks later.[32] This marked the first time that senior US government officials had ever conclusively applied the term to a current crisis and invoked the Genocide Convention.[33] Subsequently, the UN Secretary-General established a Commission of Inquiry to investigate the crimes committed in Darfur.[34] In January 2005, this Commission reported to the SC that, although it could not conclude that Sudanese government authorities had pursued a genocidal policy, other equally serious war

---

[29] NZZ, 'Haftbefehl gegen Sudans Staatschef Bashir in Khartoum gelandet' (15 June 2015), available at http://www.nzz.ch/international/al-bashir-droht-die-festnahme-in-suedafrika-1.18562523 (accessed 12 May 2016).

[30] Scott Straus, 'Darfur and the Genocide Debate' (2005) 84 *Foreign Affairs*, 123; International Commission for Inquiry on Darfur, Report of the International Commission for Inquiry on Darfur to the United Nations Secretary-General, para 50, UN Doc S/2005/60 (25 January 2005).

[31] See further Sarah M. H. Nouwen, *Complementarity in the Line of Fire: The Catalysing Effect of the International Criminal Court in Uganda and Sudan* (Cambridge studies in law and society, Cambridge University Press 2013) 262; Heyder (n 1) 651. See further for a detailed analysis of the situation of Darfur and the failure to prevent international crimes, see Grünfeld and Vermeulen (n 1). For a brief synopsis of the history and conflicts in Darfur, see Cryer (n 1) 196–98.

[32] Straus (n 30) 123.

[33] Ibid.

[34] SC Res 1564 UN Doc S/RES/1564 (18 September 2004) para 12.

crimes and crimes against humanity had been clearly committed in Darfur.[35] Consequently, the Commission recommended that the SC immediately refer jurisdiction over the crimes to the ICC,[36] citing at least six major merits such an ICC involvement would have.[37]

On 31 March 2005 the SC adopted Res 1593 referring the situation concerning Darfur to the ICC after failed attempts of the US government to gather support for a UN–AU hybrid court.[38] The US proposal remains confidential. It is clear, however, that the US did not want to be confronted with a decision on whether to veto an ICC resolution in the SC.[39]

The US did, however, secure a jurisdictional exemption similar to the one referred to in SC Res 1497 (2003). The US abstained on Res 1593, and the resolution passed 11–0–4 (Algeria, Brazil and China also abstaining) that referred the situation in Darfur to the ICC. The US administration reportedly agreed to abstain after Britain brokered a late-hour compromise adding language to the resolution which addressed US concerns about the ICC's jurisdiction over situations in non-party states.[40] This language was promoted by the US in line with its domestic legislation, which precludes contributions to UN peace operations unless the SC resolution establishing or authorizing the operation exempts US soldiers from ICC jurisdiction.[41]

Since the referral, the SC has done little to ensure Sudanese authorities cooperate with the ICC.[42]

---

35 Report of the International Commission of Inquiry (n 30) 1.

36 Ibid. para 569. Heyder (n 1) 651–52.

37 Report of the International Commission of Inquiry on Darfur to the United Nations Secretary-General, Pursuant to Security Council Resolution 1564 of 18 September 2004, Geneva, 25 January 2005, paras 571–72, 586.

38 United States Department of State, 'Gaining African Support for Sudan Action in the UNSC' (Diplomatic Cable from Secretary of State to US Embassies in Africa, 31 January 2005); See also Cryer (n 1) 201; Neuner (n 1) 322–23.

39 United States Department of State, *S/WCI Input for Press Guidance: Sudan: Accountability for War Crimes* (2005) 2.

40 Pressure mounted against the US when France introduced a resolution that would have led the US to either accept ICC jurisdiction it opposes or to exercise a politically damaging veto, see Associated Press, 'France Offers U.S. a Dilemma on Sudan' *Washington Post* (24 March 2005) A16, available at http://www.washingtonpost.com/wp-dyn/articles/A61354-2005Mar23.html (accessed 13 March 2018); Crook (n 1) 691.

41 US American Service Members Protection Act of 2002 HR 4775 Public Law 107–206, Title II (2 August 2002), Sec 2005.

42 Jared Genser, 'The United Nations Security Council's Implementation of the Right to Protect: A Review of Past Interventions and Recommendations for Improvement' (2018) 18(2) *Chicago Journal of International Law* 420–501, 461–62.

6.2.2 The SC Referral

Against this backdrop of SC resolutions attempting to shield US personnel from ICC jurisdiction, the SC, in its first ever referral, referred the situation in Darfur, Sudan to the ICC in 2005, through SC Res 1593.[43] Sudan is not a party to the Rome Statute.[44] The first SC referral to the ICC reads in the relevant parts:

> *The Security Council* . . .
> *Determining* that the situation in Sudan continues to constitute a threat to international peace and security.
> *Acting* under Chapter VII of the Charter of the United Nations,
> 1. *Decides* to refer the situation in Darfur since 1 July 2002 to the Prosecutor of the International Criminal Court;
> 2. *Decides* that the Government of Sudan and all other parties to the conflict in Darfur shall cooperate fully with and provide any necessary assistance to the Court and the Prosecutor pursuant to this resolution and, while recognizing that States not party to the Rome Statute have no obligation under the Statute, urges all States and concerned regional and other international organizations to cooperate fully . . .
> 6. *Decides* that nationals, current or former officials or personnel from a contributing State outside Sudan which is not a party to the Rome Statute of the International Criminal Court shall be subject to the exclusive jurisdiction of that contributing State for all alleged acts or omissions arising out of or related to operations in Sudan established or authorized by the Council or the African Union, unless such exclusive jurisdiction has been expressly waived by that contributing State;
> 7. *Recognizes* that none of the expenses incurred in connection with the referral, including expenses related to investigations or prosecutions in connection with that referral, shall be borne by the United Nations and that such costs shall be borne by the parties to the Rome Statute and those States that wish to contribute voluntarily;

The first SC referral to the ICC contains several specifications and elements not foreseen by the drafters concerning art 13(b), obligations of parties to the conflict and non-party states, and most controversially the jurisdictional exemption for certain categories of nationals and a statement on the bearing

43 S/RES/1593 (2005) concerning the situation in Darfur.

44 Sudan signed the Rome Statute on 8 September 2000 but did not ratify it. Later, in a communication received on 26 August 2008, the Government of Sudan informed the UN Secretary-General of the following: 'Sudan does not intend to become a party to the Rome Statute. Accordingly, Sudan has no legal obligation arising from its signature on 8 September 2000.' UN treaty collection page, available at http://treaties.un.org/Pages/ViewDetails.aspx?src=TREATY&mtdsg_no=XVIII-10&chapter=18&lang=en#8 (accessed 12 March 2018).

of the costs of the referral. Notwithstanding these issues that will be addressed below, the first referral was generally received with enthusiasm.[45]

First, Res 1593 does not contain a specific mention of art 13(b) of the Rome Statute but simply 'decides to refer the situation in Darfur since 1 July 2002 to the Prosecutor of the International Criminal Court',[46] after determining that the situation in Sudan continues to constitute a threat to international peace and security, and acting under Chapter VII of the UN Charter. The requirement in the Statute to refer a situation 'acting under Chapter VII' is thus satisfied.[47] As established above, an express mention of art 13(b) is not legally required.[48] The wording to refer the situation to the Prosecutor of the ICC must be interpreted in light of the following operative paragraph 2 in which the SC decides that the Government of Sudan and all other parties to the conflict in Darfur shall cooperate fully with and provide any necessary assistance to the Court and the Prosecutor pursuant to this resolution. Taken together, this cannot be understood as only conferring jurisdiction to the Prosecutor but also to the Chambers and the other organs of the ICC.

Next, the SC clearly circumscribes the jurisdictional authority *ratione loci* (the region of Darfur), *ratione personae* (Government of Sudan and all other parties to the conflict, while recognizing that states not party to the Rome

[45] UN Press Release SG/SM/9797/AFR/1132, 'Secretary-General Welcomes Adoption of Security Council Resolution Referring Situation in Darfur, Sudan, to International Criminal Court Prosecutor'. See also the press releases from the Darfur Consortium, 'A New Hope for Justice in Sudan'; Parliamentarians for Global Action, 'Darfur: International Parliamentary Group Welcomes United Nations Security Council Resolution 1593 and Urges All States to Fully Cooperate with the International Criminal Court'; Arab Coalition for the International Criminal Court, 'Arab Coalition for the International Criminal Court Welcomes Security Council Resolution 1593 on Crimes Committed in Darfur'; International Center for Transitional Justice, 'Security Council Referral to ICC Offers Hope for Darfur Victims'; Human Rights First, 'UN Takes Steps to End Human Rights Crisis in Darfur, But Immediate Action Is Required: US Deserves Credit for Leadership Role on Darfur'; Amnesty International, 'Sudan: Historic Referral to ICC Tarnished by Exemptions'; Human Rights Watch, 'UN Security Council Refers Darfur to the ICC'; Citizens for Global Solutions, 'US Puts Principles Over Politics'. All available at http://www.iccnow.org (accessed 24 March 2018).

[46] Operative paragraph 1 of Res 1593.

[47] Luca Schicho, 'The Security Council and the International Criminal Court: An Awkward Partnership?' (2008) 13 *Austrian Review of International and European Law* 115, 129–31.

[48] See also Frau, 'Die Überweisung der Lage in Libyen an den Internationalen Strafgerichtshof durch den Sicherheitsrat der Vereinten Nationen – zugleich ein Beitrag zur Völkerstrafrechtspraxis des Sicherheitsrates' (n 1) 281; Schicho (n 47) 129.

Statute have no obligation under the Statute)[49] and *ratione temporis* (since 1 July 2002) without making an express determination as regards the material scope of the jurisdiction. As a preliminary result, SC Res 1593 is legally conferring jurisdictional authority over the situation in Darfur to the ICC in accordance with the Rome Statute.[50]

The most controversial aspect of the referral is the jurisdictional exemption for certain categories of nationals of states not party to the ICC. The SC referral included in its operative part §6 which exempts jurisdiction of the court for certain categories of nationals of non-party states to the Rome Statute and puts them under the exclusive jurisdiction of their state of nationality; it is almost identically worded to §7 of SC Res 1497 (2003).[51] As pointed out, it was the US which pushed for such jurisdictional safeguards.[52] With this alleged deviation from the provisions of the Rome Statute, such 'exclusive jurisdiction' resulted in heavy criticism following the adoption of Res 1593 (2005) expressed by state representatives[53] and commentators[54] alike, questioning its legality under international law.[55] Given the fact that exactly the same exemption was included in the second SC referral concerning Libya, this study will address this jointly in the following sections, along with the issue regarding the financing of the referral. Suffice it to note that the practical challenge in this case has been the non-cooperation of the Government of Sudan.

---

49 Jennifer Trahan, 'The Relationship Between the International Criminal Court and the U.N. Security Council: Parameters and Best Practices' (2013) 24(4) *Criminal Law Forum* 417, 449. The phrase 'urges all States and concerned regional and other international organizations to cooperate fully' (with the ICC) cannot be read as legally binding. It is accepted that only decisions of the SC are legally binding, and the use of the word 'urges' must be interpreted as a mere recommendation and not as a legal obligation in light of art 25 of the UN Charter and the practice of the SC. Sharing this view, Dapo Akande, 'The Legal Nature of Security Council Referrals to the ICC and its Impact on Al-Bashir's Immunities' (2009) 7(2) *Journal of International Criminal Justice* 333, 344.

50 See Chapter 5.1.

51 These are 'current or former officials or personnel from a contributing State outside Sudan which is not a party to the Rome Statute of the International Criminal Court . . . for all alleged acts or omissions arising out of or related to operations in Sudan established or authorized by the Council or the African Union'. On this see also Deborah R. Verduzco, 'The Relationship between the ICC and the United Nations Security Council' in Carsten Stahn (ed), *The Law and Practice of the International Criminal Court* (n 1) 36–38.

52 Trahan (n 49) 454.

53 See UNSC Verbatim Record (31 March 2005) UN Doc S/PV.5158, especially statements of Brazil, Benin, Tanzania, Greece, France, Argentina, Denmark.

54 See e.g. Condorelli and Ciampi (n 1); Cryer (n 1) 195; Happold (n 1).

55 For a comprehensive account of the main issues raised, see e.g. Trahan (n 49).

In case that the state concerned is failing to cooperate with the Court, the RA provides in art 17:

> Where a situation is referred by the Security Council and the Court makes a finding, pursuant to article 87(5)(b) or 87(7), that a State has failed to cooperate with the Court, the Court is required by the Negotiated Relationship Agreement to inform the United Nations Security Council. Correspondingly, the Security Council is to inform the Court through the Registrar of any action taken by it under the circumstances.

In fact, the Government of Sudan failed to cooperate with the Court. On 9 March 2015, the Pre-Trial Chamber II in its unanimous decision on the Prosecutor's Request for a Finding of Non-Compliance against the Republic of Sudan, observed:

> When the SC, acting under Chapter VII of the UN Charter, refers the situation in Darfur, Sudan to the Court . . . it must be expected that the Council would follow-up by way of taking such measures which are considered appropriate, if there is an apparent failure on the part of Sudan to cooperate in fulfilling the Court's mandate as entrusted to it by the Council. Otherwise, if there is no follow up action on the part of the SC, any referral by the Council to the ICC under Chapter VII of the UN Charter would never achieve its ultimate goal, namely, to put an end to impunity . . . Since Sudan has failed to cooperate with the Court with regard to the arrest and surrender of Omar Al-Bashir . . . the Court cannot but refer the matter to the SC for the Council to take appropriate measures.

In fact, many of the detractors of the ICC and of the referral of the situation in Darfur fall within the scope of the jurisdictional exemption. Both the African Union Mission in Sudan (AMIS) and in Darfur (UNAMID) drew mainly on nationals of non-party states, including China, Egypt, Iran, Rwanda, the Russian Federation and Zimbabwe.[56]

---

[56] Contributors to AMIS (2004–07) included mainly Rwanda, a state not party, and Nigeria. Eventually, Egypt and India, as well other states parties, contributed to AMIS. UNAMID has military personnel from the following states not parties to the Rome Statute: Cameroon, China, Egypt, Ethiopia, Indonesia, Iran, Kyrgyzstan, Malaysia, Nepal, Pakistan, Palau, Rwanda, Thailand, Togo, Turkey, Yemen and Zimbabwe. See UNAMID, 'UN Mission's Contributions by Country' (30 September 2013), available at www.un.org/en/peacekeeping/missions/unamid/facts.shtml (accessed 12 June 2015). See also Verduzco (n 51) 36–38.

6.3 UN SC RES 1970

6.3.1 Factual Background

In 1969, Colonel Muammar Gaddafi gained power in a military coup against King Idris and established an authoritarian regime.[57] In early 2011, part of the so-called Arab Spring, demonstrations took place in the city of Benghazi and spread to other cities throughout Libya.[58] In response, the Gaddafi regime brutally cracked down on civilians and rebel forces,[59] ordering the air force to bomb Benghazi on 22 February.[60] On 26 February 2011, the SC adopted Res 1970 (2011), referring the situation in Libya to the ICC along with an arms embargo, travel bans and asset freezes against the government's senior leadership, explicitly citing their involvement and complicity in 'ordering, controlling, or otherwise directing, the commission of serious human rights abuses'.[61] This decision was influenced by a letter sent from the Libyan Ambassador to the UN, who expressed support for the SC referral,[62] and a resolution issued by the Human Rights Council calling on Libya to 'meet its responsibility to protect its population', noting that the government's violations potentially amounted to crimes against humanity.[63] Additionally, support for the referral came from the Arab League, the AU, and the Secretary-General of the Organization of the Islamic Conference.[64]

---

[57] Odendahl (n 1) 321.

[58] Philippe Kirsch and Mohamed S. Helal, 'Libya' in Jared Genser and Bruno S. Ugarte (eds), *The United Nations Security Council in the Age of Human Rights* (Cambridge University Press 2014) 396.

[59] For a chronology of the events see Jared Genser and Bruno S. Ugarte, ibid. 397–406. For a comprehensive analysis of the historical background of the conflict, see Cherif M. Bassiouni, *Libya from Repression to Revolution: A Record of Armed Conflict and International Law Violations, 2011–2013* (International criminal law series, Martinus Nijhoff Publishers 2013).

[60] Associated Press, 'Libya Air Force Pilots Refuse Orders to Bomb Opposition-held Benghazi' (23 February 2011, Haaretz.com), available at https://www.haaretz.com/1.5126971 (accessed 7 March 2018).

[61] Res 1970 (2011) para 22(a).

[62] Letter to the President of the UNSC, 26 February 2011, from Abdurrahman M. Shalgham, Permanent Representative of Libya to the United Nations. See also Mr. Dabbashi, the Libyan Ambassador's statement to the UN after adoption of the resolution, UNSC Verbatim Record (26 February 2011) UN Doc S/PV.6491, 7.

[63] Human Rights Council Res. S-15/2, Situation of Human Rights in the Libyan Arab Jamahiriya, UN Doc. A/HRC/S-15/2 (25 February 2011) paras 1–2.

[64] Hayner (n 1) 2; Genser (n 42) 441.

As mentioned above, the referral concerning Darfur had resulted in much criticism.[65] And even though identically worded in this respect, almost no criticism was voiced in the aftermath of Res 1970 (2011).[66] Instead, it was praised as 'a historic moment in accountability for crimes under international law'.[67] However, this initial enthusiasm faded following the NATO intervention based on Res 1973 (2011)[68] which authorized states 'to take all necessary measures, notwithstanding paragraph 9 of Resolution 1970 (2011), to protect civilians and civilian populated areas under threat of attack in the Libyan Arab Jamahiriya, including Benghazi, while excluding a foreign occupation force of any form on any part of Libyan territory'.[69] NATO's wide interpretation of this enforcement mandate was criticized by SC members such as Russia, China, India, Brazil and South Africa,[70] raising allegations of crimes relating to abuses by the opposition forces and NATO,[71] and questions about the ICC's involvement.[72]

6.3.2 The SC Referral

On 26 February 2011, the SC unanimously adopted Res 1970,[73] referring the situation of Libya to the ICC pursuant to art 13(b) of the Rome Statute. The relevant parts of the resolution read:

> The Security Council,
> *Mindful* of its primary responsibility for the maintenance of international peace and security under the Charter of the United Nations,
> *Acting* under Chapter VII of the Charter of the United Nations, and taking measures under its Article 41 . . .

---

65 See n 53. For a comprehensive account of the main issues raised, see e.g. Trahan (n 49).

66 Only the Brazilian Representative referred to its earlier concerns regarding the jurisdictional exemption; see Statement by the Brazilian Representative: UNSC Verbatim Record (26 February 2001) UN Doc S/PV.6491, 7.

67 See e.g. Amnesty International, 'Unanimous Security Council vote a crucial moment for international justice' (27 February 2011), available at www.amnesty.org/en/news-and-updates/unanimous-security-council-vote-crucial-moment-international-justice-2011-02-28 (accessed 25 February 2013).

68 UN Doc S/RES/1973 (2011).

69 Ibid. operative para 4.

70 See UNSC Verbatim Record (4 October 2011) UN Doc S/PV.6627.

71 Stahn, 'Libya, the International Criminal Court and Complementarity' (n 1) 326–27.

72 Critical David Kaye, 'Who is Afraid of the International Criminal Court? Finding the Prosecutor Who Can Set It Straight' (2011) 90 *Foreign Affairs* 118.

73 S/RES/1970 (2011); for the relevant parts see below.

ICC referral

4. *Decides* to refer the situation in the Libyan Arab Jamahiriya since 15 February 2011 to the Prosecutor of the International Criminal Court;
5. *Decides* that the Libyan authorities shall cooperate fully with and provide any necessary assistance to the Court and the Prosecutor pursuant to this resolution and, while recognizing that States not party to the Rome Statute have no obligation under the Statute, urges all States and concerned regional and other international organizations to cooperate fully with the Court and the Prosecutor;
6. *Decides* that nationals, current or former officials or personnel from a State outside the Libyan Arab Jamahiriya which is not a party to the Rome Statute of the International Criminal Court shall be subject to the exclusive jurisdiction of that State for all alleged acts or omissions arising out of or related to operations in the Libyan Arab Jamahiriya established or authorized by the Council, unless such exclusive jurisdiction has been expressly waived by the State . . .
8. *Recognizes* that none of the expenses incurred in connection with the referral, including expenses related to investigations or prosecutions in connection with that referral, shall be borne by the United Nations and that such costs shall be borne by the parties to the Rome Statute and those States that wish to contribute voluntarily;

With this, SC Res 1970 (2011) conferred jurisdictional authority to the ICC. It was expressly acting under Chapter VII of the UN Charter and decided to refer the situation in the Libyan Arab Jamahiriya (using Libya's official name) since 15 February 2011 to the Prosecutor of the ICC. As in Res 1593, the Libya referral does not contain a specific mention of art 13(b) of the Rome Statute.

Contrary to the Darfur referral, however, the SC does not expressly make a determination under art 39 of the Charter. It merely states that it is being '[m]indful of its primary responsibility for the maintenance of international peace and security under the Charter of the United Nations'. One might therefore argue that the SC resolution is not legally binding, since it does not contain an art 39 determination that is necessary for the SC to adopt Chapter VII measures.[74] However, in light of recent and accepted practice of the SC, the references in the preamble of the resolution such as 'Deploring the gross and systematic violation of human rights', 'Expressing concern at the plight of refugees forced to flee the violence in the Libyan Arab Jamahiriya', 'Expressing concern for the safety of foreign nationals and their rights in the Libyan Arab Jamahiriya' and 'Reaffirming its strong commitment to the sovereignty, independence, territorial integrity and national unity of the Libyan Arab

---

[74] See Chapter 4. For the general requirement of art 39 determinations see Frederic L. Kirgis, 'The Security Council's First Fifty Years' (1995) 89 *American Journal of International Law* 506, 512; Jared Schott, 'Chapter VII as Exception: Security Council Action and the Regulative Ideal of Emergency' (2007) 6 *Northwestern Journal of International Human Rights* 24, 29.

Jamahiriya' point to an implicit determination of a threat to the peace. This is supported by the fact that all of these grounds have been recognized as threats to the peace.[75] In particular, the wording before stating that it is acting under Chapter VII, '[m]indful of its primary responsibility for the maintenance of international peace and security under the Charter of the United Nations' must be considered an indirect determination satisfying the requirement of an art 39 determination.[76] As a result, the SC referral also satisfies the requirements under art 13(b) of the Statute.

The scope of the jurisdictional authority delegated to the ICC is determined by Res 1970 as regards jurisdiction *ratione loci*, *ratione temporis* and *ratione personae*. First, the jurisdiction *ratione loci* is limited to the territory of Libya pursuant to the operative paragraph 4 of the Resolution. Second, the jurisdiction *ratione temporis* is similarly determined therein and covers the events since 15 February 2011. Third, *ratione personae* is negatively defined as excluding certain categories of nationals of states not parties to the ICC from its jurisdiction. This will be dealt with in the following section together with the equally worded exemption in the Darfur referral.

As in the Darfur referral, jurisdiction *ratione materiae* is not expressly determined. According to what this study has established, the referral must be interpreted as providing criminal jurisdiction over the crimes included in the Statute insofar as they reflect customary international law. Additionally, it imposed cooperation obligations only upon Libya.[77]

It is important to note that several states not party to the ICC, such as Turkey, Qatar, the United Arab Emirates and the United States, undertook military operations along with states parties in Libya.[78] These operations fall under the exemption of paragraph 6 of Res 1970 (2011), to the extent that they are covered by the measures authorized by the SC Res 1973 (2011).[79] The legal effects of this exemption along with the other key issues arising out of the SC referral are addressed below.

---

[75] Frau, 'Das Völkerstrafrecht in der jüngsten Praxis des VN-Sicherheitsrates' (n 1) 787; Patrik Johansson, 'The Humdrum Use of Ultimate Authority: Defining and Analysing Chapter VII Resolutions' (2009) 78 *Nordic Journal of International Law* 309, 312–15.

[76] Frau, 'Das Völkerstrafrecht in der jüngsten Praxis des VN-Sicherheitsrates' (n 1) 787.

[77] Trahan (n 49) 449.

[78] Richard Norton-Taylor, Simon Rogers and Nick Hopkins, 'Arab states play limited role in battle against Muammar Gaddafi's regime' (*The Guardian*, 22 May 2011), available at https://www.theguardian.com/world/2011/may/22/arab-states-battle-against-gaddafi (accessed 7 March 2018). See also Genser (n 42) 401.

[79] Verduzco (n 51) 36–38.

An interesting recent question arises out of the statement of the Prosecutor assuming jurisdiction over crimes against migrants attempting to transit through Libya in 2017.[80] As pointed out, the jurisdiction of the ICC cannot be interpreted expansively and it is doubtful whether the ICC does enjoy jurisdiction in this case.[81] From the preamble of the resolution it is clear that 'situation' referred to the civil war that erupted in 2011.[82] That a situation is not encompassing automatically all crimes committed on the territory of the situation state is evidenced by institutional practice of the ICC itself. That several 'situations' may occur in one country is nothing unusual for the practice of the ICC, as the two situations in the Central African Republic show.[83]

[80] Office of the Prosecutor, Statement of ICC Prosecutor to the UNSC on the Situation in Libya (9 May 2017) paras 25–29, available at https://www.icc-cpi.int/Pages/item.aspx?name=170509-otp-stat-lib (accessed 1 June 2018); Office of the Prosecution, Statement to the United Nations Security Council on the Situation in Libya, pursuant to UNSCR 1970 (2011) (8 November 2017) para 41 https://www.icc-cpi.int/Pages/item.aspx?name=otp_lib_unsc (accessed 1 June 2018).

[81] Sharing this view Mohammed Hadi Zakerhossein, 'Crimes Against Migrants in Libya Manifestly Fall Outside the ICC Prosecutor's Jurisdiction' (*Justice Hub*, 22 May 2017), available at https://justicehub.org/article/zakerhossein-crimes-against-migrants-libya-manifestly-fall-outside-icc-prosecutors (accessed 3 March 2018). In support of the assumption of jurisdiction for policy reasons, see Thierry Cruvellier, 'Can the International Criminal Court Be Saved From Itself?' (*New York Times*, 17 December 2017), available at https://www.nytimes.com/2017/12/17/opinion/icc-symbolic-migrants-europe.html (accessed 3 March 2018); see also Itamar Mann, Violeta Moreno-Lax and Omer Shatz, 'Time to Investigate European Agents for Crimes against Migrants in Libya' (*EJIL:Talk!* Blog post, 29 March 2018), available at https://www.ejiltalk.org/time-to-investigate-european-agents-for-crimes-against-migrants-in-libya/ (accessed 30 March 2018).

[82] The preamble refers to 'the situation in the Libyan Arab Jamahiriya and condemning the violence and use of force against civilians' and 'Deploring the gross and systematic violation of human rights, including the repression of peaceful demonstrators, expressing deep concern at the deaths of civilians, and rejecting unequivocally the incitement to hostility and violence against the civilian population made from the highest level of the Libyan government'.

[83] First, the situation in the Central African Republic (ICC-01/05), which was referred to the ICC by the CAR Government in December 2004 for the conflict there since 2002, with the peak of violence in 2002 and 2003; second the situation in Central African Republic II (ICC-01/14), which was referred to the ICC by the government in 2014 relating to alleged war crimes and crimes against humanity in the context of renewed violence starting in 2012 there.

6.4 DRAFT RESOLUTION ON SYRIA: (UN DOC S/2014/348) 22 MAY 2014

The draft resolution regarding the conflict in Syria points to the continuation of the wording used in the Darfur and Libya referrals, particularly regarding the jurisdictional exemption for certain categories of nationals of non-party states and financing. On 22 May 2014, France tabled a draft resolution that would have included a SC referral to the ICC concerning the situation in Syria.[84] This was supported by a high number of states.[85] Also the UN Human Rights Council implied in several resolutions expressed support for a referral to the ICC.[86]

In the relevant parts the draft resolution provided the determination of a threat to the peace and decided to refer the situation in Syria since March 2011 to the ICC. The 'situation' is described in operative paragraph 1 as

> the widespread violations of human rights and international humanitarian law by the Syrian authorities and pro-government militias, as well as the human rights abuses and violations of international humanitarian law by non-State armed groups, all committed in the course of the ongoing conflict in the Syrian Arab Republic since March 2011.

It adds in its decision that Syria shall cooperate fully with and provide any necessary assistance to the Court and the Prosecutor a reference to the full implementation of the Agreement on the Privileges and Immunities of the International Criminal Court in paragraph 3. Another change to the previous

---

[84] UN Security Council Draft Resolution, UN Doc S/2014/348 (22 May 2014), available at http://www.securitycouncilreport.org/atf/cf/%7B65BFCF9B-6D27-4E9C-8CD3-CF6E4FF96FF9%7D/s_2014_348.pdf (accessed 12 May 2016).

[85] The draft resolution was jointly submitted by submitted by Albania, Andorra, Australia, Austria, Belgium, Botswana, Bulgaria, Canada, Central African Republic, Chile, Côte d'Ivoire, Croatia, Cyprus, Czech Republic, Democratic Republic of the Congo, Denmark, Estonia, Finland, France, Georgia, Germany, Greece, Hungary, Iceland, Ireland, Italy, Japan, Jordan, Latvia, Libya, Liechtenstein, Lithuania, Luxembourg, Malta, Marshall Islands, Mexico, Monaco, Montenegro, Netherlands, New Zealand, Norway, Panama, Poland, Portugal, Qatar, Republic of Korea, Republic of Moldova, Romania, Samoa, San Marino, Saudi Arabia, Senegal, Serbia, Seychelles, Slovakia, Slovenia, Spain, Sweden, Switzerland, the former Yugoslav Republic of Macedonia, Turkey, Ukraine, United Arab Emirates, United Kingdom of Great Britain and Northern Ireland, and United States of America.

[86] See recently, Human Rights Council Res A/HRC/31/L5, (18 March 2016) para 27. For all documents regarding the UN Human Rights Council dealing with the Syrian civil war, see http://ap.ohchr.org/documents/dpage_e.aspx?c=179&su=178 (accessed 12 May 2016).

referrals is the wording that it '*Demands* that non-State armed groups in the Syrian Arab Republic also cooperate fully with and provide any necessary assistance to the Court and the Prosecutor in connection with investigations and prosecutions undertaken pursuant to this resolution'. Paragraph 7 then includes the wording regarding the jurisdictional exemption for non-party states, and in paragraph 8 that the expenses shall not be borne by the UN.

This draft resolution was not adopted due to the negative vote of two permanent members of the SC, China and Russia.[87] According to the meeting records, the issue of the jurisdictional exemption was not addressed.[88] On these points, neither the Obama administration nor the Trump administration (at the time of writing)[89] have departed from the past US position in substance.[90] At the time of writing, a referral does not appear to be feasible in the foreseeable future, as Russia and China block any such efforts.[91]

---

[87] UNSC Verbatim Record (22 May 2014) UN Doc S/PV.7180, 4.

[88] Ibid.

[89] With the appointment of John Bolton as National Security Advisor, that position could change; see John Bellinger, 'The International Criminal Court and the Trump Administration' (*Lawfare* blog, 27 March 2018), available at https://www.lawfareblog.com/international-criminal-court-and-trump-administration (accessed 30 March 2018).

[90] See White House, 'National Security Strategy' (May 2010), available at https://www.whitehouse.gov/sites/default/files/rss_viewer/national_security_strategy.pdf (accessed 12 May 2016) ('Although the United States is not at present a party to the Rome Statute of the International Criminal Court, and will always protect U.S. personnel, we are engaging with State Parties to the Rome Statute on issues of concern and are supporting the I.C.C.'s prosecution of those cases that advance U.S. interests and values, consistent with the requirements of U.S. law.'). This position does not seem to have changed during the Trump administration. See US Department of State, 'International Criminal Court', available at https://www.state.gov/j/gcj/icc/index.htm (accessed 30 March 2018).

[91] See Human Rights Watch, 'UN Security Council: Ensure Justice for Syria Atrocities' (30 August 2016), available at https://www.hrw.org/news/2016/08/30/un-security-council-ensure-justice-syria-atrocities (accessed 3 March 2018). In 2016, the UN High Commissioner for Human Rights Zeid Ra'ad Al Hussein expressed his frustration with the lack of SC action, stating that 'the persistent failure of the Security Council to refer the situation in Syria to the International Criminal Court is an example of the most shameful form of realpolitik'. UN News Centre, "'Monstrous disregard'" for civilians, says UN rights chief, as hospitals bombed in Syria' (29 April 2016), available at https://news.un.org/en/story/2016/04/528062-monstrous-disregard-civilians-says-un-rights-chief-hospitals-bombed-syria (accessed 3 March 2018).

6.5 CONCLUSION

In conclusion, the arguably scant practice shows that SC referrals have several features. First, the SC will expressly determine the territorial and temporal scope (at least regarding the start date) of the conferred jurisdiction. The SC will clarify that the referral does not impose any obligations upon non-party states, except those addressed in the referral. Furthermore, it will not expressly provide for the material scope of the jurisdiction conferred, thus allowing for the interpretation adopted in this study to the effect that the ICC may only exercise jurisdiction over crimes included in the Statute insofar as they are recognized as customary international law. The fourth feature of SC referrals in practice points to the problematic inclusion of an exemption to the jurisdiction of the ICC concerning certain categories of nationals of non-party states. Finally, the SC will 'recognize' that the expenses of the referral shall not be borne by the UN.

Regarding complementarity, it is clear that situations referred to the ICC by the SC are subject to the principle of complementarity as provided in art 17, as has been established above.[92] In practice, the ICC has not drawn a distinction between admissibility in cases involving states parties to the ICC and those situations referred to it by the SC.

The jurisdictional exemptions are difficult to justify from a rational point of view. There has not been a threat of prosecutions against US peacekeepers in Darfur.[93] In 2005, only the AU had a peacekeeping force in place. The UNAMID, to which the US contributes through a regular UN budget, was only established in 2007.[94] However, the exemption clause has created problems of legitimacy for the ICC.[95] It highlights the application of double standards by the SC and powerful states as predicted by the statement of India after it

---

[92] Chapter 5.2.

[93] Citing data from the Coalition for the International Criminal Court, Carsten Stahn reports that in August 2003, the United States identified a concrete threat to prosecution when the SC authorized the establishment of a peacekeeping mission in Liberia through Res 1497 (2003). Therefore, it secured a clause to uphold the exclusive jurisdiction of sending states not parties over their officials or personnel. See UNSC Res 1497 (1 August 2003) UN Doc S/RES/1497, para 7; Stahn (n 11) 87.

[94] The US contributes to UNAMID through the regular budget of the UN. Consent from the host state is necessary to send troops. It is unlikely that Sudan would approve US troop contribution to UNAMID.

[95] For the resulting challenges to principles of international criminal law, see e.g. Gabriel M. Lentner, 'The Role of the UN Security Council vis-à-vis the International Criminal Court – Resolution 1970 (2011) and its challenges to ICJ' (2014) 14(2) *International and Comparative Law Review* 5 (pointing out normative challenges regarding the principle of equality before the law, the principle of universal jurisdiction

rejected the Rome Statute, since this practice suggests that the ICC can be used to prosecute some war criminals while protecting others.[96]

for international crimes, the principle of legality, and the principle of the independence of the Court).

[96] Verduzco (n 51) 36–38. See also the criticism in Aidan Hehir and Anthony Lang, 'The Impact of the Security Council on the Efficacy of the International Criminal Court and the Responsibility to Protect' (2015) 26(1) *Criminal Law Forum* 153. See further on this point Margaret M deGuzman, 'Inter-National Justice for Them or Global Justice for US?: The U.S. as a Supranational Justice Donor' (2016) 48 *Case Western Reserve Journal of International Law* 1.

7. Key issues of the Security Council referrals in practice

The practice of SC referrals raises several legal issues. This chapter will therefore analyze in turn the legal issues arising from the jurisdictional exemption, the temporal jurisdiction, the financing of the SC referrals and the question of obligations for non-party states based on the findings of the legal nature of the SC referral. Again, this study is necessarily limited to those issues that directly relate to the legal nature of SC referrals. It is important to note that to date neither the ICC nor its member states have addressed these issues directly.

7.1 JURISDICTIONAL EXEMPTION

The jurisdictional exemption included in the SC referrals is clearly intended to give exclusive jurisdiction over certain categories of nationals of states not party to the ICC to that nationals' state. The exemption in the Libya referral reads in the relevant part (as did the Darfur referral *mutatis mutandis*):

> The Security Council, acting under Chapter VII of the Charter of the United Nations
>
> . . .
>
> *Decides* that nationals, current or former officials or personnel from a State outside the Libyan Arab Jamahiriya which is not a party to the Rome Statute of the International Criminal Court shall be subject to the exclusive jurisdiction of that State for all alleged acts or omissions arising out of or related to operations in the Libyan Arab Jamahiriya established or authorized by the Council, unless such exclusive jurisdiction has been expressly waived by the State;

For several reasons, this jurisdictional exemption is hard to be reconciled with the jurisdiction regime provided in art 13(b) of the Rome Statute. As is clear from the legal considerations during the negotiation of Article 13,[1] the wording of 'situation' was specifically chosen to avoid referring only individual cases, and used with the intention of avoiding political interference by a 'pick and choose' approach, as evidenced by the drafting history, during which

[1] See Chapter 2.

the wording was changed from 'case' to 'matters' to 'situations'.[2] Indeed, the Pre-Trial Chamber of the ICC has also explained that this phrase means that a referral cannot limit the Prosecutor to investigate only crimes committed by certain persons, for example.[3]

Thus, the exemption for certain categories of nationals from the Court's jurisdiction is prima facie not in accordance with the text of art 13(b) of the Statute.[4] Also most view the exemption as providing conflicting obligations for states arising from the Rome Statute on the one hand and the UN Charter on the other.[5] Furthermore, some commentators assert that legally, the SC referral can only activate the Rome Statute as a whole and not select parts thereof.[6] Others assume that these exemptions would not withstand judicial scrutiny at the ICC itself, which under art 19(1) Rome Statute shall satisfy itself that it has jurisdiction in any case brought before it.

---

[2] Sharon A. Williams and William Schabas, 'Article 13' in Otto Triffterer and Kai Ambos (eds), *Commentary on the Rome Statute of the International Criminal Court: Observers' Notes, Article by Article* (2nd edn, C.H. Beck; Hart; Nomos 2008) para 13.

[3] *Prosecutor v Callixte Mbarushimana* (Decision on the 'Defence Challenge to the Jurisdiction of the Court' ICC-01/04-01/10-451, Pre-Trial Chamber I (26 October 2011) para 27. See also Sarah M. H. Nouwen, *Complementarity in the Line of Fire: The Catalysing Effect of the International Criminal Court in Uganda and Sudan* (Cambridge studies in law and society, Cambridge University Press 2013) 87.

[4] The RA concluded between the UN and the ICC is not insightful in that respect.

[5] See e.g. Matthias Neuner, 'The Darfur Referral of the Security Council and the Scope of the Jurisdiction of the International Criminal Court' (2005) 8 *Yearbook of International Humanitarian Law* 320, 334–39. The SC cannot bind the ICC directly; see Sebastian Heselhaus, 'Resolution 1422 (2002) des Sicherheitsrates zur Begrenzung der Tätigkeit des Internationalen Strafgerichtshof' (2002) 62 *Zeitschrift für ausländisches öffentliches Recht und Völkerrecht*, 910; Nico Krisch, 'Introduction to Chapter VII: The General Framework' in Bruno Simma (ed), *The Charter of the United Nations: A Commentary* (3rd edn, Oxford University Press 2012) para 67.

[6] Global Policy Forum, *The Relationship Between the ICC and the Security Council: Challenges and Opportunities* (International Peace Institute 2012), available at www.globalpolicy.org/international-justice/the-international-criminal-court/icc-in-the-securitycouncil-6-4/52118-the-relationship-between-the-icc-and-the-security-councilchallenges-and-opportunities.html (accessed 1 June 2018). See also D. Kaye, *The Council and The Court: Improving Security Council Support of the International Criminal Court* (Univ. of California School of Law 2013) 6, available at http://councilandcourt.org/files/2013/05/The-Council-and-the-Court-FINAL.pdf (accessed 24 April 2014). Some observers believe that if such a situation were presented to a chamber of the Court, the judges may ignore the exemption (from investigation of citizens of non-state parties) and apply the Rome Statute, assuming jurisdiction and admissibility requirements are met; see Trahan (n 6) 457.

Several points must be made here.[7] As a preliminary clarification, the jurisdictional exemption is not to be confused with immunity from ICC prosecution.[8] This is because jurisdiction precedes immunity. In the words of the ILC Special Rapporteur, 'If there is no jurisdiction, there is no reason to raise or consider the question of immunity from jurisdiction'.[9] A jurisdictional exemption, by definition, cannot be understood as establishing immunity.

Second, putting certain categories of nationals under the exclusive jurisdiction of the state of their nationality[10] means that the SC clearly sought to limit the ICC's jurisdiction to that effect. The legal nature of SC referrals reveals that since the referral is the only source of (lawful) jurisdictional authority for the ICC in case of a third states, the ICC cannot exercise jurisdiction beyond what is provided for in the resolution, irrespective of the provisions of the Rome Statute.[11] In other words, the exact scope of the conferral of jurisdiction in question therefore remains under the discretion of the SC: the ICC can only exercise such jurisdiction that is conferred to it.

This is not to say that the SC can directly modify the Rome Statute. But limiting the jurisdictional scope means that the ICC is unable to go beyond the parameters set out in the referral. The ICC is simply lacking any other basis for the lawful exercise of its jurisdiction.[12] For reasons given above, the principle of universality cannot be invoked as a jurisdictional ground.[13] As a result, the

---

[7] Regarding the situation in Libya, the US considered their operations as authorized by Res 1973 (2011), therefore the jurisdictional exemption would apply to these operations; see H. Koh, 'Statement regarding the use of force in Libya' (26 March 2011), available at www.state.gov/s/l/releases/remarks/159201.htm (accessed 1 September 2013). See also Opinions of the Office of Legal Counsel, 'Authority to Use Military Force in Libya: Memorandum Opinion for the Attorney General' (2011) 35. Contra, TV Tsentr Channel Post Scriptum, 'Transcript of Interview to Russian Foreign Minister Sergey Lvrov' (1 May 2011), available at http://www.russianembassy.org.za/IA/Brics3.html (accessed 24 April 2014); BBC News, 'Libya: Russia Decries French Arms Drop to Libya Rebels' (30 June 2011), available at http://www.bbc.com/news/world-europe-13979632 (accessed 24 April 2014).

[8] In a similar vein, Robert Frau, 'Das Völkerstrafrecht in der jüngsten Praxis des VN-Sicherheitsrates' (2011) 10 *Zeitschrift für Internationale Strafrechtsdogmatik* 784, 788.

[9] Preliminary Report of the Special Rapporteur, Mr. Roman Anatolevich Kolodkin (60th session of the ILC (2008) UN Doc A/CN.4/601 para 43.

[10] These are 'current or former officials or personnel from a State outside the Libyan Arab Jamahiriya which is not a party to the Rome Statute of the International Criminal Court . . . for all alleged acts or omissions arising out of or related to operations in the Libyan Arab Jamahiriya established or authorized by the Council'.

[11] *Nemo plus iuris transferre potest quam ipse habet, Corpus iuris civilis* (D. 50, 17, 54).

[12] See Chapter 3.1.

[13] See Chapter 3.1.

referrals concerning Libya and Darfur have therefore only conferred limited jurisdiction to the ICC.

In the next step, the referral must be analyzed for its validity under the UN Charter. Here we look at potential limits to the SC in exercising its powers. However, prima facie these resolutions must be considered intra vires, as they prima facie appear appropriate for the fulfilment of the purposes of the organization.[14] In the context of peacekeeping, it is common practice to provide for exclusive jurisdiction to states contributing to the peacekeeping operation in status of forces agreements (SOFA) that are concluded between the UN and host states.[15] It is also common practice for the SC, at the request of the GA, to provisionally apply a Model SOFA to peacekeeping operations, pending the conclusion of that agreement between the UN and the host states.[16] This has happened in all but one peacekeeping operation established after 1997.[17] The referrals are thus valid and legally binding.[18] This means that if the SC confers authority excluding certain categories of nationals as in Res 1593 and 1970, the ICC cannot exercise jurisdiction over these nationals, otherwise violating that state's sovereignty and the obligations arising from the SC resolution.[19]

Of course, it is an entirely different question whether the ICC, under *its* constituent treaty, is authorized to act upon such a conferral of only 'limited' jurisdiction.

Applying the results of this study,[20] it follows that the inclusion of art 13(b) providing for the SC referral in the Rome Statute must be read as making the SC referrals operational for the ICC insofar as the SC remains within the constitutional confines of the UN Charter generally and the conditions of Chapter

---

14 See *Certain Expenses of the United Nations*, Advisory Opinion (20 July 1962) ICJ Rep 1962, 151, 168. On the more general point on the ultra vires nature of SC measures, see Chapter 5.4 for Michael Wood's comments.

15 See UN Secretary-General, Model Status-of-Forces Agreement for Peacekeeping Operations, Annex para 47(b), UN Doc. A/45/594 (9 October 1990), available at http://www.un.org/ga/search/view_doc.asp?symbol=A/45/594 (accessed 3 March 2018).

16 See Rembert Boom, 'Special Measures for Protection from Sexual Exploitation and Abuse in UN Peacekeeping: Can the General Assembly Unite Against Impunity of Military Peacekeepers?' (*ASIL Insights* 20/13, 27 July 2016), available at https://www.asil.org/insights/volume/20/issue/13/special-measures-protection-sexual-exploitation-and-abuse-un#_edn12 (accessed 3 March 2018). See also Wood (n 14) 251.

17 Ibid.

18 Rosalyn Higgins and others, *Oppenheim's International Law: United Nations* (vol 1, Oxford University Press 2017) 352–54.

19 See however Nouwen (n 3) 88–89 (who raises the possibility that the fact that the organs of the ICC have acted upon the referrals in Darfur and Libya could support the conclusion that any elements to limit its jurisdiction would be severed).

20 See Chapter 5.1.2.

VII action, and as giving broad discretion as to the concrete parameters of the jurisdiction to be exercised by the ICC.[21] A conflict of norms can therefore be avoided by adopting the respective interpretative tools. As mentioned, this is supported by the principle of systemic integration (art 31(3)(c) VCLT *per analogiam*).[22] A presumption against conflict exists under international norm, so that the jurisdictional limitation provided for in the SC referral shall not be interpreted as contrary to the conditions of a SC referral under art 13(b). In conclusion, the jurisdictional exemption can be viewed as effectively binding the ICC.

This conclusion is however unsatisfactory to some extent. Certain powerful states may effectively tailor the referral to serve their interests and protect their nationals from international prosecution.[23] Several authors have thus provided some arguments against this result. For example, some commentators argue that the exemption is ultra vires.[24] The problem with this view is of course that it might render the entire referral ultra vires, with the result that the entire referral is simply without legal force and cannot be the legal basis for the lawful exercise of ICC jurisdiction.[25] William Schabas therefore raises the possibility of severability: the jurisdictional exemption would be excised from the resolution and the referral would take effect as if adopted without the jurisdictional exemption.[26] However, it is difficult to see how the doctrine of severability can be applied in this case. The ICC is limited in its exercise of jurisdiction to the scope as determined in the SC referral. It follows from the maxim *nemo dat quod non habet* that the ICC cannot exercise jurisdiction not conferred to it.[27]

21 Similarly, Frau (n 8) 788.

22 For an interesting discussion of this principle see Panos Merkouris, *Article 31(3)(c) VCLT and the Principle of Systemic Integration: Normative Shadows in Plato's Cave* (BRILL 2015).

23 In a similar vein, Deborah R. Verduzco, 'The Relationship between the ICC and the United Nations Security Council' in Carsten Stahn (ed), *The Law and Practice of the International Criminal Court* (Oxford University Press 2015) 36–38.

24 See on this William Schabas, *The International Criminal Court: A Commentary on the Rome Statute* (Oxford commentaries on international law, Oxford University Press 2010) 300; A. G. Kiyani, 'Al-Bashir & the ICC: The Problem of Head of State Immunity' (2013) 12(3) *Chinese Journal of International Law* 467, 481.

25 Higgins and others (n 18) 353–54.

26 William Schabas, *An Introduction to the International Criminal Court* (4th edn, Cambridge University Press 2011) 174–76. Equally, Williams and Schabas (n 2) 572–73.

27 For application of this principle in another area of international law, the acquisition of title to territory, see e.g. the *Island of Palmas case (or Miangas)* (Award) II RIAA 829, ICGJ 392 (PCA 1928) (4 April 1928). Even if this was not the case, it is not clear how the doctrine of severability could apply in the context of SC resolutions. The doctrine of severability has been developed originally by the ECtHR, in particular

The only possibility would be the acceptance of the broader jurisdiction by the state concerned by ways of acquiescence or subsequent practice.

Similarly, the RA does not resolve the issue. While it is an agreement regulating the legal relationship between the UN and the ICC, it does not address this issue and clearly does not make the SC subject to the Rome Statute.[28]

Another option could be to raise the precedent set by the Uganda referral. Uganda, a state party to the ICC, referred a situation in its own territory to the ICC. However, it only referred to the 'situation concerning the Lord's Resistance Army'. Yet the Prosecutor 'informed the Government of Uganda that it interpreted the referral to refer to all article 5 crimes of relevance to the situation.'[29] The Office of the Prosecutor thus appropriately rejected this limitation because art 14(1) of the Rome Statute permits a state party to refer a 'situation' and not only select parts thereof (specifically not only party to a conflict). The Ugandan government did not object.[30] The Pre-Trial Chamber subsequently agreed stating that 'a referral cannot limit the Prosecutor to investigate only certain crimes, e.g. crimes committed by certain persons or crimes committed before or after a given date'.[31] Here the Pre-Trial Chamber

---

in its decision in the *Belilios* case of 1988, and was later similarly adopted by the UN Human Rights Committee in its General Comment 24 (1994) with respect to reservations to the International Covenant on Civil and Political Rights. The issue of validity of reservations to human rights treaties cannot be viewed as analogical to the issue at hand, because these precedents dealt with the legal effect of reservations to human rights treaties and not to the delegation of authority from one international organization to another as in this case. Arriving at the same conclusion for slightly different reasons, see Robert Frau, 'Die Überweisung der Lage in Libyen an den Internationalen Strafgerichtshof durch den Sicherheitsrat der Vereinten Nationen – zugleich ein Beitrag zur Völkerstrafrechtspraxis des Sicherheitsrates' (2011) 49(3) *Archiv des Völkerrechts* 276, 282.

[28] Jakob Pichon, *Internationaler Strafgerichtshof und Sicherheitsrat der Vereinten Nationen: Zur Rolle des Sicherheitsrats bei der Verfolgung völkerrechtlicher Verbrechen durch den IStGH* (Max-Planck-Gesellschaft zur Förderung der Wissenschaften e.V 2011) 97. For a different view, see Luigi Condorelli and Santiago Villalpando, 'Can the Security Council Extend the ICC's Jurisdiction?' in Antonio Cassese, Paola Gaeta and John R. Jones (eds), *The Rome Statute of the International Criminal Court* (Oxford University Press 2002) 580.

[29] ICC Office of the Prosecutor, 'Draft Policy Paper on Preliminary Examinations' (2010), available at www.icc-cpi.int/NR/rdonlyres/9FF1EAA1-41C4-4A30-A202-174B18DA923C/282515/OTP_Draftpolicypaperonpreliminaryexaminations04101.pdf (accessed 1 June 2018) paras 2 and 35 (discussing the Uganda referral).

[30] Nouwen (n 3) 88.

[31] Decision on the 'Defence Challenge to the Jurisdiction of the Court', Mbarushimana (ICC-01/04/01/10-451), Pre-Trial Chamber I, 26 October 2011, para 27.

even invokes the arguments made in the Darfur referral to make this point.[32] However, the legal situation is entirely different for non-party states and therefore an analogy to SC referrals is not warranted. Legally, Uganda is bound by the provisions of the Statute because it is a state party and is thus bound by the decisions of the organs of the Court.

Another issue arises out of treaty law binding on almost all UN member states.[33] The four Geneva Conventions oblige all state parties 'to search for persons alleged to have committed, or to have ordered to be committed, such grave breaches, and [to] bring such persons, regardless of their nationality, before its own courts'.[34] The Convention Against Torture (CAT) imposes similar duties.[35] The SC referral's jurisdictional exemption imposes the obligations that are in contradiction with such duties.[36] Such a conflict of norms could be resolved by resorting to art 103 of the UN Charter, under which the obligations under the Charter and thus also those imposed by a SC referral prevail over any other international agreement.[37]

The impact of the exemptions in practice have not yet been directly addressed by the Chambers.[38] The Prosecutor only asserted that '[t]he Office does have a mandate, however, to investigate allegations of crimes by all actors',[39] not mentioning paragraph 6 of the resolution or giving any reasons

---

32 Referring to *The Prosecutor v Omar Al-Bashir*, ICC-02/05-01/09-3 para 45 'by referring the Darfur situation to the Court, pursuant to article 13(b) of the Statute, the Security Council of the United Nations has also accepted that the investigation into the said situation, as well as any prosecution arising therefrom, will take place in accordance with the statutory framework provided for in the Statute, the Elements of Crimes and the rules as a whole'.

33 Schabas (n 26) 172–74.

34 Convention for the Amelioration of the Condition of the Wounded and Sick in Armed Forces in the Field (1949) 75 UNTS 31, Art 49; Convention for the Amelioration of the Condition of Wounded, Sick and Shipwrecked Members of Armed Forces at Sea (1950) 75 UNTS 85, Art 50; Convention Relative to the Treatment of Prisoners of War (1950) 75 UNTS 135, Art 129; Convention Relative to the Protection of Civilian Persons in Time of War (1950) 75 UNTS 287, Art 146. Additional Protocol I, Article 85(1), see also Rule 157 of the International Committee of the Red Cross' rules of customary international humanitarian law.

35 Convention Against Torture and Other Cruel, Inhuman or Degrading Treatment or Punishment (1987) 1465 UNTS 85, Art 5.

36 Schabas (n 26) 172–74.

37 Ibid.

38 Carsten Stahn, 'How is the Water? Light and Shadow in the First Years of the ICC' (2011) 22(1–2) *Criminal Law Forum* 175, 179; Carsten Stahn, 'Libya, the International Criminal Court and Complementarity: A Test for "Shared Responsibility"' (2012) 10(2) *Journal of International Criminal Justice* 325, 331.

39 Third Report of the Prosecutor of the International Criminal Court to the UN Security Council pursuant to UNSCR 1970 (2001), May 2012, para 55.

for this assertion in his Third Report to the UN SC concerning the situation in Libya.

It must be noted, however, that the practical effect of this exemption has been limited. To date, no foreign national that would fall into the exempted category has been subject to ICC proceedings (at least publicly).[40] The Pre-Trial Chamber has asserted full applicability of the Statute with respect to SC referrals, arguing that

> by referring the Darfur situation to the Court, pursuant to art 13(b) of the Statute, the Security Council of the United Nations has also accepted that the investigation into the said situation, as well as any prosecution arising therefrom, will take place in accordance with the statutory framework provided for in the Statute, the Elements of Crimes and the Rules as a whole.[41]

It could be implied from this wording that the ICC would apply the entire Statute, thus effectively carving out the jurisdictional exemption.[42]

The reactions of states to the exemption is also interesting. While extensive debates questioned the legality and effect of paragraph 6 following the adoption of the Darfur referral, no such reactions came after the Libya referral, which was adopted unanimously. Such continued practice could point to developing acceptance or acquiescence of such troubling SC practice.[43] However, with only two instances of such practice it is difficult to argue that these instances developed into legally relevant subsequent treaty practice. One solution for the ICC could be, as suggested by William Schabas to 'sen[d] the Resolution back, telling the Security Council that it was impossible to proceed on such a basis, and to reprise the adoption without paragraph 6'.[44] Until then, it will be interesting to see how states react should the ICC Prosecutor indict exempted nationals.

---

[40] Abdullah Al-Senussi, against whom an arrest warrant has been issued in the Libya situation would meet the first criterion of the exemption clause, since he is a foreign national of Sudan, a non-state party. However, he does not fulfil the second requirement since his actions did not relate to operations authorized by the SC. See Nouwen (n 3) 89 at fn 212.

[41] *Prosecutor v Omar Hassan Al-Bashir, Situation in Darfur* (Decision on the Prosecution's Application for a Warrant of Arrest against Omar Hassan Ahmad Al-Bashir) ICC-02/05-01/09-3 (4 March 2009) para 45.

[42] In a similar vein, Verduzco (n 23) 36–38.

[43] Such practice is important since legal defects might be cured by operation of acquiescence or acceptance; see Jan Klabbers, *An Introduction to International Organizations Law* (3rd edn, Cambridge University Press 2015) 186.

[44] Schabas (n 26) 172.

7.2 TEMPORAL JURISDICTION

At present, SC referrals have always been retroactive. The referral of the situation in Darfur was adopted on 31 March 2005 but refers to the situation from 1 July 2002. The referral of the situation in Libya was adopted on 26 February 2011 and refers the situation to the Court back to 15 February 2011. Some of the arrest warrants that emerged from these referrals indeed concerned conduct occurring before the adoption of the referral. For instance, Omar Al-Bashir, the Head of State of Sudan, is indicted for crimes committed between April 2003 and July 2008.[45] Furthermore, in the Libyan situation, the arrest warrants against Muammar Gaddafi, Saif Gaddafi and Abdullah Al-Senussi were for crimes committed between 15 February 2011 and 28 February 2011.[46] Finally, the draft resolution to refer the situation in Syria to the ICC, presented before the SC in May 2014, proposed that the Court's jurisdiction extend back to March 2011. Also, the GA urged the SC in a (non-binding) resolution to refer the situation in North Korea since 1 July 2002 to the ICC.[47] This followed a UN Commission of Inquiry report issued in February 2014 documenting crimes against humanity committed in North Korea reaching as far back as the 1950s.[48]

As established above,[49] SC referrals without containing language to the contrary must be interpreted to only confer criminal jurisdiction over crimes recognized as part of customary international law at the time of the commission of the crime binding on the state concerned or otherwise applicable through binding treaty obligations.[50] This also means that in theory the SC could refer a situation involving crimes committed before the entry into force of the Rome

---

45 *The Prosecutor v Omar Hassan Ahmad Al-Bashir,* Warrant of Arrest for Omar Hassan Ahmad Al-Bashir ICC-02/05-01/09-1 (4 March 2009); *The Prosecutor v Omar Hassan Ahmad Al-Bashir,* Second Decision on the Prosecution's Application for a Warrant of Arrest ICC-02/05-01/09-94 (12 July 2010).

46 *The Prosecutor v Saif Al-Islam Gaddafi*, Warrant of Arrest for Muammar Mohammed Abu Minyar Gaddafi ICC-01/11-01/11-2 (27 June 2011); *The Prosecutor v Saif Al-Islam Gaddafi*, Warrant of Arrest for Saif Al-Islam Gaddafi ICC-01/11-01/11-3 (27 June 2011); *The Prosecutor v Saif Al-Islam Gaddafi*, Warrant of Arrest for Abdullah Al-Senussi ICC-01/11-01/11-4 (27 June 2011).

47 GA Press Release GA/11604.

48 See Report of the detailed findings of the commission of inquiry on human rights in the Democratic People's Republic of Korea, UN Doc A/HRC/25/CRP.1 (7 February 2014).

49 See Chapter 5.1.3.

50 See, however, Robert Frau, who argues that from the time of the SC referral the ICC may prosecute crimes in accordance with its Statute including those that go beyond customary international law; Frau (n 8) 789.

Statute since it would only provide for jurisdiction over crimes recognized as part of customary international law at the time of their commission. No reasons are apparent why the SC would be barred from referring a situation involving crimes committed before the entry into force of the Rome Statute, as long as it does not decide to retroactively apply ICL that way. While one commentator recently raised the issue of a potential problem regarding 'retroactive' exercise of jurisdiction,[51] this seems to be a rather theoretical question as states seem to be reluctant to confer such broad jurisdictional reach for the ICC anyway.[52]

The question of retroactive application of criminal law, though, is not merely an academic issue. Regarding North Korea, for example, among the various acts amounting to crimes against humanity that the Commission of Inquiry reported, gender-based persecution was singled out in this context.[53] In its report it stated that '[t]he Rome Statute introduced gender-based persecution as a crime against humanity, which was not yet included in the statutes of the ICTY and ICTR. In the opinion of the Commission, this norm is crystalizing into customary international law'.[54] It is not the purpose of this study to identify the status of customary international law in this respect, but suffice it to note here that failing a treaty obligation of North Korea, the ICC would only be able to prosecute crimes against humanity as it is recognized under customary international law at the time of the commission of the offence. Still, courts naturally enjoy wide discretion in determining the status of customary international law crimes[55] and the ICC could view this as an opportunity to

---

[51] See on this question Michail Vagias, 'Retroactive State Criminal Jurisdiction under International Law' (2018) 7(1) *Cambridge International Law Journal* 122. However, such an approach seems to conflate the actual enforcement of ICL (by courts that only recently gained judicial jurisdiction over such cases) with retroactive application of substantive criminal law, the former not being a question of retroactivity.

[52] It has been pointed out that '[t]he ICC's inability to address past atrocities may be viewed as a deficiency that would limit the success of the Court's mission of ending impunity. Still, practical considerations supported this limitation on the Court's jurisdiction. It is doubtful that an agreement could ever have been reached on the establishment of a permanent court if it had the power to delve into the history of state parties. Nor is it likely that all of the current state parties would have joined the Statute under such terms. Additionally, a broad temporal jurisdiction would have overburdened the Court with complicated investigations into historical events'. Yuval Shany (ed), *Assessing the Effectiveness of International Courts* (Oxford University Press 2014) 238.

[53] Report of the detailed findings of the commission of inquiry on human rights in the Democratic People's Republic of Korea, UN Doc A/HRC/25/CRP.1, 7 February 2014, para 1059.

[54] Ibid. para 1576.

[55] See the development of ICL by the ICTY, see e.g. Robert Cryer and others, *An Introduction to International Criminal Law and Procedure* (3rd edn, Cambridge

clarify customary international law (and perhaps even a prospect for the progressive development of ICL), while still honouring the principle of legality.[56]

7.3 FINANCING OF THE SC REFERRALS

Another key legal issue raised by the SC referral practice relates to the financing of the SC referrals. Both SC referrals to date contain the following clause:

> *Recognizes* that none of the expenses incurred in connection with the referral, including expenses related to investigations or prosecutions in connection with that referral, shall be borne by the United Nations and that such costs shall be borne by the parties to the Rome Statute and those States that wish to contribute voluntarily;

The intention of the SC is clearly that the referral shall not be funded through the general budget of the UN. This is illustrated by the statement the US delegate made when the first referral was adopted:

> We are pleased that the resolution recognizes that none of the expenses incurred in connection with the referral will be borne by the United Nations and that, instead, such costs will be borne by the parties to the Rome Statute and those that contribute voluntarily. That principle is extremely important and we want to be perfectly clear that any effort to retrench on that principle by this or other organizations to which we contribute could result in our withholding funding or taking other action in response. That is a situation that we must avoid.[57]

It is difficult to justify such an approach. The SC uses the ICC to fulfil its responsibility for the maintenance of international peace and security, but does not want to provide the necessary funding. As one commentator put it, 'the Council borrowed the funding scheme for the ICC as an independent criminal court in an attempt to have its cake and eat it too'.[58] There are other reasons, too. Beside the political rationale behind this approach, the US Consolidated

University Press 2014) 137. For criticism that the ICTY has been too quick to decide on the customary nature of crimes, see Guenael Mettraux, *International Crimes and the Ad Hoc Tribunals* (Oxford University Press 2005) 13–18. See also Kononov before the ECtHR.

56 On the relation between the principle of legality and the progressive development of ICL, see e.g. Mohamed Shahabuddeen, 'Does the Principle of Legality Stand in the Way of Progressive Development of Law?' (2004) 4(2) *Journal of International Criminal Justice* 1007.

57 UNSC Verbatim Record (31 March 2005) UN Doc S/PV.5158, 3–4.

58 G. P. Fletcher, 'The ICC – Two Courts in One?' (2006) 4(3) *Journal of International Criminal Justice* 428, 430.

Appropriations Public Law of 2000 prohibits any funds from being 'obligated for use by, or for support of, the International Criminal Court'.[59]

The legal qualification of this clause included in the operative part of the SC referrals is less clear. First, the wording that the SC 'recognizes that none of the expenses incurred in connection with the referral . . . shall be borne by the United Nations' is ambiguous. The word 'recognizes' usually indicates that this is to be interpreted as not legally binding.[60] Next, according to art 115 of the Rome Statute, the expenses of the ICC shall be provided by contributions made by states parties and under (b) by funds provided by the UN, subject to the approval of the GA, 'in particular in relation to the expenses incurred due to referrals by the Security Council'. As this provision rightly points out, the budgetary authority within the UN system rests with the GA pursuant to art 17 of the UN Charter.[61] The SC is not authorized to make a decision on the budget. In any case, nothing in the Statute prevents the ICC from accepting referrals even if the UN does not pay for the expenses resulting from SC referrals.[62]

Furthermore, lacking the qualification of a binding decision of the SC under Chapter VII, the RA concluded between the UN and the ICC is relevant but does not specify the matter.[63] According to its art 13 '[t]he United Nations and the Court agree that the conditions under which any funds may be provided to the Court by a decision of the General Assembly of the United Nations pursuant to article 115 of the Statute shall be subject to separate arrangements'. No such separate arrangements exist.[64]

Commentators have thus rightly criticized this approach towards financing the SC referrals. For example, Luigi Condorelli comments:

---

59 Consolidated Appropriations Fiscal Year 2000, Public Law 106–13, Sec 705 (29 November 1999) and amended by the Hyde Amendment (US House Amendment, 10 January 2002).

60 See Michael Wood, 'The Interpretation of Security Council Resolutions' (1998) 2 *Max Planck Yearbook of United Nations Law* 73; *Namibia Case* (Advisory Opinion) [1971] ICJ Rep 1971, 53.

61 *Certain Expenses Case* (Advisory Opinion) [1962] ICJ Rep 151. See also Jennifer Trahan, 'The Relationship Between the International Criminal Court and the U.N. Security Council: Parameters and Best Practices' (2013) 24(4) *Criminal Law Forum* 417, 451; Higgins and others (n 18) 1351; Kenneth S. Gallant, 'The International Criminal Court in the System of States and International Organizations' (2003) 16(3) *Leiden Journal of International Law* 553, 575.

62 Mahnoush H. Arsanjani, 'Financing' in Cassese (n 28) 325.

63 In case of a binding measure under Chapter VII of the UN Charter, the obligations arising therefrom would prevail over any other international agreements pursuant to art 103 of the Charter, thus in theory it would prevail over the RA concluded between the UN and the ICC.

64 Verduzco (n 23) 38.

> [t]he Security Council's unilateral ruling out of the provision of funds by the United Nations to the Court in connection with Darfur is thus at odds not only with the decision to refer, but also with the duty of good faith negotiations, which flows from the obligation mutually agreed upon between the ICC and the United Nations. The position of the United Nations is unlikely to be flexible on this point.[65]

However, during the debates in the SC, none of the SC members raised this issue. As William Schabas noted, '[l]ike most initiatives in the Security Council, the resolution was a diplomatic compromise. Those States favouring referral to the Court must have felt they had the better of the Americans, and that the toxic paragraphs injected by the latter did not fatally compromise the referral itself'.[66]

Legally, it is clear that the SC cannot bar funding for the ICC, since it is the UN GA that has the budgetary authority. In practice the UN has not contributed to the ICC.[67] The ASP of the ICC addressed this with respect to the funding necessary for the Libya referral and sought to engage with the GA of the UN to explore options to cover the financial burden of future referrals.[68] The only discussion with respect to funding at the UN level takes place in the context of the negotiation of the annual GA resolution on the ICC.[69] This forum offers limited opportunity. For instance, UNGA Res 67/295 (2013) simply notes in a preambular paragraph 'the need for funding of expenses related to investigations or prosecutions of the International Criminal Court, including in connection with situations referred to the Court by the Security Council',[70] while referring to the reimbursable nature of the cooperation in an operative paragraph.[71]

---

[65] Luigi Condorelli and Annalisa Ciampi, 'Comments on the Security Council Referral of the Situation in Darfur to the ICC' (2005) 3(3) *Journal of International Criminal Justice* 590, 594.

[66] Schabas (n 26) 174–76. Equally, Williams and Schabas (n 2) 572–73.

[67] See Contingency Fund request for extra resources for the Libya situation for May to December 2011, Letter from Mr Marc Dubuisson, Director of Court Services, on behalf of the Registrar to H E Mr Santiago Wins, Chair of the CBF (2011/09/1A, 27 April 2011), referred to in Proposed Programme Budget 2012, ICC/ASP/10/10, 21 July 2011 (Tenth Session of the Assembly of States Parties) Table 1.

[68] See Report of the Committee on Budget and Finance on the Work of its Sixteenth Session, ICC–ASP/10/15, 17 June 2011 (Tenth Session of the Assembly of States Parties) para 23. See also Budget Res, ICC–ASP/11/Res.1, 21 November 2012 (Eleventh Session of the Assembly of States Parties), sec J. See also Budget Res, ASP/10/Res.4, 21 December 2011 (Tenth Session of the Assembly of States Parties), sec G.

[69] Verduzco (n 23) 38–42.

[70] UNGA Res 67/295 (22 August 2013) UN Doc A/RES/67/295, preamble.

[71] Ibid. para 17.

The funding issue does constrain the Office of the Prosecutor and is thus negatively affecting her prosecutorial independence.[72] In November 2011, for example, the Office of the Prosecutor reported to the SC after the end of the NATO campaign in Libya that the scope of investigations and prosecutions, including of potential crimes by 'all parties to the conflict [would depend] on the funds available to the Office to conduct the Libya investigation'.[73] This would of course potentially challenge the independence of the ICC in practice.[74]

From these facts on the financing of the ICC one might be able to deduce a general trend of a shifting of leadership in ICL (as represented by the ICC) from the US to Europe and Asia.[75]

7.4 OBLIGATIONS OF OTHER NON-PARTY STATES AND STATES PARTIES

7.4.1 Obligations of Other Non-Party States

In principle, a SC referral as a Chapter VII enforcement measure is addressed to all UN member states.[76] This is important because the SC referral is the only possible source for obligations to cooperate with the ICC for states not parties to the Rome Statute.[77] However, the SC referrals to date have adopted a rather narrow approach, emphasizing that non-party states have no obligations to cooperate with the Court, except for the situation state concerned and parties to the conflict. In the relevant passage the SC provided in the Darfur referral,

---

[72] In the same vein see Verduzco (n 23) 38–42; Stahn, 'Libya, the International Criminal Court and Complementarity' (n 38) 328. On the general issue of limited financing of international criminal courts and tribunals, see Mahnoush H. Arsanjani and W. M. Reisman, 'The Law-in-Action of the International Criminal Court' (2005) 99 *American Journal of International Law* 385, 402.

[73] See OTP, Second Report of the Prosecutor of the International Criminal Court to the UN Security Council pursuant to UNSCR 1970 (2011), 2 November 2011, para 53.

[74] Verduzco (n 23) 38–42. For the financial details of the ICC see Sigall Horovitz, Gilad Noam and Yuval Shany, 'The International Criminal Court' in Shany (n 52) 247.

[75] Making this argument see Stuart Ford, 'How Leadership in International Criminal Law is shifting from the United States to Europe and Asia: An Analysis of Spending on and Contributions to International Criminal Courts' (2011) 55 *Saint Louis University Law Journal* 953.

[76] Verduzco (n 23) 42.

[77] See above Chapter 4. Annalisa Ciampi, 'The Obligation to Cooperate' in Cassese (n 28) 1608–09; Annalisa Ciampi, 'Current and Future Scenarios for Arrest and Surrender to the ICC' [2006] *Zeitschrift für ausländisches öffentliches Recht und Völkerrecht* 719–36, 731.

> *Decides* that the Government of Sudan and all other parties to the conflict in Darfur shall cooperate fully with and provide any necessary assistance to the Court and the Prosecutor pursuant to this resolution and, while recognizing that States not party to the Rome Statute have no obligation under the Statute, urges all States and concerned regional and other international organizations to cooperate fully.

In the Libya referral, the wording did not change except that it only referred to the Libyan authorities and not to other parties to the conflict.

This clear wording points to the conclusion that non-party states are under no obligation to cooperate with the court, except for those states that are addressed in the referral directly (Sudan and all other parties to the conflict in Darfur; and Libya). It follows that a general obligation to cooperate cannot be inferred from the referral alone.[78] As a result, non-party states not addressed in the referral to the ICC are under no legal obligation to give effect to the ICC's decisions (such as enforcing an arrest warrant issued in a situation that was referred to the ICC by the SC).[79] It is interesting to note that the SC's narrow approach was debated during the Argentinian presidency at the SC (in October 2014) regarding the question of whether or not to oblige all states to cooperate with the ICC when referring a situation.[80] It remains to be seen if this practice will change in the future.

The ICC itself has affirmed that no obligations for non-party states exist under the Statute without any special agreement and that hence no legal basis exists for the ICC to demand the enforcement of the arrest warrants from non-party states.[81] As a result, the Chambers have been reluctant to accept the

---

[78] Verduzco (n 23) 42; Alexandre Galand, 'Security Council Referrals to the International Criminal Court as Quasi-Legislative Acts' (2015) 19 *Max Planck Yearbook of United Nations Law* 142, 168. On the other hand, an early commentator has suggested that the obligation of cooperation could be implicit in the referral; see P. Gargiulo, 'The Relationship between the ICC and the Security Council' in F. Lattanzi and W. Schabas (eds), *The International Criminal Court: Comments on the Draft Statute* (Il Sirente 1998) 101.

[79] As Verduzco notes, this failure of the SC to create obligations on cooperation for non-party states 'runs against the very raison d'etre of the system of referrals'; see Verduzco (n 23) 42.

[80] See e.g. United Nations Security Council Verbatim Records, UN Doc S/PV.7285 (23 October 2014) Resumption 1 and 5.

[81] Decision on the request of the Defence of Abdullah Al-Senussi to make a finding of non-cooperation by the Islamic Republic of Mauritania and refer the matter to the Security Council, *Gaddafi and Al Senussi, Situation in Libya*, ICC-01/11-01/11-420 (28 August 2013) paras 13–14 (footnotes omitted); *Prosecutor v Omar Hassan Ahmad Al-Bashir* (Decision Regarding Omar Al-Bashir's Potential Travel to the United States of America) ICC-02/05-01/09-162 (18 September 2013) para 11; *Prosecutor v Omar Hassan Ahmad Al-Bashir* (Decision Regarding Omar Al-Bashir's Potential Travel to

Prosecutor's filings to inform the SC of travels of fugitives to non-party states, since the SC has merely 'urged' non-party states to cooperate with the Court.[82]

The related question is whether a non-state party to the ICC would be authorized to enforce an arrest warrant. In March 2016, Sudanese President Al-Bashir (against whom the ICC issued two arrest warrants) visited Indonesia, a state not party to the ICC.[83] The answer depends on the legal relationship between the states concerned and the rules of general international law. In that case, for reasons given above,[84] Indonesia as a non-state party is required under the customary international law rules on personal immunity to respect the immunity of the head of state of Sudan.[85] The SC referral does not change that.[86]

This conclusion would only be different if the wording 'urges' was treated as an authorization. It is generally accepted that authorizations by the SC acting under Chapter VII are also subject to the supremacy clause of art 103 of the UN Charter.[87] It might seem plausible to interpret the fact that the SC is not imposing an obligation but 'urging' all states to cooperate with the court as the SC implicitly authorizing all UN member states to set aside personal immunities. However, as Dapo Akande correctly notes, the word 'urges' merely suggests a recommendation or exhortation to take certain action and the referral also clearly says as much when it recognizes 'that states not party to

---

the Federal Republic of Ethiopia and the Kingdom of Saudi Arabia) ICC-02/05-01/09-164 (10 October 2013) para 8.

[82] *Al-Bashir, Situation in Darfur* (Decision Regarding Omar Al-Bashir's Potential Travel to the Federal Republic of Ethiopia and the Kingdom of Saudi Arabia) ICC-02/05-01/09-164 (10 October 2013) para 8.

[83] See http://www.reuters.com/article/us-sudan-indonesia-idUSKCN0W80YH (accessed 1 June 2018). For a full list of Al-Bashir's travels since 2009 see http://bashirwatch.org/ (accessed 1 June 2018). Of these, seven countries (Chad, Democratic Republic of Congo, Djibouti, Kenya, Malawi, Nigeria and South Africa) are ICC members. Countries such as Kenya, Nigeria and South Africa have reversed their stand on arresting Al-Bashir in light of the rise of the 'pan-African' opposition to the ICC. Notably, these countries had in the past (2009–2011) denied entry to Al-Bashir onto their territory, but have subsequently invited him to state level events such as swearing in ceremonies (Kenya, 2013) and African Union Summit (Nigeria, 2013; South Africa, 2015).

[84] See Chapter 5.1.5.

[85] See Chapter 5.1.5.

[86] For the contrary view see Frau (n 8) 790–91; Dapo Akande, 'The Legal Nature of Security Council Referrals to the ICC and its Impact on Al-Bashir's Immunities' (2009) 7(2) *Journal of International Criminal Justice* 333.

[87] Wood (n 14) 253. Although it is disputed whether art 103 of the UN Charter also applies to conflicting customary international law, good arguments favour such an interpretation, see Akande (n 86) 348. For the contrary view see R. Liivoja, 'The Scope of the Supremacy Clause of the United Nations Charter', 57 *International Comparative Law Quarterly* (2008) 583.

the Rome Statute have no obligation under the Statute'.[88] Therefore, non-party states are under no obligation to arrest Al-Bashir (or the other accused persons sought by the ICC in the situation of Darfur).[89]

The Pre-Trial Chambers do not share this view. In the *Al-Bashir* case, the Pre-Trial Chamber II invited the competent authorities to surrender him to the ICC, considering non-party states authorized to do so.[90] In that case, the state in question, by enforcing the arrest warrant, would be violating the personal immunity of the accused.

In case of non-cooperation of the non-state party, it is not violating obligations arising out of the Rome Statute directly but rather through its obligations arising out of art 25 of the UN Charter to give effect to the SC referral.[91] The conferral of power to the ICC means that the non-state party is bound by the specific decisions and orders of the ICC, be it through the Office of the Prosecution or the Chambers.

7.4.2 Obligations of States Parties

In practice, the Pre-Trial Chamber II urged for the arrest of President Al-Bashir on his travels to states parties to the ICC.[92] However, there have been already numerous cases of non-execution of the ICC's order for the arrest and surrender of Al-Bashir, namely by Kenya, Djibouti, Chad (twice), Malawi, Nigeria, the Democratic Republic of Congo and South Africa.[93] In contrast to non-party states, the obligations to comply with the ICC's orders stem from the Rome Statute, even though, in cases of SC referrals of situations in non-party states,

[88] See Res 1970 (2011) and 1593 (2005).

[89] Akande (n 86) 344.

[90] Decision Regarding Omar Al-Bashir's Travel to the United Arab Emirates and his Potential Travel to the Kingdom of Saudi Arabia, the State of Kuwait and the Kingdom of Bahrain (Pre-Trial Chamber II) ICC-02/05-01/09-224 (24 February 2015) 6–7; Decision Regarding Omar Hassan Ahmad A1-Bashir's Travel to the Kingdom of Saudi Arabia and the Arab Republic of Egypt (Pre-Trial Chamber II) ICC-02/05-01/09-232 (24 March 2015) 5–6.

[91] Faustin Ntoubandi, 'Towards Ending Impunity in Darfur: The ICC Arrest Warrant of 27 April 2007' (2009) *Zeitschrift für ausländisches öffentliches Recht und Völkerrecht* 123–54, 148.

[92] For a chronological listing of PTC II decisions relating to Al-Bashir's travel, see https://www.icc-cpi.int/en_menus/icc/situations%20and%20cases/situations/situation%20icc%200205/related%20cases/icc02050109/court%20records/chambers/ptcII/Pages/index.aspx (accessed 20 April 2016).

[93] Dire Tladi, 'The Duty on South Africa to Arrest and Surrender President Al-Bashir under South African and International Law' (2015) 13(5) *Journal of International Criminal Justice* 1027, 1028–29. On the legal issues surrounding South Africa's obligations see ibid.

personal immunities remain opposable to authorities of ICC member states for the reasons given above.[94] The ICC member states concerned are thus faced to choose which obligation to honour, those stemming from the Rome Statute to disregard personal immunities, or those stemming from customary international law obligations.[95]

7.5 CONCLUSIONS

This chapter has demonstrated that applying the results of this study on the legal nature of the SC referral is important to understand the key legal issues raised by practice. States not party to the ICC that are directly addressed in the referral, such as Sudan and Libya, are bound to accept the jurisdiction of the ICC and the legality of the Court's operation in accordance with its Statute as determined by the SC referral.[96] Key differences flow from the fact that the source of obligation is not the Rome Statute directly but the UN Charter on which the SC referral is based.[97]

This chapter has also made apparent the unsatisfactory consequences of the jurisdictional exemption and the financial constraints imposed by the SC referrals. Of particular practical importance is the fact that, as it stands, the personal immunities of heads of state are still applicable even with respect to states parties to the ICC. Of course, personal immunities are only a procedural bar to prosecution. After the removal from office, the accused would not be able to invoke personal immunity. Still, this is a very unsatisfactory result. But at least it is laying bare an inconvenient truth about international criminal justice: the ICC is an over-ambitious project that perhaps cannot meet the exaggerated expectations it has created. In other words, what we witness here is that '[t]he idea of universal justice . . . has met with the reality of power politics'.[98]

---

[94] See Chapter 5.1.5. In a similar vein, Paola Gaeta, 'Does President Al-Bashir Enjoy Immunity from Arrest?' (2009) 7(2) *Journal of International Criminal Justice* 315. Contra Akande (n 86).

[95] The issues surrounding conflicting obligations also played a role in the withdrawal strategy announced by the AU. The AU's Withdrawal Strategy Document states that 'the effect of being legally bound by a decision of the UNSC to a Statute that a country has not even ratified is not acceptable'; Withdrawal Strategy Document (Draft 2, 12 January 2017) annexed to the Draft Decision on the International Criminal Court, Doc. EX.CL/1006(XXX), African Union, Assembly of the Union, Twenty-Eighth Ordinary Session, 30–31 January 2017, Addis Ababa, para 4.

[96] Similarly Akande (n 86).

[97] Similarly ibid. 342.

[98] Hans Köchler, 'Justice and Realpolitik: The Predicament of the International Criminal Court' (2017) 16(1) *Chinese Journal of International Law* 1, 1.

In an overall assessment of the legal issues, one may identify other challenges the SC referral practice poses to the ideal behind the creation of the ICC, i.e. that no one shall enjoy impunity for the most serious crimes of concern to the international community as a whole.[99] First, the SC referral is inherently selective since veto-yielding states are likely to protect their own or their allies' citizens from the jurisdiction of the ICC.[100] The SC referral practice has aggravated this inequality further due to the jurisdictional exemption provided in the SC referrals. For instance, two individuals who have committed the same crime in the same place at the same time may be treated differently, one surrendered to the ICC and the other not, solely on the basis of their different nationalities.[101] Perhaps, some states' nationals are more equal than others.[102] Such practice seriously impedes the development of ICL on its path to a truly international criminal *justice* system that applies to all actors in the world equally. In conclusion, it appears that the historical criticism of double standards in international criminal justice still holds true today. Only this time, it presents itself as 'Council's justice'.

---

[99] See Preamble to the Rome Statute of the International Criminal Court. The Rome Statute itself is flawed in this respect due to the rejection of the proposal to provide the Court with universal jurisdiction. See also Claudia Fritsche, 'Security Council Resolution 1422: Peacekeeping and the International Criminal Court' in Jochen A. Frowein (ed), *Verhandeln für den Frieden: Negotiating for peace: Liber Amicorum Tono Eitel* (Beiträge zum ausländischen öffentlichen Recht und Völkerrecht vol 162, Springer 2003) 118.

[100] Vera Gowlland-Debbas, 'The Relationship between the Security Council and the Projected International Criminal Court' (1998) 3 *Journal of Conflict and Security Law* 97, 114. The situation in Syria is a case in point, in which the SC referral was vetoed by China and Russia. The situation in North Korea is another example that is blocked by the threat of a veto by China.

[101] Fritsche (n 99) 117; Salvatore Zappala, 'Are Some Peacekeepers Better Than Others? UN Security Council Resolution 1497 (2003) and the ICC' (2003) 1 *Journal of International Criminal Justice* 671, 675.

[102] Robert Cryer, 'Sudan, Resolution 1593, and International Criminal Justice' (2006) 19(01) *Leiden Journal of International Law* 195, 217.

8. Conclusions: The Janus face of the International Criminal Court

This study has demonstrated that the legal nature of the SC referral to the ICC involving states not party to the ICC must be conceptualized as a conferral of powers from the SC to the ICC. In analyzing the legal nature of the SC referral to the ICC, I have pointed to important legal differences between the establishment of the ad hoc tribunals and the referral. Because the general justification for such exercise of the SC's powers as provided for in the *Tadic* case cannot, therefore, be applied, it was necessary to scrutinize the Chapter VII powers of the SC to do so.

In that respect, I have demonstrated that it is not easy to establish binding limits in abstract terms to SC measures under Chapter VII. However, it is clear that the SC is not unbound by law and I have argued that the SC is bound inter alia by the principle of legality, and that a cautious approach is warranted with respect to quasi-legislative measures in the field of international criminal law affecting individuals.

Applying these findings to the SC referral practice, this study has shown that the legal issues raised are better understood and analysed by reference to the legal nature of the SC referral. We have thus seen why the ICC is bound by the jurisdictional exemptions included in the SC referrals since it cannot exercise jurisdiction in non-party states that go beyond the conferred jurisdictional authority provided for in the referral.

In a concluding reflection of these results, it becomes apparent that the source of ambiguities and legal uncertainties in this regard stem from the complex ICC–SC relationship consisting of the interlocking of a consent-based system of the Rome Statute as a separate multilateral treaty with the power of mandatory decision making of the SC. Thus, it might be helpful to conceptualize the court as functionally two in one.[1]

---

[1] G. P. Fletcher, 'The ICC – Two Courts in One?' (2006) 4(3) *Journal of International Criminal Justice* 428, 428–33. See also Jessberger and Geneus, who consider the ICC as having three distinct functions, namely the ICC as a 'criminal court', a 'watchdog court' and a 'security court'; Florian Jessberger and Julia Geneuss, 'The Many Faces of the International Criminal Court' (2012) 10(5) *Journal of International Criminal Justice* 1081.

In this sense, the SC referral mechanism reveals the 'Janus face' of the ICC:[2] when jurisdiction is conferred to the Court by a state party, it is an independent judicial body in the pure spirit of the Rome Statute financed by the ASP pursuant to art 115. When 'leased'[3] by the SC, however, it is primarily used as an instrument to maintain or restore international peace and security and not necessarily to advance international criminal justice.[4] This separate nature is further evidenced by art 115(b) of the Statute which provides for the UN to fund the expenses incurred by the referral.[5] Hence, depending on how a case is brought before the Court, then, it can be either an independent criminal court, or prosecute criminals as an instrument to advance the SC's security objectives:[6] when acting under a SC referral, the ICC becomes an altogether different entity.[7]

This legal relationship links the peace and security mandate of the SC to the justice mandate of the ICC. On the one hand, this constitutes a potentially serious impediment to the independent functioning of the ICC.[8] On the other hand, this dichotomy lies at the heart of international criminal justice: prosecuting individual suspects yet receiving cases only when collective security demands it.[9] And instead of strengthening the universal reach of international criminal law, the SC as a political organ sets dangerous precedents by insisting on jurisdictional exemption for certain states. The SC missed opportunities to strengthen the court's authority and undermined its legitimacy by applying

over-statement?

---

[2] In a similar vein see Abdoulaye Tine, 'Article 13' in Julian Fernandez and Xavier Pacreau (eds), *Statut de Rome de la Cour pénale internationale: Commentaire article par article* (Pedone 2012) 614. See also Carsten Hollweg, who foresaw a double function for the ICC – on the one hand as a court of law, on the other as a subsidiary organ of the SC; Carsten Hollweg, 'Vom Jugoslawientribunal der UNO zum allgemeinen Internationalen Strafgerichtshof? Der schwierige Prozess der Schaffung einer internationalen Strafgerichtsbarkeit' (1994) 112 *Schweizerische Zeitschrift für Strafrecht* 281.

[3] See W. M. Reisman, 'On Paying the Piper: Financial Responsibility for Security Council Referrals to the International Criminal Court' (2005) 99(3) *American Journal of International Law* 615, 615–18.

[4] Primarily as an instrument to maintain or restore international peace and security, not necessarily to advance international criminal justice.

[5] Reisman (n 3), 615–18; Fletcher (n 2) 430. It must be noted however, that the SC also attempted to blur this distinction by insisting that none of the expenses relating to the referrals shall be borne by the UN. See Chapter 7 above on the financing of the SC referrals.

[6] Fletcher (n 1) 430.

[7] Ibid. 429.

[8] Dan Sarooshi, 'The Peace and Justice Paradox: The International Criminal Court and the UN Security Council' in Dominic McGoldrick, Peter Rowe and Eric Donnelly (eds), *The Permanent International Criminal Court: Legal And Policy Issues* (Hart Publishing 2004) 100.

[9] Fletcher (n 1) 433.

double standards in ICL. As a result the very project of international criminal justice as international *justice* is called into question.[10] The true tragedy of the ICC is that it is a court that cannot conceivably exercise political jurisdiction over great powers, creating a permanent two-tier justice system in which powerful states use global institutions to discipline the weak – the SC referral only adds to that.[11]

[10] Otfried Höffe, 'Konfuzius, der Koran und die Gerechtigkeit' (24 August 2015), available at http://www.faz.net/aktuell/politik/die-gegenwart/recht-und-moral-konfuzius-der-koran-und-die-gerechtigkeit-13753298.html?printPagedArticle=true#pageIndex_2. (accessed 30 March 2018).

[11] Stephen Hopgood, *The Endtimes of Human Rights* (Cornell University Press 2013) 167. Looking at this question more comprehensively, see Christopher Rudolph, *Power and Principle: The Politics of International Criminal Courts* (Cornell University Press 2017). But see also the general critique of B. S. Chimni, 'International Institutions Today: An Imperial Global State in the Making' (2004) 15(1) *European Journal of International Law* 1, 13–14.

Index

Jain, N. 86, 93
Jallow, H. 91
Jessberger, F. 204
Johansen, R. 24
Johansson, P. 72, 179
Johnstone, I. 86